MW00648231

Ann Walker

Ann Walker

The Life and Death of Gentleman Jack's Wife

Rebecca Batley

PEN & SWORD
HISTORY

First published in Great Britain in 2023 by
Pen & Sword History
An imprint of
Pen & Sword Books Ltd
Yorkshire – Philadelphia

ISBN 978 1 39909 928 8

A CIP catalogue record for this book is
available from the British Library.

Typeset by Mac Style
Printed in the UK by CPI Group (UK) Ltd, Croydon, CR0 4YY.

Pen & Sword Books Limited incorporates the imprints of Atlas,
Archaeology, Aviation, Discovery, Family History, Fiction, History,
Maritime, Military, Military Classics, Politics, Select, Transport,
True Crime, Air World, Frontline Publishing, Leo Cooper, Remember
When, Seaforth Publishing, The Praetorian Press, Wharncliffe
Local History, Wharncliffe Transport, Wharncliffe True Crime
and White Owl.

For a complete list of Pen & Sword titles please contact

PEN & SWORD BOOKS LIMITED
47 Church Street, Barnsley, South Yorkshire, S70 2AS, England
E-mail: enquiries@pen-and-sword.co.uk
Website: www.pen-and-sword.co.uk

Or

PEN AND SWORD BOOKS
1950 Lawrence Rd, Havertown, PA 19083, USA
E-mail: Uspen-and-sword@casematepublishers.com
Website: www.penandswordbooks.com

This book is dedicated to my Mum and to my loyal secretary Jem –
I love you more than anything in the entire universe.

Contents

Acknowledgments

No book is written in isolation and many people have helped me in writing *Ann Walker: The Life and Death of Gentleman Jack's Wife*. First and foremost I would like to acknowledge and thank Diane Halford for her support, encouragement and the time she has taken to discuss all things Ann with me. I would also like to thank everyone at In Search of Ann Walker, who have been unfailingly supportive and for their kind permission to quote research. In particular I would like to mention Alexa Tansley for permission to use her photographs and Ivana Nika, for discussing her research on Ann's education with me.

I also want to acknowledge the help and support of the staff at WYAS Calderdale, in particular archivist Ruth Cummins who has answered my multitude of questions. Likewise the staff at Shibden Hall and in particular I'd like to thank Chris for answering my many emails and for permission to reproduce the image of Shibden Hall.

I particularly wish to thank Ian Philp, Chair of the Friends of St Matthew's Churchyard for answering my dozens of emails with great patience and assisting me with photographic permissions, it was much appreciated. Likewise I wish to thank David Glover for answering my questions regarding Ann and Cliff Hill.

I would also like to thank the members of Anne Lister Italia, especially Francesca and Lucia who kindly discussed John Walker's time in Italy. Likewise, thanks go to Olga Khoroshilova for allowing me access to her work on Anne Lister in Russia.

I also acknowledge and thank Dr Dan O'Brien for taking the time to answer my questions on nineteenth-century burial practises, as well as Dr Jennifer Wallis for her opinions on nineteenth-century medical matters.

Biljana Popovic has been very kind in allowing me to reproduce her artwork and interpretation of Ann and Anne's coat of Arms – thank you so much. Thanks also to Lynn Shouls for taking the time to discuss Ann and Anne's heraldic pedigree with me and for allowing me to quote from her research.

Thanks to Ann Boyens, who found documents relating to Ann's time in the asylum and took the time to respond to my queries and Dan at the North Yorkshire County Record Office for assisting me in obtaining permission to reproduce a page from the asylum records.

I also wish to acknowledge the assistance of Jim MaKay of the Kirkmichael trust who helped me with my research into the Sutherland's and Ann's time in Scotland. Thanks also to Pat Metcalfe, who was kind enough to respond to my message regarding the Ladies of Llangollen and the nature of nineteenth-century female sexuality.

Thanks are also due to Kelly at Crow Nest Golf Club, for taking the time to answer my questions and for her assistance in gaining permission to reproduce images of Crow Nest. The website 'Packed with Potential' has proved an invaluable resource and I would like to thank Marlene Oliveira in particular for her advice regarding referencing. Likewise I want to thank each and every Anne Lister transcriber, whose invaluable work is bringing Anne Lister to a wider audience. In a similar vein, this book would not have been possible without the remarkable Anne Lister researchers who have gone before; Jill Liddington, Anne Choma, Phylis Ramsden, Muriel Green and Helena Whitbread, the latter of whom was kind enough to offer me words of encouragement.

My friends have been amazing and supportive during the writing of this book, but very special thanks must go to Louise, Tak for alt my dearest friend, Toyah, who has listened to me patiently talk about Ann every day for the past two years, and Amy – it's been fun; your help and support has meant so much.

I would also like to take this opportunity to thank my family for their unfailing support, chief among them being my wonderful Mum, without whose unfailing support and endless encouragement this book would never have been written – I appreciate and love you. My final thanks must go to my long-suffering secretary Jem, for sorting my papers, only mildly grumbling about my disorganisation, and wielding a stapler like a pro.

List of Figures

Dramatis Personae

Ann's Family:
John Walker 1753–1823: *Ann's father. A Halifax merchant, he married Mary Edwards of Pye Nest. He left his children well provided for and appointed his brother-in-law Henry Edwards, and William Priestley, as trustees of the estate.*

Mary Walker née Edwards 1763–1823: *Ann's mother, the daughter of John and Elizabeth Edwards of Pye Nest, she married John Walker in 1795.*

John Walker 1804–1830: *Ann's only surviving brother and their parents' heir. He died while on honeymoon in Naples.*

Frances Esther Penfold – 'Fanny' 1803–1838: *John Walker's wife and Ann's sister-in-law. Her son by John was stillborn after his death in 1830. She later married Courtney Kenny Clarke in 1832 and by him had two daughters.*

William Walker 1798: *Ann's eldest brother who died at three weeks old (before her birth).*

Mary Walker 1799–1815: *Ann's eldest sister, who died aged 15.*

Elizabeth Sutherland née Walker, 1801–1844: *Ann's elder sister. Married Captain Sutherland in 1828 and had six children – Ann's nieces and nephews were: Mary 1829–1845, George 1831–1843, Elizabeth 1832–1872, John 1834–1836, Evan Charles 1835–1913 and Ann 1837–1917.*

Captain George MacKay Sutherland 1798–1847: *Ann's brother-in-law, married Ann's sister Elizabeth. He mistrusted Anne Lister's motives. Ann largely lived with him and his family after the Lunacy Commission. He remarried after Elizabeth's death.*

Aunt Mary Walker 1747–1822: *Ann's spinster Aunt Mary. Daughter of William Walker. She and Aunt Ann Walker moved into Cliff Hill around the time their brother John Walker and his family moved into Crow Nest.*

Aunt Ann Walker 1757–1847: *Ann's spinster Aunt Ann. Youngest daughter of William Walker.*

William Walker 1749–1809: *Ann's uncle, her father's elder brother. His death meant that her father inherited the bulk of the Walker estate.*

Elizabeth Priestley 1750–1829: *Ann's aunt. Married to John Priestley of Sowerby Bridge.*

Henry Edwards (the elder) 1775–1848: *Ann's uncle and trustee of Ann's fathers will. Lived at Pye Nest and was a member of the Halifax Tory elite.*

Henry Edwards (the younger) 1812–1886: *Ann's cousin. He proposed to her sometime after her brother's death. Lived at Pye Nest. Tory.*

William Priestley, 1770–1860: *Ann's cousin and co-trustee of her fathers will. Married Eliza Priestley in 1808. Lived at New House Lightcliffe.*

Delia Priestley Edwards, 1807–1892: *First cousin and friend of Ann. She accompanied Ann's brother John on his honeymoon. She married Fanny's widower Courtney Kenny Clarke after Fanny's death and they had three children.*

Elizabeth Edwards Aitkinson 1764–1834 (and husband): *Ann's Aunt Elizabeth and uncle. Elizabeth was Ann's mothers sister. Lived in Huddersfield*

Lucy Edwards Plowes 1796–1868: *Ann's aunt, lived in London.*

Christopher Rawson 1777–1849: *Halifax banker, and Deputy Lieutenant of Yorkshire. Lived at Hope House. He came into conflict with Ann (and Anne) on numerous issues.*

Thomas Groves Edwards 1783–1855: *Ann's uncle, he lived near Regent's Park in London.*

Harriet Edwards Dyson 1778–1865: *Ann's aunt. She became more involved in Ann's care after the death of Elizabeth and Captain Sutherland.*

Eliza Priestley: *Married William Priestley of New House. Initially a confidante of Anne Lister.*

Stansfield Rawson, 1778–1865: *Of Gledholt, Huddersfield, who bought land and built in the Lake District.*

Catherine Rawson: *Daughter of Stansfield Rawson. Cousin and close friend of Ann.*

Delia Rawson: *Daughter of Stansfield Rawson, sister to Catherine Rawson. Cousin and friend of Ann.*

Romantic Interests:
Anne Lister 1791–1840: *Ann's wife. Lived at and later inherited Shibden Hall.*

Andrew Fraser: *Ann seriously considered marrying him and called him the 'best of men'. Died July 1832.*

Reverend Thomas Ainsworth: *He wanted to marry Ann after his wife's sudden death. Prior to his wife's death he and Ann had several physical encounters. He gave her a ring and books, but she did not welcome his advances.*

Alexander MacKenzie: *A Cousin of Captain Sutherland's. Proposed as a suitor and husband for Ann.*

Doctors:
Dr Henry Stephen Belcombe: *Treated Ann in the 1830–40s. Friend of Anne Lister and brother to Mariana Lawton.*

Dr Jubb: *Doctor in Halifax and to Shibden Hall and Ann.*

Dr Kenny: *Halifax doctor. Ann felt his questions to be inappropriate and urged Anne not to trust him. He was a friend of Marian Lister's.*

Dr Double: *Parisian doctor who saw and treated both Ann and Anne.*

When Travelling:
Prince Golitsyn: *Governor-General of Moscow.*

Princess Sophia Radzivilli: *Daughter of Prince and Princess Ourosoff. Her flirtation with Anne Lister in Moscow deeply upset Ann.*

Mrs Howard: *Owner of the hotel, at which Ann stayed in Moscow 1839–40.*

Charles Stuart de Rothesay 1779–1845: *British Ambassador to Paris and later to St Petersburg.*

Mr and Mme de Fischer de Waldheim: *Acquaintances of Ann and Anne. Their son ran the botanic garden in Moscow.*

Count Gustav Carl Frederik von Blucher 1798–1864 and Countess Emily von Blucher 1802–1885: *Chamberlain to the Danish court and acquaintances of Anne and Ann in Denmark.*

Count and Countess Panin: *Moscow acquaintances involved in the Moscow University.*

Madame Tchekmarev: *Friend of Ann's, met while travelling. Ann admired her style of dress.*

Charles
Adam   *Guides employed by Anne and Ann while travelling.*
Moshe

Employees/Servants:
John Booth: *Servant at Shibden Hall.*

James Briggs: *Lister Steward, died 1832.*

Gross and Grotza: *German manservant and maid.*

Cookson: *Shibden servant. Ann did not get along with her.*

Cordingly: *Shibden servant.*

James: *Ann's Manservant at Lidgate.*

George Playforth: *Manservant and Groom at Shibden.*

Rachel: *Shibden Kitchen maid.*

Samuel Washington: *Ann's estate Steward.*

Josephine: *Appointed as a maid/nurse for Ann on her travels.*

Eugenie Pierre: *Anne Lister's French maid.*

Jane Chapman: *Servant/Maid of Ann's. Ann suggests that she would go with her if she moved to London or Paris.*

Others:
Thomas Adams: *Partner of Robert Parker Halifax layer at 6 The Square.*

Miss Bentley: *Sister to Reverend Ainsworth's wife and friend of Ann.*

John Bottomly: *Anne's tenant at Brierley Hill. Could vote in the Halfiax elections.*

Miss Bramley: *Governess and friend of the Walkers.*

Mr Brown: *Ann's drawing master.*

Lady Vere Cameron: *Lover of Anne. Married Captain Donald Cameron in 1832.*

Jonathan Gray: *Ann and Anne's York lawyer.*

Aunt (Anne) Lister, 1765–1836: *Anne Lister's unmarried aunt. Lived at Shibden Hall.*

Mr (Jeremy) Lister, 1752–1838: *Anne Lister's father and brother to Aunt Anne Lister.*

Marian Lister 1797–1882: *Anne Lister's younger sister, Ann acted as a buffer between them.*

Reverend Wilkinson: *Headmaster of Heath Grammar School and curate at Lightcliffe Church.*

Lydia Wilkinson: *Daughter of Rev. Wilkinson and friend of Ann.*

Robert Parker: *Halifax lawyer, partner of Thomas Adams at 6 The Square. He was Anne Lister's lawyer and worked for Ann. Instrumental in bringing about Ann's removal from Shibden.*

John and Mrs Carr: *Owned the White Swan Inn in Halifax.*

Mariana Lawton, 1790–1868: *Anne Lister's long term lover, married Charles Lawton in 1816.*

Rev Samuel Knight: *A vicar in Halifax, he taught many young people in the area.*

Isabella Norcliffe, 1785–1846: *Previous lover of Anne Lister, Ann visited the family several times with Ann.*

James Stuart Wortley: *Tory candidate in Halifax, elected in the 1835 window smashing election but defeated two years later.*

Mr William Duffin, 1747–1839: *York surgeon, he was a friend of Anne Lister and later knew Ann.*

Eliza Raine 1791–1860: *Anne Lister's first lover. In 1816 she was declared a lunatic and lived in York asylums.*

John Abbott: *Halifax Woolstapler and Marian Lister's suitor.*

James Hinscliffe: *Local coal merchant.*

Emma Saltmarshe née Rawson: *Ann visits her when she is sick. Married to Christopher Saltmarshe of a local mercantile family. Members of the Tory elite.*

Elizabeth Firth 1797–1837: *Kept a diary and was Anne Brontë's godmother.*

Harriet Parkhill: *A friend of Ann's.*

John Snaith Rymer 1806–1876: *Ann's solicitor during the Lunacy Commission proceedings, initially convinced she was well, a meeting with her dramatically changed his mind. He became interested in spiritualism and emigrated to Australia.*

Samuel Waterhouse: *A local magistrate who attempts to help Ann upon her return to Shibden.*

Caroline Walker: *Distant relation of Ann's; she kept a diary.*

Mrs Todd: *Member of staff at Dr Belcombe's private asylum. Talks Ann into leaving Shibden.*

All transcriptions of Ann Walker and Anne Lister's diaries were undertaken by myself unless otherwise stated. Any errors are therefore my own.

Nearly all the names and places mentioned have a variety of spellings in the documentation, for example Cliff Hill can also be spelt as Cliffe Hill. For ease and uniformity I have adopted a standardised spelling in all cases.

Introduction

It is both a universal truth, and a personal bugbear of mine, that throughout history women have been defined by the people they loved, rather than by their own achievements. Even when talking about Elizabeth I, arguably England's greatest monarch, more academic ink has been spilt on the issue of whether or not she and Robert Dudley ever slept together than on the details of her education. It therefore feels wrong to begin a biography of Ann Walker by mentioning Anne Lister, the woman whom she married – but it is unavoidable.

Until recently, Ann has only spoken to us through the eyes of her wife, via her now infamous diaries filled with sex, passion and scandal. I first encountered Ann when watching the BBC's 2010 production *The Secret Diaries of Miss Anne Lister,* which primarily tells the better known story of Anne Lister's long term love affair with Mariana Belcombe/Lawton.[1,2] In the series, Ann appears only as a bit-part player, the wan, quiet heiress, valued for her wealth and little else. In general culture she tends to be simply referred to, when she is mentioned at all, as 'Anne Lister's lunatic wife', and I remember thinking: surely there has to be more to her story than that?

Ann was a person in her own right and the Ann Walker I have come to know during the course of writing this book is quite different to the one I imagined before I began my research. Not in the sense that I had a clear view of who she was, but that she has become very real. Far from being a romantic interlude in the life and career of her famous wife, she has leapt off the page for me through her own letters, the recollections of her friends and family and of course through her diary. This small, blue-marbled notebook was discovered in 2019 by the remarkable Diane Halford, while hunting though the veritable treasure trove of papers relating to the families of Lightcliffe held at the West Yorkshire Archives in Calderdale. This document, more than any other, had allowed Ann to speak to us directly: undiluted and extraordinary.

Ann owned a vast amount of land and cared deeply for those who lived on it. She opened a school for local children, at which she taught and took a keen personal interest, and frequently spent her evenings knitting or sewing clothing for friends, children and the poor. Ann was also a passionate artist, reader, collector of books, traveller, and mountaineer, she rode well enough to impress the Cossacks and frequently hiked for miles. She thrashed the fiercely intelligent Anne Lister often at backgammon and was not afraid to stand her ground when she thought she was right. Alongside all of which she was a peacemaker, shopaholic, animal lover, cook and student of languages and history.

However, Ann wrote no books; her diary gives us no salacious details of her sex life to titillate, nor did she broadcast her participation in the first historic same-sex marriage, all of which which has allowed her to slip through the cracks of history. Yet in the words of George Eliot, 'the effect of her being on those around her was incalculable', her kindness and her courage deeply affected all those who knew her.[3]

The courage Ann displayed when pursuing a marriage with Anne cannot be underestimated. Society in the nineteenth century in general was far less worried about lesbianism than male homosexuality. It wasn't pursued under law in the way that male homosexuality was, and would continue to be. This is at least in part due to the fact that many didn't consider sex between two women possible. In the words of Ladies of Llangollen expert Pat Metcalfe, lesbianism wasn't really heard of, rather it was classed as romantic friendship.[4]

Ann's marriage though was no friendship, she moved into Shibden Hall, considered herself as married in the eyes of God, and gave her wife a 'husband's' interest in her money and estates. For these actions Ann was ostracised by society, she was attacked by her family, threatened, and her whole sense of faith and self was challenged.

In the course of writing this book I have spoken to a great many people interested in, and researching, Ann. The portrayal of Ann by Sophie Rundle in Sally Wainwright's hit TV show *Gentleman Jack* has ignited many people's interest in her life.[5] Everyone has an opinion on her character and on the issue of her mental health. I certainly do not claim here to be presenting a definitive picture of Ann, this necessarily is Ann's story as I have interpreted it, but I fervently hope that I have done her – and the remarkable courage she displayed – some justice.

Chapter 1

The Asylum Road

On 17 July 1843, Robert Parker, a solicitor in the northern town of Halifax, sat down at his desk in the window of Number 6, The Square, and began to draft a letter.

It was a letter he had thought long and hard over writing. He had consulted legal texts and communicated with the doctors of the town, but now there was nothing left to do but sit and write.

This letter was addressed, in his looping hand, to Mrs Elizabeth Sutherland and in it he conveyed to her the procedure that would be necessary, to have a woman declared a 'lunatic' against her will by her family.[1] Robert Parker explains clearly the steps that would need to be taken given recent changes in the law. First, Elizabeth's personal authorisation would be needed, then they would require two certificates from two separate doctors who had seen the patient at least seven days prior to her removal to any asylum. It seems the procedure was not quite as straightforward as Elizabeth had hoped, for she had agonised long and hard before making this enquiry, and now faced with the reality of her role in it, she just wanted the whole affair over with.

The Dangerous Lunacy Act of 1843, 'made provision for the safe custody and prevention of offences by persons dangerously insane and for the care and maintenance of persons of unsound mind', but it required doctor certification for the safety of any potential patients.[2]

In practice, however, the system was often abused, and it opened the door for the committal of women to asylums against their will on the say-so of doctors who were sometimes paid, or bribed, by the woman's husband or family.[3]

There was no danger of such misuse here though, Elizabeth Sutherland was determined that her sister would get the best possible care and that everything would go through official channels. The image of the feeble 'lunatic' woman had long pervaded Victorian culture, one only has to open a novel by writers such as Charles Dickens or Wilkie Collins to be exposed to female nerves, swooning and hysteria.[4] At the time religious obsession, illness, grief or unsuitable love affairs were all deemed as causes of female 'madness'. A woman's sexuality and childbirth, or the lack thereof, was the key focus of Victorian psychiatrists as they sought to understand the nature of 'madness'.

At the time Parker was writing his letter, many doctors felt the asylum was the best place for women who transgressed the social norms, declaring their 'madness' to be a consequence of unnatural behaviour.

Once Parker had written his letter, events for the intended patient, Miss Ann Walker of Shibden Hall, moved at frightening speed.

Elizabeth Sutherland genuinely believed that her younger sister, Ann Walker, fulfilled all the criteria for insanity. Ann had suffered from religious mania, crippling grief, and had above all transgressed the norms of society by marrying a woman. She had alienated everyone in her life and mismanaged her estates. For years Elizabeth had been kind, patient, and had sought medical help but now Ann had gone too far and she had to act.

On 11 August she wrote a reply to Parker stating that she would be putting into motion the steps he had outlined, and that to do anything else would be neglecting her duty.[5] She felt that out of 'kindness' and to 'prevent further exposure' they must do something. In this letter she also expresses her fervent hope that her sister will be restored to health by treatment in the asylum. Elizabeth instructed Parker to speak with her uncle Henry Edwards of Pye Nest, a fine Jacobean mansion that once lay between Halifax and Sowerby Bridge, as to how everything must be managed. Henry Edwards was one of Halifax's great Victorian gentlemen and he had served the town as its MP for many years. His father had been a brother to Ann and Elizabeth's mother and it was through this familial relationship that he now found himself embroiled in Elizabeth's action.

Elizabeth wrote again on 17 August and placed the whole matter into the hands of Parker and Edwards.[6] She would, she wrote, approve whatever they decided – a fact she reiterated on the 21st, although as her frequent letters testify, she found it impossible to step back entirely. Elizabeth offers the suggestion that Drs Belcombe and Jubb could be applied to carry out the examination of her sister.

A tall, handsome man with an interest in psychiatry, Dr Henry Stephen Belcombe had treated Miss Walker for many years. He was familiar with the family and, Elizabeth felt sure, could be trusted to act with sensitivity. Following her advice it was Dr Belcombe that Parker now approached, stating that Miss Walker now required further help and asking his advice as to how to proceed. Elizabeth was correct, Dr Belcombe both knew Ann Walker well and cared for her welfare. He replied immediately, telling Parker that he feared Miss Walker would refuse their help and:

> her refusal might lead to an examination before the Lord Chancellor and his sending down someone to manage the property ... I confess I am by no means sanguine of the success of this and I fear you will have to resort to the [lunacy] commission unless she can be made sensible that it will be wiser for her to submit to our friendly advice.

Ann had previously proved, on occasion, to be resistant to his treatment and he thought their best chance of gaining her cooperation was to scare Ann into compliance.[7] Ann valued Shibden and her independence; by threatening her, both men felt that they could convince her to voluntarily seek treatment. Both feared the practical and social consequences of her refusal, or of a protracted legal case, and their fears were well justified. Many would have welcomed the chance to manage the Shibden lands, which were already embroiled in several legal disputes, and gossip about Miss Walker's health was rife in Halifax, but as it turned out they had no time to convince her.

On 8 September, Dr Belcombe wrote to Parker informing him that Captain Sutherland, Elizabeth's husband, now wanted the matter dealt with immediately.[8] Out of time, they quickly planned to get Mrs Carr, the matron at Clifton House/Green, Dr Belcombe's private institution, to go to Ann at Shibden with a constable and persuade her to leave with her. A coach would be waiting to whisk Ann away. Mrs Carr found Ann alone, without even servants, and Ann admitted her. Exactly what she said to Ann can only be guessed at, but it seems likely that to Ann – increasingly anxious, embattled by lawyers and alienated from her family, and isolated from even her servants – the idea of help was welcomed and accepted. She had after all been treated for her mental health by Dr Belcombe many times before, and although they had grown rather estranged, perhaps crucially in Ann's mind, his advice had been sought and approved by her late wife. Did Mrs Carr allude to this? We shall never know.

What we do know is that Parker's plan worked and on 9 September Ann was removed from Shibden Hall. She did not know it, but she would never live there independently again. Ann now found herself removed 'to the neighbourhood of York', under the care of Dr Belcombe. Parker and Captain Sutherland wasted no time travelling to Shibden Hall after Ann's removal, reaching it by 10.30 in the morning. Once inside they found every room 'locked except the little dining room, the hall, the kitchen and the butler's pantry'. When they found Miss Walker's Red Room also locked, they took the door off its hinges to gain access. The idea that Ann made a 'last stand' inside this room before being dragged from it by her family and doctors entered into local legend, as we have seen, Ann was already out of the house when Sutherland and Parker arrived at Shibden.

Inside they found it to be 'filthy ... on the side of the bed there was a brace of loaded pistols ... the shutters were closed ... an old dirty candlestick near the bed was covered in yellow tallow ... papers were strewn about in confusion [and] many handkerchief were splattered all over with blood'. Parker took care to note all these things down in detail, they would be needed by the commission.[9] There was then, as now, believed to be a correlation between the state of a person's living conditions and the state of their mind. The chaos at Shibden Hall was therefore useful evidence to argue for Ann's 'lunacy'.

Ann seems to have travelled easily enough to York, we do not know where she spent her first night, but two days later she was admitted to Terrace House at Osbaldwick. The owners of Terrace House described it as a 'retreat', in reality it was a private asylum, which according to its advertisement was set up for the treatment of 'persons mentally afflicted'.[10] It was managed at the time by Mrs Elizabeth Tose, who was extremely proud of the fact that her establishment had been placed on the Lunacy Commissions list of recommendations for private asylums. All such private asylums had to meet the criteria of the Private Lunacy Asylum Act of 1832 and were inspected regularly. We know from the report of one such inspection that took place just prior to Ann's arrival that the inmates 'appear[ed] in good health and none [were] under restraint'. In addition, 'prayers were said night and morning and as such [the inmates] are fit to attend divine service on a Sunday'. The building was described as 'very airy, clean and comfortable', rooms were generously proportioned, for those who could pay, and the whole environment was welcoming and comfortable.[11]

The treatment plan for patients once there was one of kindness. They could expect a 'bountiful table and rational amusements', which were in keeping with the moral treatment system popular at the time under which patients were treated as largely rational beings.[12] It was a non-restraint treatment, so long as the inmates were not violent, which had been pioneered at an institution called The Retreat near York, founded by William Tuke in the late 1700s. His grandson Samuel had more recently written a book outlining his moral approach to 'lunatic' care which had gone a long way to popularising his more gentle treatment. Patients under his plan were expected to 'dine at table, make polite conversation over tea and do regular chores'.[13] The role of the doctors being largely to promote and supervise such civilised behaviour. One downside of this human approach was that it requires the patients to be constantly supervised. This required large numbers of staff and as such corners were often cut in treatment to reduce this requirement.

Establishments such as Terrace House were regularly inspected and when the commission came in 1843, Ann Walker was listed on the register as an inmate. The admission book entry tells us she was 40 years old at the time, a single spinster, admitted on 12 September on the authority of Mrs Elizabeth Sutherland, her sister. It is also noted that at that time, she had not yet been found to be a 'lunatic' by the commission. Others included on the same page of the register include Jane Skelton, age 30, admitted on the authority of her mother, and Hannah Gordon, age 41, admitted on the authority of her brother. None of these women, however, were present when Ann was admitted. Only one other woman was confined to Terrace House in 1843: Ann Barstow, who had been admitted in March at 66 years of age.[14]

What is not clear from Ann's admission entry is exactly what her symptoms of lunacy were considered to be. Dr Belcombe frequently writes about Ann's 'melancholia', but what is interesting is that on the Terrace House register both the Ann's admitted in 1843 were considered to have had a 'hereditary preposition to insanity',[15] This is an interesting point, as it is unclear how this conclusion was reached, or what proof Ann Walker's family might have offered to support such a conclusion. A genetic inheritance of insanity was considered under the Lunacy Act to be one of the qualifications for an official diagnosis. A family history of insanity was therefore one of the points that was always explored in relation to the patient. It was not unusual for 'insane' aunts, uncles or even distant cousins to be produced for a lunacy trial, but as far as it is known, Ann Walker's family contained none of the above, which raises the question of where this assumption originated. It also raises the possibility that Ann's family were actively seeking additional evidence for any future lunacy commission hearing.

Ann, although now removed from her home and under medical care, was not yet considered of unsound mind and, as such, was still able to legally act on behalf of, and manage, her own interests. She had recently appointed a new legal counsel, Mr Rymer, from the law firm of Murray, Rymer and Murray based in London, who had been acting and advising her in relation to several pressing legal matters concerning Shibden. Mr Rymer was fairly astonished to learn in a letter from Parker that Ann was now under psychiatric care and wrote that although he had found Ann Walker to be 'eccentric' he had seen no evidence of madness.

By October, however, this had all changed; he had requested and been granted three interviews with Ann at Terrace House and these meetings radically changed his opinion of her health and abilities. So much so that he considered her from this point on totally unfit to manage her own concerns.

What did Ann do or say to so radically alter his opinion? Sadly we can never know, they were private meetings and the only records from this time suggest she was suffering from severe melancholia but nothing more. That Ann was experiencing melancholia was nothing new, and there is earlier evidence that Ann had previously feared it would at some point overwhelm her. Feeling her illness to be serious she had, many years earlier, spoken to her wife's lawyer, Jonathan Gray, as to what would happen if her 'indifferent health' should prevent her from carrying out her duties as a landowner. All of which begs the question as to what extent Ann was willing to consent to the arrangements her family was now making.

Whatever Ann said, Rymer immediately wrote to Elizabeth informing her that Ann should in his opinion now be regarded as 'totally unfit to manage her own affairs and that she would not now be able to avoid the Lord Chancellors (lunacy) Commission'.[16] There was after all, he went on, a large amount of money and property involved and for Ann's sake as well as everyone else's, the affair had to be dealt with firmly and correctly to avoid 'exposure or waste of money and property'.

Elizabeth was upset by his letter but not shocked, and she sent a letter to Parker to authorise him to give evidence to Rymer's law firm, in order to prepare a petition for the Lord Chancellor so that he might grant them permission to involve the Commission to determine Ann's state of mind once and for all. Ann's sister and brother-in-law now determined that Ann was going to be formally and officially assessed by the newly formed Lunacy Commission, an official procedure through which the Chancellery would be able to monitor both her health and any actions taken by her estate, meaning that her guardians would be monitored and not simply able to assess her money freely. It seems that in this matter her family were determined to act in a way that offered Ann the most protection.

Ann seems to have been completely unaware that this process was underway. She clearly knew she was not considered well but there is no evidence she was aware that things had gone quite so far in the opinion of her family and friends. Ann still had access at this point to both money and legal professionals but she did not act. Whether this was because she was being kept largely in ignorance of the legal process, or due to her health, we can never know.

The legal request was drawn up quickly and signed by Captain and Elizabeth Sutherland, stating that:

> The said Ann Walker now is and for sometimes past hath been so far deprived of her reason and understanding as to render her altogether unfit or unable to giver herself or manage her affairs as by the affidavits hereunto annexed appears. Your petitioners therefore pray your lordship that a Commission in the nature of a Writ de Lunatico Inquirendo may issue to enquire of the lunacy of the said A.W.[17]

Attached were numerous affidavits which contained the evidence amassed, including witness statements, doctors accounts and records of actions undertaken by Ann. The Lord Chancellor responded quickly, given the nature of the estate involved, and it was determined that Ann's lunacy commission hearing would be held at the Royal Oak hotel, Halifax. The Royal Oak was a well known local landmark, built in 1809 to serve people travelling on the newly built railway, and was close to Brighouse Railway station for ease of access. Twenty-four jurors were assembled for the hearing, and they were required to be 'honest men' who lived locally to the proposed lunatic; because the estate in Ann's case was so large these jurors would have been selected from a special list of suitable candidates and paid 1 guinea each for their trouble. Back in York, sitting and taking tea, Ann was left in the dark. She should have been informed by letter that an enquiry was taking place, but it appears that Ann was issued with no such notice.

Rymer opened the commission by stating that, 'A more perfect evidence of unsound mind [cannot] I think be imagined' than in the case of Ann Walker.[18] He went on to calmly produce doctor and witness testimony, which collectively painted a picture of a woman deeply troubled and who had lost her grip on reality to the point of insanity. Ann, they said, was a woman plagued by religious mania, and a melancholy that years of treatment had failed to resolve. More than that she was no longer willingly accepting their help, and in refusing to do so was threatening her own financial security and the stability of her estates. The jury also met with Ann, as was their duty under a law which clearly stated that the proposed lunatic must be examined in all but the most dangerous of circumstances. The precise nature of these examinations in Ann's case is not known, but they would almost certainly have spoken to her alone, observed her interactions with others as well as talking to her doctors personally. To a woman who was largely unaware and unprepared, the shock of this must have been great. There is, however, no hint of mistreatment or mismanagement outside of the missing legal notification, nor were Ann's circumstances unusual; although lunatic hearings could be opposed in reality they rarely were.

Out of the twenty-four jurors who heard Ann's case, seventeen declared her to be insane and seven objected; there was, therefore, some doubt as to the verdict but it didn't matter. Ann had been certified by the majority as a lunatic of unsound mind and a document certifying the fact was issued by the Commission and backdated to 15 October 1841.[19]

Ann's fate was now sealed and she would never again be allowed to manage her own affairs; instead, a committee would now do this on her behalf. Ann would not be able to choose where she lived, nor live independently. From this moment on she had no power of decision even over her own person.

For the rest of her life Ann would remain a 'lunatic'.

Ann's fate has traditionally been met with outrage by modern readers and viewed as the wrongful imprisonment of a woman who was unwell, not mad – and they would be right, but that is a modern judgement with the wealth of knowledge and understanding we as a society now possess regarding mental health. Ann's doctors, we must remember, simply did not have the knowledge or the skills to help her.

The society in which she lived had already condemned and mistrusted her as a single, financially independent woman, who not only had rejected marriage to a man with all the protection it would have offered her, but who had actually followed her heart and instead chosen a marriage – unlawful, but still in her mind sanctified – to a woman. This transgression both made her 'mad and bad' by contemporary thinking, and all of those involved believed they were acting in Ann's best interests. There is no doubt that Ann was genuinely unwell and struggling to cope. That we now judge their actions to have been misguided in a modern-day context should not detract from the nature of that intention.

Ann could not, or would not, speak for herself at the commission that was to take away her autonomy and her freedom. Earlier in her life her brother-in-law or cousins had spoken for her, later in life her wife, Anne Lister, took on that role. It is through Anne Lister's now infamous diaries that we see Ann most clearly, but never before have we heard Ann speak for herself. Yet in her diary, she has plenty to say. It is time we listen to Ann and let her speak for herself.

Chapter 2

Lustum perficito nihil timeto – 'Do what is right and fear nothing'[1]

Ann Walker was born on 20 May 1803 to John Walker and his wife Mary (née Edwards). Ann was Mary's fourth child, she had already given birth in 1799 and 1801 to daughters Mary and Elizabeth respectively, and in 1798 she also bore a son, William, who died at 21 days old. A victim of infant mortality rates that saw one in three infants die before their fifth birthday.[2] Mary was therefore experienced in childbirth by the time she went into labour with Ann, but this did not protect her from the dangers inherent with it in the 1800s. There are few reliable records concerning maternal mortality prior to the later eighteenth century but estimates place the number at around 20 per cent, making childbirth by far the most common cause of female death. Death in childbirth at the time was generally caused by a form of Puerperal pyrexia, an infection of the placental bed and often caused by attendants. As early as the 1770s, physician Alexander Gordon had advocated hand washing, the burning of women's bloody bed clothes after delivery and the fumigation of rooms, but few listened.[3] Haemorrhage, due to infection, placenta previa or the failure of the placenta to deliver fully were other threats, as was pre-eclampsia, the diagnosis of which, without the ability to take blood pressure, would not be possible for nearly a hundred years. A combination of all four meant that the novelist Jane Austen would lose four sisters-in-law to childbirth in the same era.[4]

Yet for all its risks, childbearing was considered to be the natural female condition; by bearing children Mary was doing her duty, by her husband, her family and society.[5] Prior to the 1730s, if births were attended at all it was almost almost exclusively by midwives, but from the 1730s more male physicians took on this role. Partly this was due to 'fashion and forceps': surgery was becoming more and more fashionable just as forceps were created in the 1730s, and the combination of the two meant that a male birthing practitioner assumed a position of high status. As a result, from 1750–1800, more men established themselves as proper attendants for births. At the time of Ann Walker's birth, therefore, more options were available to women than in previous centuries, but the majority of deliveries were still either unattended or attended by a local midwife. Not just because of the expenses associated with medical treatment, but also because there was still a deep-seated trust in female midwives that was not easily superseded by 'trained' male doctors.

We do not know who attended Mary at Ann's birth, but it seems likely that a midwife was present as would have been usual for a woman of her class. When Mary Wollsencraft had gone into labour six years earlier, her husband wrote that she was 'taken in labour … attended at home by a midwife'.[6]

In 1803 natural childbirth was the only option, and it would remain so until 1847 when Dr James Simpson first used chloroform.[7] The only form of pain relief available to women like Mary was opium, usually given in the form of the draught laudanum. Following Ann's birth Mary would have had a lying-in period, which would have lasted for up to six weeks.[8] The medical view at the time was that an extended period of rest was necessary to help protect women from postnatal dangers. The truth of the matter though is that the close confinement that many women endured postnatally left them open to infection. Doctors such as the reformist Charles White were beginning to oppose a claustrophobic confinement during which 'by the heat of the chamber amid the breath of so many people the whole air is rendered foul and unfair for respiration'. Change however was slow and it was probably in a hot, closed-off chamber that Mary rested.[9]

Ann was born at Cliff Hill, a mansion that was part of her family's Lightcliffe estate. Her father, John Walker, is mentioned as being 'of Cliff Hill' in newspaper articles either side of her birth in 1799 and 1805.[10] Mary Walker was 39 years of age at the time of Ann's birth, which would not have been considered unusual in an age where the idea of contraception, or sexual abstinence, was seen as an affront to God. Mary had been 35 when she had her first child, quite old by the standards of the time, and the fact she successfully came through childbirth on several occasions speaks to her overall health as well as to the privilege of her position in society – she would have had access to good food, sanitary conditions and clean water. As the baby Ann was her parents' third daughter, it is safe to assume that her gender was a disappointment. Sons were the means by which a family's future would be assured. Daughters were often viewed less favourably as both mouths to feed and, in the future, a draw on the family resources. The mercurial Branwell Brontë is the perfect example of the hopes that were instilled in male heirs, especially when there were a multitude of women to support.[11]

If Ann's sex made Mary and John feel a pang of disappointment, they would nonetheless have been thrilled that Mary had safely come through childbirth and that this infant was alive and strong.

At the time of Ann's birth, a book for nursery maids suggested that a new baby be 'very comfortably laid upon a cushion, where it can be in no danger of falling', and that it should be 'constantly attended by someone to divert and cheer it if necessary'.[12] Ann had the advantage of being born in the spring, avoiding the biting Yorkshire winter. The autumn/winter of 1802–3 had proved unusually wet with the Commons chamber stating that the 'harvest was unfavourable owing to bad weather'.[13] Parliament, however, had more important things to discuss than the weather; just a few days after Ann's birth the Napoleonic Wars began when France refused to withdraw from Dutch Territory.[14]

The baby Ann was descended on both sides from industrious and enterprising Yorkshire families. Her mother was the daughter of John Edwards (b. 6 February 1737). John had been born in Birmingham, and as a young man was full of ambition; he began to operate as a merchant and at some point became friends with Joshua Hudson, an ironmonger of Halifax. Joshua Hudson was a friend of the Lees family who owned Lower Willow Hall, and they employed John, who moved to Halifax to work at their cotton mill at Sowerby Bridge. While there, John met and married Samuel Lee's daughter, Elizabeth. He was a man on the rise and this is clearly seen when in 1769 he was chosen to attend an official enquiry called by the Marquess of Rockingham to discuss a local criminal case: the murder of William Deighton.[15] William Deighton had been an excise officer sent to Halifax to investigate a group of coiners. One of these coiners turned the king's evidence and betrayed the group, leading to one David Hartley being arrested. In revenge, his brother Isaac offered a reward of £100 for anyone who killed Deighton. Deighton was duly 'fired upon by a person or persons unknown' and killed. The crime drew national attention and the government was outraged; Rockingham, the Lord Lieutenant for the West Riding, was sent to see that justice was served. John Edwards was present at the enquiry which saw David Harley sentenced to be hanged at Tyburn; such an appointment speaks to the regard in which John Edwards was held.

John and his wife Elizabeth went on to have six children, Mary being born in 1763. To accommodate his family John built Pye Nest house, designed by the architect John Carr on land he bought from Japhet Lister.[16,17] John's cotton spinning business was increasingly prosperous and he was rapidly becoming one of Halifax's foremost citizens. He served as Justice of the Peace for Yorkshire and was a leading subscriber to the Leeds Infirmary. In 1806 he hosted William Wilberforce, MP for Yorkshire, at Pye Nest, who was there to speak to a crowd at Halifax Piece Hall.[18] Wilberforce was greeted enthusiastically by the cheers of 'an immense multitude' of local people, and the following year he would achieve his life's goal and see the Abolition of Slavery Bill passed.

John and Elizabeth's daughter Mary was considered to be an excellent match for John Walker, the second son of a wealthy Halifax family, and Mary Edwards duly married John Walker in 1798.

The Walker family had been living in the district of Lightcliffe, Halifax since at least 1714 when William Walker of Crow Nest is mentioned in the York probate index.[19] However, William was far from the first Walker to live in the wider area. In 1654, William Walker (born 1596) bought Waterclough Hall, a handsome property just to the south east of Halifax dating to 1379. William Walker had two sons, William and Abraham; Abraham lived at Waterclough Hall while William moved to Lower Crow Nest. However, in 1692 there is also a reference to Abraham Walker of Crow Nest, so exactly how the inheritance was split is unclear. It is clear, however, that in 1714 there was a William Walker living at Crow Nest, and that he had a younger brother, Richard. Richard Walker's family took in and adopted one Jack Sharp, a man who, when he lost a legal challenge to inherit the estate over his young cousin, vowed revenge. To this end, in 1778 Jack Sharp built Law Hill a mile down the road, and from there he enticed his cousin to ruin. Law Hill went on to become a school and it was the building in which Emily Brontë would teach in

1837–8, leading many to speculate that Jack was the inspiration behind the Byronic character of Heathcliff.[20]

William Walker married Sarah Mortimer in 1686 and together they had five children. Of these children the eldest son, William, married Elizabeth Haigh of Honley in 1708. Elizabeth was the daughter of wealthy mill owner George Haigh and she brought to her marriage several mills as her dowry. The wool trade was the basis of the Walker and Edwards' family fortunes. During the eighteenth century the output of cloth from the West Riding of Yorkshire equalled that of any other area in England.w By the time of Ann's birth in 1803, the cloth manufacturing districts of Leeds, Bradford, Halifax, Huddersfield and Wakefield had taken shape with families like the Walkers leading the way in production.

It would be wrong to assume that everyone was making or manufacturing cloth the same way though. By the time of Ann's birth a number of separate industries had developed within the Yorkshire textile industry and had begun to transform the industry and landscape. An important distinction in relation to Ann's story is that between the manufacturer of wool and of worsted, the Walkers were primarily woollen manufacturers. Wool involved the bulk cross-meshing of fibres which traditionally required the cloth to be 'fulled', as was the case in the mill at Sowerby. Worsted manufacturer, meanwhile, was a more recent development that involved longer stapled wool and the additional straightening out of the fibres prior to spinning a finer yarn. For practical purposes the finer Worsted fabric could not be produced on the hand jenny, and required mechanised spinning on machines.[21] Worsted fabric was generally associated with merchants who had capital to invest. A more fashion-conscious market hastened the development of worsted and by the turn of the nineteenth century, more and more mills in the area were being converted from cotton spinning to worsted manufacture. It was against this backdrop of investment and industry that families such as the Walkers and Edwardses, as well as other related families such as the Rawsons and Priestleys, had made – and would continue to make – their fortune.

Together William and Elizabeth had four children: Elizabeth 1710, Sarah 1711, William 1713, and Haigh 1714, who were all baptised at the local Eastfield Chapel. The chapel was built in 1529 on land donated by local landowner Richard Rooks; suffering damage in the Reformation, it was repaired in 1598. In 1680 it was endowed for baptisms and burials and by 1714 the churchwarden for the chapel is listed as being 'William Walker for Crow Nest'.[22] It was his eldest son William (b. 1713) who inherited Crow Nest, and in the 1770s he funded the building of St Matthews Old Church, the church in which Ann would be baptised, on the site of the Eastfield chapel. William brought the timber for the church from the Baltic, to use both for the church roof and for the refurbishment of Crow Nest and Cliff Hill, which he had recently acquired. It is possible that he went to the Baltic to personally supervise the timber selection, and it was one of the first large loads to travel on the Aire Calder Navigation canal system. It is a testament to the family's wealth that William was able to afford such an undertaking. This William Walker was Ann's grandfather, though she would never know him as he died in 1786. He was married twice, his first wife Mary Wainhouse had died after only a few years of marriage. His second was Elizabeth Caygill, whom he married on 6 November 1746. Elizabeth was from a very wealthy family indeed, and she brought some of her family's fortune to her marriage. Her brother, John Caygill, was an extremely wealthy wool merchant who owned most of Halifax and gave the land and money in order that the Piece Hall might be built.[23] William and Elizabeth were therefore very wealthy, and when William's father died, as the eldest son he inherited the Walker Lightcliffe estates, meaning that they became wealthier still.

All this meant that they were well able to support their growing family which consisted of two sons, William (b.1749) and John (b. 1753) alongside three daughters, Mary (b.1747) Elizabeth (b.1750) and Ann (b.1757.) The eldest son, William, never married, but he inherited the bulk upon the death of his father in 1786, and it was his younger brother John who was to become Ann's father.

Mary and Ann Walker never married, becoming Ann's sometimes irritating, sometimes beloved Aunts, but Elizabeth did. In 1776 she married John Priestley, and they went to live near Sowerby Bridge. It seems that the unmarried siblings William, Mary and Ann lived at Crow Nest, whose rebuilding William undertook in the mid-1770s. He had been so impressed by Pye Nest that he asked that architect Thomas Bradley replicate the design.[24] Meanwhile, William's younger brother John and his wife Mary went to live at Cliff Hill, the house in which they were residing when Ann was born.

Chapter 3

3 Girls and a Boy

The baby Ann was baptised on 1 July 1803 in St Matthews church.[1] Baptism was, for most of the population at the time, a key Christian rite instituted by Christ for human salvation. For Ann, her journey with Christianity which began that day was one that would have a profound influence on her life.

Ann was born at a time when views about childhood were in a state of flux. A hundred years earlier the puritanical view that humans were born into sin as a consequence of man's 'fall' had been the prevalent one, and led to the belief that childhood was a perilous journey. Children had been viewed as miniature adults to be influenced by harsh instruction in which the focus should be the salvation of the soul. By 1800 however, all this had begun to change, largely due to the philosopher Jacques Rousseau, whose views became increasingly widespread throughout the 1800s. His book *Emile*, published in 1762, not only rejected the view of original sin but also maintained and promoted the view that children were innocent, and only ever became corrupted by their experiences of the world.[2] Rousseau's views soon found their way into works all across Europe. Artists like William Blake and William Wordsworth picked up on this theme and created works such as Blake's *Songs of Innocence and of Experience* that were also widely reproduced, and helped to spread the idea that childhood was a time of innocence, when souls were particularly close to God. It became a stage of life to be celebrated and cherished – at least among those who could afford to do so.[3] For Ann this would have meant that she joined her two older sisters in a nursery that was likely much gentler in its approach than it would have been a generation earlier. Now the prevalent thinking was that children were blank slates and as such many new products tailored to this halcyon age began to flood the market. For children there were now books available, especially written for their entertainment. In around 1744 the celebrated pioneer John Newbury published his first book quaintly called *A Little Pretty Pocket-Book, intended for the Amusement of*

Little Master Tommy and Pretty Miss Polly.[4] The children's book business he founded continued to flourish into the 1800s and at the time of Ann's birth it was booming. Perhaps the infant Ann was given one such book; she would certainly have encountered them alongside dolls, blankets and toy animals.

Very little is known of Ann's childhood aside from the fact that the first six years of it were spent at Cliff Hill, the house in which she was born. The first really significant event in her young life occurred there in her second year when Mary gave birth to a son and heir, John, who joined Ann and her sisters in the nursery. It is important to remember that Ann did not grow up in isolation; along with her siblings, the large Walker and Edwards clans also supplied her with a multitude of cousins. One such cousin was Delia Priestley Edwards, born in 1807. She was the daughter of Ann's uncle Henry Lees Edwards and Thea Priestley. Henry was Mary's sister and the families appear to have been close. Henry, who was director of the Halifax and Huddersfield Union Bank, would later be named as a trustee in the teenage Ann's affairs. Delia was far from Ann's only cousin though; Henry and Lea had ten children, many of whom played roles in Ann's life. Mary also had other siblings; her sister Harriet married John Dyson of Willow Hall and had four children, and another sister Elizabeth married Law Atkinson, who co-owned Atkinson's Mill in Colne Bridge. John also was not short of siblings and his sister Elizabeth, who had married John Priestley in 1776, provided Ann with cousins.

With such an extended family living in close proximity there would have been no shortage of playmates for the young Walker children, and there were also friends to be found outside the family. Friends such as Lydia and Mary Wilkinson, who were the daughters of the Reverend Robert Wilkinson, the curate of Lightcliffe. Lydia and Ann became early and lifelong friends, and Ann had two older sisters for companionship. Sibling relationships are often overlooked by biographers yet it has been well established that they play one of the most important roles in a child's formative years.[5] Elder siblings are the means by which behaviour is learnt and copied, they are often looked to for affection as well as being playmates. Younger siblings are often the target of intense affection or indeed intense rivalry. Ann's earliest relationships would therefore have been formed with her siblings. Mary was 4 when Ann was born and Elizabeth 2, and as they were so close in age it seems likely they would have shared rooms, and beds, as well as the nursery. Later in life Ann would recall that she had been made to walk very early, something that she blamed her back pain on. Perhaps her impatient elder siblings had held her up, dragging her around as they played.

When Ann was 6 years old John Walker's elder brother died and he inherited a large sum of money. Ann's parents had not been poor initially, but this inheritance greatly improved all of the children's prospects as well as their day to day lives. The most obvious consequence of this inheritance is that the family moved into Crow Nest. This was the mansion her grandparents had rebuilt in the 1770s and existing photos show us that it was a large, symmetrical building in the classical style. Thirteen windows were cut into the front facade which would have flooded the interior with light. To reach Crow Nest, Ann would have travelled down the Coach Road, a winding lane flanked by foliage. According to local legend this lane is haunted by a white lady and headless horseman, who appear at midnight on clear nights. Once through the gates the house was approached down a long drive, past manicured lawns and it was flanked by two large wings, as well as cut paths and beautiful flower beds. Cottages stood a little distance away, home to the servants and estate workers. Ann would have already been familiar with the house, having visited her uncle and aunts there, but did she feel a pang when moving? The answer seems to have been yes, for although she grew to like Crow Nest, it was to Cliff Hill that she felt a lifelong attachment.

Ann's father John Walker is an enigmatic figure; he was well respected locally, but perhaps a tantalising clue to his character appears in Anne's Lister's diary where she writes that William Priestley told her in 1822 that John Walker was a spoilt 'madman' who 'blackguarded his wife and daughters'.[6] Much has been made of John as the 'evil' that cast a long shadow over Ann's early life, but it seems that jealousy was behind William Priestley's blackening of John's character, and Ann herself tells us that her father was a kind man.

John's inheritance was also more than sufficient for all his children to be educated in any manner that he and Mary wished. We know that all the Walker children were indeed educated, though how and where Ann received her education is unclear. Since the 1790s the education of girls and women had become an issue that was increasingly on people's minds. A changing society and social pressures were beginning to give credence to the views of campaigners such as Mary Wollsencraft, that equality of education was, or could become, the means by which they gained independence.[7] Alongside this however, the conformist view that men were the breadwinners while women managed the domestic sphere was beginning to become more and more entrenched, with many believing that women simply did not need much of an education to fulfil their role in society. As a consequence of this we see women at the time, 'increasingly and generally excluded from public life and were expected to concentrate their attention on their domestic responsibilities which were being increasingly viewed as moral duties'. [8] As such, the early 1800s is sometimes seen as a period during which female education actually suffered as families stopped educating their daughters alongside their sons. Girls were increasingly being educated separately and in different subjects.

John and Mary would therefore have followed convention at the time and set out to provide Ann and her sister with a typical female education, designed to prepare them for their future roles as wives and mothers. This would typically have included such subjects as reading, writing, French, needlework, drawing and music. Basic arithmetic, geography, and history would be offered at various levels for girls and offered alongside lessons in etiquette, social graces and household management. Such an education would also have been deeply rooted in religious teaching and worship. Regular church attendance was very much expected of all citizens and the Walkers attended like clockwork, with the family maintaining a pew at St Matthews as befitted their social status.[9]

Ann was certainly educated in all of these subjects, but it is not known if she or Elizabeth attended a school. For girls of Ann's social class there were two options available for their education, they would either attend a girls' 'dame' school, which were usually boarding schools, or be educated by a governess and tutors at home. We know that in the York area at the time there were many schools set up for this purpose, such as Aldwark National School which opened in York in 1813 and was the first of its kind for girls.[10,11] It proved popular and by 1819, 233 girls were enrolled there. We know that Anne Lister attended a 'dame' school, but we also know that Anne regarded Ann's 'new' self-made money and corresponding social class as inferior to her own position as a member of the ancient landed gentry. Such distinctions seem meaningless today, but they would have had a tangible social effect that was reflected in spheres such as education. There was a social distinction, acknowledged or otherwise, and so we cannot assume that because Anne attended school, Ann did also.

Yet John and Mary Walker were ambitious for their children. Ann's brother John almost certainly went to a local boarding school before he later enrolled at Brasenose College, Oxford, in January 1822 at the age of 17.[12] He therefore must have received an education that made him capable of assuming such scholarship.

Given Ann's significant accomplishments it does seem likely that she, Mary and Elizabeth at least had a governess. We know that Ann's close friend Catherine Rawson had one, a Miss Holmes, as did the Norcliffe sisters, whose former governess Miss Fryer later opened a school in Leeds.[13,14] While Jane Eyre immediately comes to mind for most people as being the stereotypical nineteenth-century governess, in reality at the time many governesses came from a background of breeding and privilege but had been forced to seek 'respectable' employment by circumstances. The range of experience of governesses was vast; some were treated as part of the family and paid as much as £200 a year by aristocratic families.[15] Such positions were naturally much sought after and on 17 September 1819 Anne Lister records that one of her acquaintances was offered such a position when 'Miss Merienne the Ricket governess ... had the fortune of being summoned by her grace the duchess of Cambridge' to take up a position.[16] More usually though, governesses found themselves working for families such as the Walkers or Rawsons, where they would have been paid about £20 a year, which, while not being a fortune, was a decent wage.

The increasing availability of books and resources available to young women also made a governess's training and life easier. Ann certainly would have had access to educational books. Isaac Dalby's *A Course of Mathematics*, Webster's *Mechanical and Chemical Philosophy*, Neilson's *Greek Idioms, Leçons de l'histoire and Gibbon's History* were all popular study books at the time, and on 30 May 1818 Anne Lister had spent the afternoon reading Gibbon before Mrs Walker of Crow Nest called interrupting her, perhaps she recommended that she bought the book for her daughters.[17]

If Ann did have a governess, one possible candidate is a Miss Bramley, because in 1823 Ann's mother was searching for a new governess position for her. Miss Bramley was an acquaintance of Anne Lister but frustratingly she never specifies whether Miss Bramley was a governess to the Walker girls, only that it was Mary who was seeking her new employment. Anne was, however, happy to help Mary and promised to 'mention Miss Bramley to my friends as being in want of a situation'; it was a promise that Anne kept and she mentioned the fact in a letter she wrote the same day to Isabella Norcliffe.[18] Ann's mother and Anne exchanged many letters on the subject and on 28 May 1818 Anne visited Willow Field and finding Mary there she 'mentioned the contents of Miss Marshes letter about Miss Bramley', who had written to her that Mrs Thompson of Sheriff Hutton had been asking for Anne's opinion. Indeed, the only opinion we have of Miss Bramley is Anne's and she describes her as being 'as clever as a girl at 16 or 17, when I spent ten days in the same house with her that she was at that time amiable and certainly like a gentlewoman'; she was not, however, very impressed with her grammar.[19] Mary Walker was happy to help Miss Bramley when she needed assistance and went to some trouble to do so, which does suggest a fairly close relationship; however, the fact that Mary does not provide Miss Bramley with a reference herself likely indicates that she was in fact a friend or acquaintance rather than a former employee. The task of providing a reference was left to a Miss Hoyle and Anne Lister, who writes on 30 May 1818 that 'Mrs Walker (Crow Nest) called about 5 and sat 1/2 an hour to talk over what I should say about Miss Bramley, Miss Hoyle [also] recommends her.'[20] Anne later burns the letters she and Mary wrote at this time so the precise nature of Miss Bramley's role in Ann's life is sadly likely to remain a mystery.

If the Walker girls did indeed have Miss Bramley as a governess, then the timing of her departure for a new position would make sense. By 1818 Ann would have been 15, the age at which a young woman was expected to take her education under her own advice and the employment of tutors was increasingly expected to be used in place of a governess to advance the basic understanding that had been imparted by her.

If Ann did not have a governess, perhaps she was privately tutored; there were many such teachers around. Both Anne Lister and Catherine Rawson received lessons from the Reverend Samuel Knight – who taught

Arithmetic, Mechanics, Geometry, Rhetoric, Greek and Latin.[21] We know that he taught many young women in the narrow world of Halifax society. Catherine Rawson had 'been 5 years with Mr Knight – seldom missed a day'.[22] Frustratingly, there is once again no mention of Ann or Elizabeth Walker having been tutored by him, but it does indicate the options that would have been available to them. Catherine Rawson was, in 1818, of a similar age to Ann and had just finished reading 'Demosthenes and was now reading Anacreon', given that they were very much of the same social circle it is likely that Ann studied along similar lines.[23]

Ann loved books and reading. Popular books at the time included Lord Byron's *Childe Harold's Pilgrimage* (published from 1812–1818) – although to what extent Byron was thought suitable reading for a respectable young lady is open to debate. Leigh Hunt's *The Story of Rimini* was also published in 1816 and Ann would have been the perfect age to be swept away by his tale of Francesca de Rimini; likewise the works of Shelley, Keats, and Walter Scott were very popular at the time. Other books, less well known today, would also have been available to Ann; novelists such as Anne Hatton, who under the name 'Anne of Swansea' wrote fourteen novels between 1810 and 1831, were wildly popular and sold large numbers of copies, feeding the popular taste for romantic, gothic fiction. Such was the Walker sisters' enthusiasm for reading that when Ann was 17 she and Elizabeth raised the idea of starting a book society, as 'it was so long before they could get proper new works from the Halifax library'.[24] The idea was that there would be twelve subscribers who each paid 'one guinea per annum each, the books to be disposed of every year to the highest bidder of the subscribers'. We cannot be sure whether Ann and Elizabeth's scheme ever got off the ground but we can determine from this that not only did they read excessively but that they were frequent callers at the Halifax library. There were also numerous bookshops for Ann to frequent in Halifax. Bookselling in Halifax dates from the late seventeenth century, when several book shops were recorded as having been in business and *Baines' History, Directory and Gazetteer* in 1822 lists eight booksellers, stationers and binders and four book binders.[25] In addition to this, books were frequently bought there by auction; between 1750 and 1781 there were thirty-one book auctions, illustrating the demand for books in Halifax during this time. Perhaps Ann's grandfather attended one to purchase books and begin the lost library that we know existed within the various Walker properties. Halifax was also a place of bibliographical renown due to the presence there of William Edwards booksellers in the Old Market. By 1820 this had a national reputation as bookseller, publisher and binder, so much so that they were able to open a premises in London six years later. In their general catalogue in 1815, Edwards had 7,282 titles, many of which were religious and classical works, but there were also titles covering mathematics, arts, sciences, natural history, maps, history, voyages and travels.[26] Ann would undoubtedly have visited the shop regularly, if not to purchase then to peruse the titles available.

Alongside all this reading, Ann learnt to play the piano very well and she seems to have enjoyed it, happily playing when an adult for the distraction and entertainment of her friends. She also leant to draw and paint, something that she was regarded as being quite skilled at and which she linked to her interest in botany. Ann also began to learn French, and was extremely keen on the subject though she lamented her lack of skill, indeed her French was never fluent, suggesting she did not learn regularly from a young age. Alongside all of this formal education Ann would have learnt sewing and needlework, a necessary skill for any woman regardless of her rank. Ann was taught to cut and sew clothing as well as make repairs. She also learnt to knit, and spent many an evening knitting baby clothes, socks and scarves for the local poor.

Ann's childhood was shattered in early 1815 when, at just 15 years old, her sister Mary died.[27] The loss of her sister must have been devastating for Ann, her confidante, playmate, and the sister she looked up to, was gone. Following Mary's death Ann would have donned black mourning and she would almost certainly have accompanied her sister on her final journey to St Matthew's Churchyard. Of the eight burials listed between that of Mary and the end of February 1815, all but two were those of children. We should not, however, assume that the frequency of such childhood deaths made the loss of children any more devastating for a family. Ann would have been guided to 'find consolation in a humble resignation to God's will', and to view her and Mary's separation as a merely physical one. She would have had faith that they would be reunited in heaven. It does not follow though that such acceptance came easily to a more religious society, as Elizabeth Gaskell would famously write in *Wives and Daughters*, when the squire addresses the loss of his eldest son: 'God's will be done … but it is harder to be resigned than happy people think.'[28]

As she enters her teenage years, Ann begins to feature more frequently in the letters and diaries of her friends and relatives and a picture emerges of her as an intelligent, thoughtful and well educated young woman. There was, however, another aspect to her character that was emerging: she appears to have already been suffering from bouts of the crippling self-doubt and low self-esteem that would plague her throughout her life.

Ann and Elizabeth were both described as being 'sickly' by observers, but it does not follow that they were 'sick' in the way that we understand it today. Strong physical health was more luck than judgement without either vaccinations or antibiotics and many young women suffered from what was then termed 'green or virgin sickness', leaving them pale and weak.[29] People expected young girls to be weak and frail and this often became a self fulfilling prophecy as young ladies sought to conform to this stereotype by staying indoors, out of the sun and taking little food. There is no direct equivalent of this disease today, but it is considered as having corresponded to anaemia and the historian Helen King likens it to certain aspects of anorexia.[30] When Ann and Elizabeth are described as sickly therefore, it does not necessarily have negative connotations, it could merely be telling people that they conformed to the early nineteenth-century feminine ideal.

Chapter 4

Bright Young Thing

On 19 May 1818, the day before her fifteenth birthday, perhaps as a birthday treat, Ann attended a lecture on the courses of the seasons alongside Mrs John Priestley, her mother, sister, Miss Armytage, the two Miss Hudsons, the Miss Listers, the Hipperholme boys and numerous other young men.[1] Such lectures were considered both educational and social occasions at which young people could be seen and admired. Anne was to declare that it was a rather boring evening, but as we shall later see in her journal Ann did not always agree with her – we must not make the mistake when searching for Ann Walker, of assuming that Anne Lister's views were hers. Anne Lister's diary offers us glimpses into Ann Walker's life, but she does not speak for her.

A couple of weeks later on 5 June, Mrs William Rawson, Ann's cousin Mary Priestley and her daughters came to Crow Nest for a dinner at which Ann was present.[2] A dinner at the time for a family of the Walkers' social standing would have been, by our standards, a fairly extravagant affair. Guests would have been seated around a large table in the dining room, which would have been one of the most lavishly decorated rooms in the house. Later photographs of Crow Nest reveal the dining room there to have been large, richly carpeted, with a fireplace and chandelier suspended from the ceiling. The doorways were surrounded by ornate plasterwork, giving an impression of wealth and opulence.[3]

The dinner table would have been 'covered but not crowded.'[4] and the first course would usually have been soup, with chestnut, artichoke, vegetable and white soup all being popular choices. Roast meat would have been served next possibly alongside game, fish or pies. Vegetables would also have been served, often in a rich butter sauce or lightly pickled. A dessert would then be served, of tarts, custards and cakes. Fruit pyramids were extremely fashionable, and Ann loved fruit, especially berries and stone fruit such as apricots or peaches. That June evening there would have been such offerings from the gardens at Crow Nest, with their spacious hot houses. All this would have been followed by treats such as marzipan, considered a good way to round off a meal as sugar was believed to aid digestion. For the same reason a warm sugary, spiced drink at the end of the meal would also feature frequently on menus.

Dressing for dinner was also very much a social convention, and fashions during Ann's teenage years leaned towards classical comfort. She was fortunate in that the period from 1795–1820 was defined by more relaxed and comfortable clothing than those of any decades before or after. Dresses were inspired by neoclassical tastes and often made from soft muslins that clung to the frame. Evening dresses were still fairly comfortable but also often trimmed with lace, ribbons or netting. They were often low cut with short puff sleeves, and women's arms would then be covered by long white gloves. Our Lady of Distinction, however, cautioned that care should be taken and that 'the bosom and shoulders of a very young and fair girl might be displayed without exciting much pleasure or disgust'.[5] Usual colours for a girl Ann's age would have been pinks, whites, blues or lilacs. Ann would have avoided deeper colours which were more often associated with older, married women.

We know that Ann had 'pretty flaxen hair', which she would have worn pinned up, curled and sometimes dressed with flowers or beading. It is curious that in a surviving painting of Ann's sister Elizabeth she has light hair, when hers was said to be darker than Ann's. If the sitter is indeed Elizabeth, then Ann's hair must have been very light indeed.

A week on from that dinner there was a huge storm over Lightcliffe when an 'electric cloud burst over Mr Walker's house between Whitehall and Mr Hudson's ... [it] struck dead a young man of 16, severely injuring a young woman and stupefied for some minutes an old woman'.[6] Ann was afraid of storms and perhaps it was her witnessing or hearing of this incident that contributed to that fear. It was very much the subject of local gossip among Anne Lister's circle and we know that at this time Ann's aunts and cousins were all visitors to Shibden Hall. Ann's family was out and about paying calls on a daily basis in each other's company and Ann herself is rarely glimpsed during these years without either her sister or a friend at her side. One of her closest friends was Miss Rawson, with whom, on 14 July 1818, she spent one of what was no doubt many evenings out socialising.[7]

The focus of that evening was music, and later in August there was a music festival held at Lightcliffe, which we can assume Ann attended. Music was an important part of Halifax life, and Ann's second cousin William Priestley was at the very heart of it. William was the son of Ann's Aunt Elizabeth Priestley and had grown up in the household of his uncle, William Walker, at Crow Nest. He was a renowned musician who played woodwind well and possibly founded the Halifax Choral Society.[8] William had married in 1808 and lived at New House Lightcliffe.[9] He travelled widely and collected musical manuscripts one of which, a manuscript score of Handel's *Judas Maccabaeus*, which has been suggested bears evidence of arrangement by Mozart.[10] William frequently held well attended musical evenings and Ann's regular attendance at such evenings was almost certainly the origin of her musical acumen. Later in life, she is not reticent when forming a judgement on musical performances and had a deep respect for musical talent.

On 10 August 1818 we find Ann once again in company; when she called upon her aunt Mrs Priestley she found both Delia Walker and Anne Lister already there taking tea.[11] She joined them for a time and it is impossible not to wonder what the 15-year-old Ann made of the formidable Miss Lister, who already had a reputation in the neighbourhood as both being eccentric and unconventional.

A week later, 'Mrs Walker (Crow Nest) and the 2 Miss Walkers of Cliff Hill' called at Shibden to inform Anne of the outcome of the Miss Bramley governess saga.[12] She was finally to take a position near Cambridge that had been recommended by the Reverend Charles Hoyle and was to leave 'anytime after Thursday'. If Miss Bramley had been Ann's governess, she must surely have felt a pang at her departure which helped to signal the end of her childhood.

Around this time Ann would also have been entering puberty, with 14 being the average age for a girl's period to begin in the early 1800s.[13] We know that Ann suffered from severe menstrual pain and heavy periods throughout her life which were often accompanied by premenstrual tension. Her periods would not have arrived with the monthly regularity which we have come to expect today. In a pre-antibiotic age, a lack of nutritional understanding, vitamin deficiencies and diseases were much more prevalent, a regular cycle was more an oddity than the norm. As early as 1671 a midwife called Jane Sharp noted that 'sometimes they flow too soon, sometimes too late ... strange things (clots) can be sent from the womb', and sought to understand the reasons .[14] To deal with her bleeding Ann would have worn 'clouts' – handmade menstrual pads beneath her clothing, also called sanitary napkins. Drawers had first made their appearance in 1806 and by the time Ann was a teenager they were beginning to gain in popularity; wearing them helped to hold protection in place.[15] For a woman such as Ann, who suffered from heavy bleeding, there was also the option of a 'tampon or plug [which] may be linen rag, cotton or sponge, in the form of a ball and introduced into the vagina like a pessary ... not introduced more than two inches for fear of inflaming the mouth of the womb which is very sensitive.'[16] Popular physician opinion at the time depicted women suffering from gynaecological issues as either victims of 'hysteria', or entirely unaffected by menstrual hormonal fluctuations. Ann, like most women, fell somewhere in the middle, in suffering from moderate hormonal symptoms and physical pain during her cycle and nor was she alone; Anne Lister's friend Lady Gordon 'had her cousin all day and was rather hysterical', and Miss Hobart was described as being 'very low and nervous [when] had her cousin.'[17,18] Menstruation as a whole was very poorly understood at the time, and the more it was studied the stranger medical understanding seems to be to modern eyes. In 1869 Dr James MacGregor Allan would tell the Anthropological Society of London that menstruating women were 'unfit for great mental or physical labour', advising that they rest and not be allowed to make decisions during such times.[19] It was also thought that menstrual suppression could cause illnesses and as such, women with irregular or erratic periods were often bled to try to induce menstrual bleeding. We now know that the absence of menstrual bleeding is a symptom of diseases such as cancer or tuberculosis rather than a cause, but in the 1800s this was treated as a disease itself. Ann may well have been told therefore, from an early age, that she was unwell.

Ann's teenage years followed a pattern familiar to women throughout England. She rode often and well, she also spent a good deal of time, as all young people do, in cultivating her own friendships and she had many friends that she considered to be close. One of these was Lydia Wilkinson, with whom she was regularly seen. Lydia Wilksinson was seven years older than Ann and she was the fourth daughter of the Reverend Robert

Wilkinson and his wife Sarah Robinson. Robert Wilkinson is described as being 'of Hipperholme' on his marriage certificate, and became the curate of Lightcliffe upon the death of the previous curate in 1782.[20]

Lydia herself had gone to school at Crofton Hall near Wakefield where she became friends with Elizabeth Firth, who would later become Anne Brontë's godmother.[21,22] Elizabeth's diary for 1815 reveals that Lydia enjoyed going to the Assembly Rooms and that she kept up a correspondence with Elizabeth, writing frequently.[23] The average turnaround between their letters was just three days at one point in August, and we can suppose that she extended this diligence to her communications with Ann. Elizabeth's diary also offers us a clue as to what a young woman such as Ann might have been spending her allowance on. Her shopping list for 1818, included a bonnet, white silk, needles, worsted stockings, two pairs of gloves, silk handkerchief, pink ribbon, postage and 'Jaconet muslin'.[24] With her family's large income such fripperies were well within Ann's reach. All young women were encouraged to donate money to charitable causes by the church. In Elizabeth's case that meant donating 3s 6d for 'the collection for the Jews', and 1s 6d for 'the collections for missionaries', and the teenage Ann no doubt followed this example, beginning her lifelong concern in philanthropy.[25]

Ann and Lydia spent a good deal of time together paying calls, taking tea and visiting the library. Lydia's circle of friends were keen on reading novels such as *Pride and Prejudice*, and it seems likely that Ann shared similar reading habits.[26] Ann also was growing increasingly close to Catherine Rawson, her distant cousin, and the two young women frequently visited each other.

Outside of this friendly familial social circle however, the Walkers were treated by some with a certain level of disdain in the local area. They were 'new' money, and money made from trade at that and therefore not to be considered as the equal of the older, landed families of the neighbourhood. Ann's father also suffered from having a reputation for commercial aggression, which was considered distasteful. When his 'great fondness for money made him indifferent to decorum', he found himself somewhat ostracised by society.[27] The Walkers were therefore excluded from intimate circles of women such as Anne Lister. Mary Walker and her daughters, as we have seen, were called upon, but they did not become intimate friends. This distance is clearly seen when, on 1 May 1820, Ann and her mother, sister, coachman and footman were quite frightened when their coach overturned on the way home. They were rescued by the Lister family but although they were kindly offered wine, cloaks and lanterns, they were not invited to stay the evening and nor did the incident lead to a deepening of their acquaintance.[28] 'Their hothouses and footmen could never disguise the vulgar taint of trade', wrote Anne Lister, and this seems to have been the prevalent view of Ann's family.[29]

In around 1820 Ann fell ill, the exact nature of this illness is not specified, nor is it easy to pin down precise dates for its first occurrence, but it led to Ann being regarded as having 'a gradual tendency to mental derangement'.[30] Whether this was a real physical illness leading to psychological trauma, or whether it was a bout of mental illness is not certain. Adolescence is described by the World Health Organisation as a 'uniquely formative time', and one during which a large number of mental health conditions begin to manifest themselves.[31] One theory is that Ann did in fact suffer from a neurological imbalance and that this illness of 1820 was the first manifestation of a condition such as chronic depression or bipolar disorder. Another is that at some point 1820, she suffered from a real and serious physical illness, leading to what we would today term as a near death experience, after which she suffered a crisis of religious faith that shook the very foundations of her world at a crucial stage of childhood. Given that Ann's episodes of mental illness consistently feature 'religious mania' on the natures of life, death and most importantly sin, what we can be certain of is that her faith was of profound importance to her.

Whatever the precise nature of Ann's illness, and we shall never know for certain, she seems to have recovered fairly quickly, although the episode was serious enough to make her the subject of family gossip. It marked the beginning of her family's attitude of overprotectiveness towards her, from now on Ann was to be considered 'delicate'.

Physically Ann was slender but strong, and on 12 June 1821 she ran after a somewhat bemused Anne Lister, who was walking that day along the New Road towards Crow Nest.[32] Ann ran 'herself almost out of breath' in order to catch her, and the women walked together: 'as far as the Lidgate entrance to their [Crow Nest] grounds'. Anne writes that she:

made myself, as I fancied, very agreeable and was particularly civil and attentive in my manner. I really think the girl is flattered by it and likes me. She wishes me to drink tea with them … after parting I could not help smiling to myself and saying the flirting with this girl has done me good. It is heavy work to live without women's society and I would far rather while away an hour with this girl who has nothing in the world to boast and good humour, than not flirt at all.[33]

What can we conclude from this incident? Firstly it is clear that Anne has caught Ann's attention, she would later recall this incident with something like embarrassment at her eagerness to be in Anne's company. It is hard to escape the impression that she had at the back of her mind the desire to know Miss Lister better and impulsively seized the opportunity to speak with her alone when it presented itself. The whole episode conjures an image of Ann having experienced something like a schoolgirl crush, or 'pash' of admiration for an older woman and it made her brave enough to extend an invitation to Crow Nest without the presence of her mother or elder sister. The other inescapable impression of Ann here is that she was happy, laughing and maybe even flirting back. Anne returned to Shibden that night and thought little more of Crow Nest's youngest daughter over the next few years. When she did run into Ann and Elizabeth the following year she was less impressed, described Ann as a 'stupid vulgar girl', and Elizabeth as 'deadly stupid' – neither a fitting epithet.[34] Ann had far more important things to worry about than Miss Lister's opinion of her though, for her world was about to come crashing down.

The year 1823 dawned for Ann much the same as any other with a round of social calls, local lectures, philanthropic works, punctuated by her attendance at the occasional ball. Her world seemed stable and her future predictable. Halifax was undergoing the beginnings of what would prove to be a substantial economic boom, but there were not as yet any dramatic changes to either town or landscape. While locally families such as the Ackroyds were leading the charge towards industrial development by installing worsted power looms as early as 1822, the Walker lands and estates continued as usual, with John Walker reluctant to invest in new technology until its effectiveness had been proven.

For the Priestley family the year did not get off to an auspicious start. In February the counting house at Thorpe Mill, owned by them, was broken into and a number of banknotes were stolen from the safe. John and William Priestly were so incensed that they offered the substantial reward of 100 guineas to anyone who offered information that led to the capture of the thieves.[35] For the Walkers though, the year would soon turn deadly. Sometime in early 1823 Ann's father fell mortally ill, and page 73 of the burial register for St Matthews Lightcliffe records his burial on 29 April.[36] Ann's father was 70 years old, and his death was followed in November by Ann's mother, who died unexpectedly in November, aged 60.[37]

At the age of 19, Ann had lost both of her parents in the space of eight months and must have become used to callers coming up and down the long drive at Crow Nest to pay their condolences. One of which was Anne Lister, who writes that she called to pay her condolences to the 'Walkers of Crow Nest' in the evening following the death of John Walker.[38] There's no mention of Ann, but it is not much of a leap to picture the three Walker women sitting in the parlour at Crow Nest, pale and dressed in black. Ann and Elizabeth perhaps flanking their mother. It was a scene that would be repeated, minus Mary Walker, on 13 November, when Anne called again at Crow Nest 'in consequence of the death of Mrs Walker'.[39]

The Priestleys, Mrs Priestley in particular, rallied around Ann and Elizabeth, helping them to sort out the necessary arrangements and on 20 November Ann, Elizabeth and John made the sad trip up to Lightcliffe in high winds and pouring rain as their mother made her last journey. 'The vault at Lightcliffe was opened' Anne Lister records, and Mary Walker was laid to rest alongside her husband and eldest daughter, before her children, damp and cold, made their way back to Crow Nest.[40]

As eldest son, John inherited his family land and properties but John Walker's will was very complex.[41] With a strict inheritance entail in place the estate passed to John Walker as tenant for life, but there were also to be trustees with the power to administer the trust. Settlements and entails were hugely complex documents, so much so that it was claimed that few people in the whole country had the ability to properly interpret them. Settlement was designed to keep an estate together while still providing for one's children, it was relatively unusual for 'traders' to use an entail, more usually it was the landed gentry with their particular attachment to their ancestral lands that used them. John Walker had gentrified ambitions in life, which manifested in his will. The document itself is forty-eight pages long and full of now outdated and complex legal jargon. The key facts as far as Ann is concerned were that he had entailed the chief of all the Walker property on her brother John, with Henry Edwards of Pye Nest and William Priestley as trustees. John Walker's inheritance included an estate of well over 500 acres of land as well as numerous properties and business interests. John Walker also proved himself a caring father to his daughters. Ann and Elizabeth were each left stocks in the canals, and a capital sum that would be paid to them annually when they were 21 years old. John also added clauses that his daughters' property was for their 'sole and separate use' – it was not for the use of their future husbands. Such care to safeguard his daughters' inheritance was not usual at the time, and perhaps speaks to John's fear that upon his death his daughters would be in the sights of many a fortune hunter – and he would be proved right.

Once the mourning period was over, life at Crow Nest took on a new lease, John was a fun-loving young man with plenty of Oxford friends. In 1825 he held a ball at Crow Nest, which was termed a 'coming of age', and was attended by Ann. Balls in the early 1800s were social affairs, a chance to see and be seen by the neighbourhood. An 1825 engraving in *The English Spy* shows dozens of colourfully dressed men and women dancing at just such a ball. Books such as the 1816 *Companion to the Ballroom* were widely circulated and taught readers both how to dance and how to behave at a ball.[42,43] Balls were regarded as the pinnacle of society and were the highlight of the social calendar. It was also often the scene of a heady courtship at which women could dance with different men, a ball being one of the few places in which the two sexes could both be in close physical proximity and speak freely. We only have to look at the novels of the time to know that they were hotbeds of flirtation, romance and sometimes scandal. They were also dominated by the dancing and at Crow Nest that evening they danced the newly fashionable quadrille. A dance that consisted of a chain of four to six contredanses, and which had been introduced to England by the infamous Lady Jersey.[44] The quadrille was a craze that swept through England, and Ann certainly would have learnt to dance it. It was reported that there was scarcely a woman in the country from countess to kitchen maid that did not know the steps. Typically, a ball would have begun at 9 or 10pm and gone on until 5am. Ann, one can imagine, fell into bed the next morning, happy but exhausted.

Outside of such events the business of managing the Walker estates rolled on, though it seems Ann took little part in it. Her brother also took less part than some had hoped, and by 1828 several buildings had been allowed to fall into disrepair. He was also pulled up for not maintaining Walker social obligations within the neighbourhood.[45]

John's pretty and wealthy sisters, now of perfect marriageable age, soon became, as their father had feared, a target for fortune hunters and by 1828 Elizabeth's eye had fallen on the handsome Captain George Mackay Sutherland of the 92nd Highlanders, His portrait shows a smooth-faced man, with bright auburn hair, sharp eyes, an unsmiling mouth, and wearing the infamous Redcoat of the British Army.[46] Captain Sutherland was born at Uppat House in Scotland in 1798 and was by all accounts a stranger to Halifax.[47] Elizabeth met him at one of the balls now frequently held at Crow Nest and she was quickly smitten. Her family was far less so, to such a degree that Elizabeth at one point felt it necessary to plan to marry him in secret – plans she no doubt shared with Ann. If secrecy had been her intention she was to be disappointed, her uncle Henry Edwards wrote to her that her engagement was 'the common topic of conversion in the neighbourhood'.[48] The focus of this gossip boiled down to one key fact: that George Sutherland had no fortune.

While on a personal level this was true, he was far from being a pauper; Captain Sutherland was one of the heirs of his uncle Robert Sutherland who held great estates in St Vincent which produced large profits thanks to the 400 enslaved people who worked the land there. This steady income would continue until the 1833 Emancipation of Slaves Act severely affected it.[49] The most damning evidence that Captain Sutherland was in fact primarily a fortune hunter can be found among his own surviving papers, which prove that he was very quick to consult lawyers regarding what claim he would have to Elizabeth's inheritance upon their marriage. After many letters back and forth he was eventually told that he could ask her to grant him any of her personal or unentailed inheritance, but her entailed inheritance was another matter. He also tried to persuade Elizabeth to act without her trustees' consent, fearing that they would never grant him access to her money if they could help it. He was quite right, Henry Edwards was deeply concerned about Elizabeth's attachment to him and he spilt a good deal of ink trying to safeguard her fortune as best he could. For despite her father's care, his will failed to protect a large part of Elizabeth's money should she choose to grant it to her husband.

While busy trying to protect Elizabeth, Henry Edwards' attention was also drawn to his younger niece Ann who was once again unwell, plagued by thoughts of her 'wicked life', so much so that her mind was 'warped by religion', her family feared permanently.[50] This time the focus of her family's concern was very much on Ann's mental rather than her physical health and after consulting doctors, Henry Edwards tried to persuade Ann that she should go abroad for a change of air. Was the prospect of change, or maybe even a future marriage that unsettled Ann's mind this time? Whatever the reason her illness kept Ann from going to church for over a year, she remained at home while the rest of the family attended Sunday services.

All of Henry Edwards' efforts to prevent Elizabeth's marriage proved to be in vain, like many a young woman whose head had been turned by an unsuitable young man, opposition only strengthened Elizabeth's resolve and on 29 October 1828 she married him.[51] Ann was well enough to attend and it was the first time Ann had been to church in over a year. Her aunt Ann travelled with her and the day went smoothly. Anne Lister stopped by to have a piece of the bride cake and she recorded that back at Crow Nest Captain Sutherland proved to be rather 'better' than she, or the gossip she had heard, had led her to expect.[52] Elizabeth was to travel to Scotland with her new husband and she would live there for most of her marriage. Within a year she had given birth to her first child. Up near Inverness, surrounded by her husband's family, Elizabeth missed Ann as much as Ann missed her and they wrote to each other constantly.

Elizabeth's departure left Ann the only Walker heiress in Lightcliffe and largely dependent on her family, especially Aunt Ann, for company. She did have one other source of companionship though. A niece of the Priestley's, one Fanny Penfold, had travelled north from her home in Sussex and was now employed as a companion to Aunt Ann, whose health was not strong. Ann and Fanny spent a good deal of time together at Cliff Hill and seem to have become friends, but even as their lives settled down after Elizabeth's departure, change was once again on the horizon and hints of it were to be found in Fanny's heated cheeks whenever John was at home.

Chapter 5

Tragedy

Legend tells that the beautiful church of St Matthew and St Cuthman in Steyning, Sussex, was first founded during the Saxon period when a shepherd boy, who was wheeling his sick mother along in a wheelbarrow with rope around his shoulders to help take the strain, felt the rope break. This boy, Cuthman, believed that this was a sign from God that he was to build a church on the very spot that the rope had broken. There is no evidence today for that Saxon church, but a Norman one was built on the site and on 28 July 1829 it was bathed in summer sunshine. It was the perfect day for a summer wedding and there was quite a party from Halifax who had travelled down to attend. The groom was Ann's brother John, the Walker heir; he was marrying Frances Esther Penfold. Fanny was the daughter of the Reverend John Penfold and his wife Charlotte Jane Brookes.[1] Fanny's aunt, Mary Ann Brookes, her mother's sister, had married Christopher Rawson, connecting them to the Rawson family in Halifax. It is through this connection that Fanny ended up as a companion to Ann's aunt at Cliff Hill, where she met John Walker. Fanny was, like Ann, 26 years old and the two women would have known each other well.

The wedding party consisted of Christopher Rawson's wife, Mary Ann, Fanny's aunt, Fanny's sisters Catherine and Charlotte Penfold, Delia Priestley Edwards, Ann's and John's cousin who, demonstrating the often complex nature of marital and familial relations would, in later life, marry Fanny's second husband, as his second wife. The wedding was also attended by Ann Walker.[2] Unfortunately it is not certain whether it was Ann Walker of Crow Nest or her aunt Ann of Cliff Hill who had travelled down from Lightcliffe. However, given the general age of the party it seems likely that it was indeed Ann who went to her brother's wedding. Especially as she had initially planned to accompany the newlyweds on their honeymoon journey. Ann was close to her brother, referring to him as her 'dear brother John', and maybe they took a moment together to speak and mourn their parents' absence amid the excitement.[3] After the service Ann attended the wedding breakfast, which contrary to its name could take place at any time of day.[4] It simply referred to the first meal the married couple would take together.

At the time it was also customary for a female companion to accompany the newlyweds, and Delia Edwards stepped into that role after Ann turned it down. By the 1820s honeymoons were becoming hugely fashionable and popular destinations included Rome, Venice or Paris. The Grand Tour had made such destinations increasingly desirable as reports flooded English newspapers of sunny climes and romantic ruins. Taking a Grand Tour was very much the fashion for wealthy young men, who would travel around Europe when they came of age at around 21. Accounts of these tours, such as William Bexford's *Dreams, Waking Thoughts and Incidents* were very popular.[5] John was in the fortunate position of being able to afford to take such a journey without financial strain.

Ann doesn't seem to have regretted not accompanying them, maybe feeling that her duty lay with her Aunts, Aunt Ann in particular, who had just been deprived of her companion. Her eagerness for travel a few years later, however, was perhaps a consequence of not accompanying her brother on his journey.

Ann returned north and the newlyweds set off at the beginning of August and by the 21st they had reached Paris, where John went to the bank Laffitte and drew a draft there for the value of £280.[6] In today's money such a sum was worth a huge £31,000, giving a good indication of just how much money John had to spend. At the time it was usual to use circular letters to obtain money when travelling abroad. The letter of credit was one of the oldest ways of transporting money and had been developed by European bankers just prior to the Renaissance when travel was increasing exponentially. John and Fanny's drafts were all drawn on the Glyn, Mills and Co, Bank on Lombard Street, London, and were all paid back by July 1830 from his bank account in Rawson's Halifax.[7] By 31 August, the honeymooners were in Basel and a month later they were in Geneva, before travelling on to Livorno.[8] From Livorno they travelled south making for Florence, that city where 'everything seems to be coloured with mild violet like diluted wine'.[9]

Earlier that year the city had witnessed the birth of Florence Nightingale, and was part of the Grand Duchy of Tuscany which had replaced the Florentine Republic in 1569. It was ruled by King Leopold II who was an unpopular but liberal ruler and his reign had seen an influx of foreign visitors who had heard of his city's beauty and were eager to see for themselves the dome of Santa Maria de Fiore. Naples though was John and Fanny's destination and they travelled on through a chilly December via Milan. Upon arrival at Naples they would have been greeted, then as now, by the sight of mighty Vesuvius rising up into the sky. The volcano was a subject that had caught the public imagination during the 1820s and many travelled to see its steaming crater.

Largely due to the city's crucial role as a port in the Mediterranean, it was home at the time to a thriving British diplomatic and social community. For aristocrats such as Sir George Talbot and his two daughters it was the ideal residence, with frequent visitors, beautiful scenery and long hot summers. The journal of his daughter Marianne paints a vivid portrait of the city's effervescent social life: Naples was the place to be seen.[10]

We know from Ann's diary that John and Fanny first went to a hotel but as they 'could only have a back room' they tried to take a house.[11] After having no luck with that either they took rooms at the Riviera di Chiaia 276, which had 'a good view of the bay'. It was a lovely location near to the Villa Comune di Napoli, gardens which had been built in the 1780s by Ferdinand IV. Unfortunately John was not able to enjoy the location for long as at some point after their arrival he fell ill. Initially his illness doesn't seem to have caused particular concern, but this changed when he worsened and on 18 January Caroline Walker records that 'five physicians attended him at the hotel'.[12] Naples in 1829 had a thriving medical community, but its position as a centre of learning was undermined by the fact that the city was also large, overcrowded and poor, with outbreaks of diseases such as cholera frequently being reported. In addition, people suffering from tuberculosis or 'consumptions' were sent to resorts such as Naples in the hope that the change of air would aid their recovery.

Back in the Walker's apartment the 'five physicians' all pronounced that John was expected to 'recover with care', perhaps they bled him or left him with laudanum.[13] Given the speed of John Walker's decline there are several possibilities for his illness, one being that he had contracted cholera. Cholera was ever present in the city and his 'rapid decline' perhaps has echoes of the infamous masked ball in Paris two years later, as recorded by the German poet Heinrich Heine, where an outbreak of cholera led to half the guests dying almost before they left the ballroom.[14] Tuberculosis is another possibility and in support of this Ann later makes a reference to her brother having been 'afflicted with delicate lungs'.[15] If John was already tubercular and he encountered a different strain upon arrival in Naples then it may have reactivated the disease. It was not unheard of for a patient to die quickly if this was the case, however it is doubtful that if he were coughing up blood any physician would have predicted his recovery, even with their treatment. There is also the fact that neither Fanny nor Delia caught it, neither would go on to display signs of the disease and we know that John and Fanny were sleeping together in the fullest sense of the word right up until John's illness. This does not discount tuberculosis as the cause entirely, some people have a natural immunity. Charlotte and Patrick Brontë, for example, would escape the infection that ravaged their family with frightening efficiency; but equally, it does cast serious doubt. It could be that John simply succumbed to one of the many Mediterranean fevers or winter infections such as typhus that ran rampant during the European chill prior to the advent of antibiotics.

Whatever the cause, by 3pm on 19 January John Walker was dead: he had been married less than six months. If Catherine's account is accurate, then Fanny was in the room at the time, reading a letter from Ann that John had just finished looking over, when he died. They had only been in Naples for three weeks, and now John would never leave.

The first thing to be considered was the funeral, and a death certificate was issued the day after John's death in swirling Italian lettering it states that 'Signore Giovanni Walker of Halifax, Yorkshire, England, 25 and of wealthy profession … husband of Francisca Penfold, 23' died, 'at his residence Riviera di Chiaia 276,' and that the British Consulate was informed.[16] John was buried in the Old Protestant Cemetery within the grounds of the Santa Maria Della Fede church. Simple in its form with a high altar dating to 1741, Fanny would have entered beneath a painting of the Virgin Mary and a gleaming white cross which mounts the typically eighteenth-century facade. Set in the midst of the city it must have felt a very long way from the rolling wild green of Yorkshire.

John's death left his widow and cousin, for although there is no mention of Delia it is assumed that she was still with Fanny, practically alone in Naples. The day after his death Fanny went to the Messieurs

Falconnet and Co. bank and drew a draft for £150, presumably to pay for the doctors, funeral and other expenses.[17] She would remain in Naples for a month during which time British newspapers reported that Vesuvius was spewing forth fire and stone, it was quite a spectacle but it's unlikely Fanny enjoyed it.

The news of John's death would have taken several days to reach England. The shock and horror of his family can hardly be overstated. We have no record of Ann's reaction, but five years later she would still sadly recall him on the anniversary of his death writing 'five years today since I lost my poor brother'.[18] Perhaps she was comforted by the thought that he had read words from his family, before his death. The whole Walker family would have once again gone into mourning. As it was Ann's brother and the family heir who had died, deepest mourning would have been appropriate. Ann's clothing would therefore have been black, symbolic of spiritual darkness. Such dresses would usually have been made from dull rather than reflective silk, or bombazine trimmed with black crepe. Fanny would have ordered a similar outfit in Naples, as a widow; a period of two years mourning was prescribed, for Ann it would have been six months. Mourning dress was usually ordered new upon each bereavement as it was a long-held belief that keeping mourning dress in the house was bad luck.

Fanny (and Delia) left Naples sometime after 20 February. She spent March in Rome and it is likely that it was around this time that she realised she was pregnant with John's child. It took her six weeks to reach England, travelling via Lyon and Paris.[19] It would have been a very different Fanny Walker who arrived back in Paris eight months after she had first seen the city with her new husband, but it was also a different Paris. Revolution was brewing and there was tension on the streets, just nine weeks after Fanny's departure the July Revolution would take place which led to the overthrow of Charles X and the succession of his cousin Louis Philippe, Duc d'Orleans.

Keen to leave an uneasy city that seemed to echo the uncertainty of her own life, Fanny arrived back in Dover on 8 June 1830.[20] The news of her pregnancy had already reached the Walkers and Ann Walker, in this instance most likely Ann's aunt, went down to Dover to meet her. The child Fanny was carrying stood to inherit the bulk of the Walker estate. Exhausted, Fanny hired a carriage to take her back to her parents at Steyning. This journey cost her £59, 4s 6d – it was an enormous sum but after such an ordeal Fanny simply wanted to get to her mother. She remained with her parents at the vicarage in Steyning awaiting the birth of her child. It is unlikely that she would have felt up to any further travel even if she had wished to return to Halifax. In early October she went into labour and on 10 October, she gave birth to a stillborn boy.[21] Stillbirth was far from an uncommon occurrence during this period, but for Fanny the loss of her son, all that she had left of her husband, must have felt like the cruellest of blows.

The death of John and Fanny's son was a personal tragedy for Fanny; for the Walker family it threw everything into yet more uncertainty.

Walker had died intestate, that is without having written a will. His son would have inherited if he had lived, and Fanny's pregnancy was therefore of the greatest interest to the Walker family. When his son died, discussions began in earnest about who would inherit the lands and businesses. Fanny, as John's widow, would have been entitled under law to her 'widow's right', which the Statute of Distribution stated meant that 'a widow could claim ⅓ of an estate as of legal right if there was an heir and ½ if there was not'.[22] This was not always legally enforced, or indeed enforceable, we are after all fifty years too early for the Married Women's Property Act. John's father had made provision in his will to protect the estate from the claims of any future widows or widowers. Fanny's brother stated that the Walkers exhibited a want of 'delicacy of feeling' when it came to dealing with Fanny in the aftermath of her son's death, and he even went to Crow Nest to search for a will, in case John had made one secretly that might have left everything to Fanny.[23] Despite this ill feeling, Anne Lister's diary suggests that a payment of £25,000 was eventually made to Fanny, which was raised from the sale of Walker shares in the Calder and Hebble and Barnsley navigation companies and of turnpike shares.[24] Money was also given to Samuel Washington, presumably to discharge any debts John had owed him and £100 was given to Fanny's brother James to cover the expenses that he incurred while assisting Fanny and dealing with matters relating to John's estate in the south of England. Fanny commissioned a monument to her husband that was erected on the southern wall in St Matthew's church close to one of the pulpits.[25]

The issue of who would now inherit what was complex and much time was devoted to the re-reading of the wills of Ann's father and grandfather. As we have seen, her father's complex forty-eight-page will had been designed with the aim of ensuring the Walker estate would be kept together, but John hadn't considered that his only son and heir would die so soon, and without issue.

Ultimately, it was decided that Ann and her sister Elizabeth would jointly inherit the estate, a fact that in Elizabeth's case caused the family further consternation. Captain Sutherland had been quick off the mark and had consulted his lawyer, already seeking confirmation that Fanny, as John's widow, could not prevent Elizabeth from inheriting her share of the property. Assured of this fact, Captain Sutherland persuaded Elizabeth, by now pregnant with her second child, to sign a deed that placed 'the property coming to [her] as one of the coheiresses of [her] brother at the complete disposal of Captain Sutherland'; Henry Priestley was furious and repeatedly warned Elizabeth about the danger of granting her husband such liberties, but she did not listen.

The will basically stated that Crow Nest and lands were left 'to the use of my daughter Elizabeth Walker', while 'Upper and Lower Cliff Hill and all such other of my lands ... to the use of my said daughter Ann', but the specifics were left to interpretation.[26] The family quickly began to split into factions with Ann, Elizabeth and Captain Sutherland on one side and the trustees of the estate on the other, while the lawyers of all parties rubbed their hands in glee at the prospect of so much business. It is clear that Ann sided with her sister in these matters, largely due to her dislike of Henry Edwards, whom she distrusted, but also due to the fact that around this time his son – her cousin, another Henry Edwards – proposed to her. Ann did not welcome his advances and rejected his proposal, so personal and family awkwardness may have played a part as well. This did not, however, mean that she agreed with her sister and brother-in-law absolutely.

Outside of these legal transactions it is difficult to reach Ann herself among all the disputes; her grief led Elizabeth to express a deep and genuine concern for her sister. She worried about leaving Ann all alone when she returned to Scotland, and feared that her tendency towards melancholy would return. To address this we know that in 1831 Ann was invited to visit Elizabeth in Scotland and Captain Sutherland came down to accompany her north. They travelled via Edinburgh and stayed for several days.[27]

All this death had focused Ann's thoughts to the future and she drafted her will in late 1831, perhaps to try to spare any future descendants the ordeal being experienced by her family.[28] She left almost everything in trust to her infant nephew. The entailed property would pass to him as of right, but Ann's valuable un-entailed inheritance was hers to leave as she wished and she chose to leave it to him in the event she had no children. Their brother's death had made them two of the wealthiest heiresses in the north of England, and with Elizabeth already spoken for, it was now the unmarried Ann who was a financial prize worth catching.

Chapter 6

Miss Walker for Miss Lister

F ollowing her brother's death, Ann lived at Crow Nest, adjusting to her new position and status. At some point she engaged Samuel Washington to manage her lands, and through his records we know that Ann was involved in the running of her estates, she met regularly with him, issued orders and gave opinions. During this period she also undertook a series of visits to friends and family. On one of these visits Ann stayed with Mr Ainsworth and his wife, who was a long-standing friend of hers; on this occasion however, Mr Ainsworth made advances towards Ann. The precise nature of what occurred between Ann and Mr Ainsworth is unclear, but Ann later told Anne that they kissed and enough passed between them physically for her to consider herself 'compromised'. He certainly pressed her to have full intercourse, but their interactions seem to have stopped short of that. Ann later makes it clear that she did not welcome his advances, and she was tortured by the fact that she had not managed to stop him. Mr Ainsworth's married kisses offended God and Ann was plagued by the idea that she had sinned and that God would punish her. It is clear that by the standards of today that Ann was sexually assaulted by her friend's more experienced husband, but back then the church taught that the fault for any sexual indiscretion lay with the woman, and Ann duly blamed herself.

In late 1831 Ann moved to Lidgate, a smaller house on the Walker's Crow Nest estate.[1] An early photograph of Lidgate shows a handsome brick building, covered in ivy, with large windows and four white steps leading to a door. On a smaller scale than Crow Nest, it was inviting whilst not being ostentatious, and welcoming rather than intimidating. It had been part of the Walker lands since the early eighteenth century and Washington's later estate records confirm that it was part of Ann's inheritance.[2] The house was set in gardens and surrounded by fields, a fact that appealed to Ann with her interest in horticulture and she soon set about planning improvements. Ann was also regularly seeing Dr Kenny, who continued to treat her for various ailments including a painful back and bowel troubles.

It was in the midst of all this Ann formed a serious attachment to a Mr Fraser, who she calls 'one of the best men', and by whom her 'affections had been engaged'.[3] We do not know how or when they met, but the relationship was serious. It seems clear that Ann was considering and planning a conventional marriage. Unfortunately the only evidence we have for this attachment to date comes from the diary of Anne Lister, which records when Ann told Anne of her former attachment.

Whatever hopes or dreams Ann may have been harbouring during this period sadly came to nothing. The death of Mr Fraser in July 1832 crushed all her hopes for the future. Suddenly there was no prospect of filling her house with children and nothing stretched out before her except a life in which there was only philanthropic works and religion to give her life meaning. Lidgate must have felt very empty indeed.

It was from Lidgate that on 6 July 1832 a smartly dressed Ann went out.[4] She was accompanying her Aunt and Uncle Aitkinson on some social calls, one of which was to be to Shibden Hall where they hoped to find the family at home. They were in luck, and Ann was received by the Listers very civilly. They would have most likely been shown into Shibden's panelled dining room or parlour, and the fifteen minutes that Ann stayed was more than enough time for Anne to joke with her about 'travelling together', which is perhaps the first hint of flirtation between them.[5] Ann was delighted to meet with Anne Lister once again, but the woman who Ann called upon that day was not the one of her memories. Anne was tired and recovering from bitter disappointment. Two months earlier she had returned to Halifax and her aunt had been shocked to find her so despondent.

Bruised by her love affair with Mariana Lawton, Anne had earlier that year courted Vere Hobart and determined that she would be the one with whom she could build a real life. The two women had stayed together in Hastings where, Vere observed, they spoke more like lovers together than like friends. What Anne had no way of knowing was that Vere had chosen to go to Hastings because she had another, male, suitor waiting in the wings. His name was Donald Cameron of Lochiel, a hero of the Napoleonic wars who had fought bravely as a member of the Grenadier Guards. Plans for Vere to marry him, driven by Vere herself, had long been underway. Anne had not been aware of this and was hurt when she realised the truth, feeling that 'she [Vere] might have been more candid with me'. Anne, though, was determined to press her suit.[6] Vere liked and respected Anne, but in a rare moment of clarity Anne acknowledged that Vere felt her to be 'more man than woman'. A kiss on New Years Eve 1831 caused friction between the two women and Anne's lack of femininity – something of a tender spot for her – increasingly bothered Vere.[7] Any hopes Anne still harboured that Vere would agree to be her life partner were ended in January 1832 by the reappearance of Donald Cameron. Whether or not Vere knew of the pain she was inflicting is open to debate; for her, the idea of living with Anne outside the bounds of society never had been a real prospect. Vere seems to have been genuinely attracted to Anne and she missed her love and affection, but equally she was simply not willing to risk everything to keep it and Anne had been a secret too many times before, she wanted her love to be acknowledged in the light not simply to exist in the shadows.

The rejection Anne felt was all consuming, she could not sleep and railed against the failure of yet another love affair. In misery, Anne went to visit Mariana Lawton and the two women slept together but Anne's heart was no longer in it; she found their physical interaction only 'tolerable'. This visit was in many ways the end of an era, Mariana had been the love of Anne's life, but now she found her to be 'altered and fine … this has destroyed our chance of being together, she could live and die where she is'.[8] Everyone, it seemed, had the life they wanted except for her, and Anne limped back to Halifax exhausted. It was this despondent and tired Anne Lister that Ann Walker called upon at the beginning of July. Ann would not have been surprised when Anne returned the call a week later, to do so was only polite. Ann had company at the time, having spent the morning with Mr and Mrs Priestley and the Atkinsons.

Despite regular visits from her friends, family and her drawing tutor Mr Brown, who instructed her, Ann was lonely. At the end of the day she was alone and she was feeling the weight of her inheritance during this period as family pressures grew. In addition to 'advice' regularly coming in from the Priestley's and Rawsons, Captain Sutherland had begun to press Anne to consider a husband from within his family. Perhaps it was a subject Ann discussed with Anne that day as they looked over her vast inheritance; after all, it was one of the things they both had in common.

Anne, like her, had only inherited the Shibden estate after the death of her brothers. It is clear that Ann welcomed Anne's company, ten years earlier she had been intrigued by the sophisticated Miss Lister. Now a real friendship was being offered and it is clear that Ann wanted to encourage it.

Anne was not overawed by viewing Ann's lands that day, she spends more time describing the weather – heavy rain – than she does the Lightcliffe estate, but surely she felt a pang of envy. To an outsider, Ann's position must have seemed charmed. Shibden was suffering from the latest of a series of financial difficulties, Ann meanwhile had at least £2,500 a year easily at her disposal.[9] An absolutely enormous sum when you consider that the average household income at the time was no more than £70. Anne at Shibden only had somewhere in the region of £830–40.

The overprotective nature of her family may have shielded Ann from the reality of the power of her present position but she was not entirely ignorant of it, nor did she forget her duty to help those less fortunate than herself. In particular, she began to take a more active interest in the education of local children that would eventually lead to her opening a school.

Her fortune continued to present her as an eminently marriageable prospect and her family, especially the ever interested Mrs Priestley, contrived to keep a close eye on her. Captain Sutherland and his mother were by now pressuring Ann to marry Sir Alexander MacKenzie, a relative of the Sutherlands who had fallen on hard times.[10] The enterprising Mrs Sutherland was hoping that Ann's fortune would restore his position, and she dangled as an incentive the fact that if she married him Ann would inevitably spend more time with her sister. With this prospect on her mind Ann was at home on 10 August when Miss Lister once again called and Ann showed her into the parlour to take tea. Ann had been anticipating her visit and was eager to talk, much of her previous reserve gone. She had determined to ask Anne's opinion on Doctor Kenny, who she felt had been asking her 'queer questions', with which she was not comfortable.[11] Ann was aware that he was also a friend of Marian Lister, so hoped that Anne would be able to offer her advice. Ann felt that Dr Kenny was crossing professional boundaries with her, and Anne was happy to listen to her concerns. The two women passed a very 'civil and agreeable' 1¾ hours together.

Smothered by her family, people with whom she could talk to impartially and openly were in short supply. Ann did not go out again that day, spending the afternoon drawing and reading. Anne, on the other hand, left Lidgate that day nursing plans to develop a romantic future with Ann. She had thought of Ann – and her fortune – many times before, but usually in an abstract sense, but now she considered it more seriously. 'Should I try and make up to her?' she asked in her diary that evening.[12]

There is no doubt that Ann welcomed Anne's company, but did she have any indications of Anne's intentions? We cannot be sure, but we can be certain that she wished Anne to call again. She was eagerly awaiting her the following week when Anne came to see her having cut short a visit with Mrs Priestley so that they could spend the afternoon together, Anne's scarcely concealed impatience seems to have aroused Mrs Priestley's suspicions.

Ann hosted Anne for three hours, and as they talked she shed the last of her restraint and launched a rather vehement attack on William Priestley and Mr Edwards, who she felt, in their capacity as trustees of the Walker estate, had 'not behaved as gentlemen'.[13] Ann argued that 'he [was] not really a man of business, things went better without him'. Ann was horrified to hear that Anne had planned to make Mr Edwards executor of her Will, declaring herself 'astonished and grieved'.[14] Whatever had passed between their families in the years that followed John's death Ann was clearly not willing to either forgive or forget.

The two women spoke of business and estate finances, Ann was well aware of Miss Lister's financial concerns, her aunt Mrs Priestley having filled her in on how matters sat with the Shibden estate. The fact that Mrs Priestley had done so suggests that she both trusted Ann with the information and wished to subtly warn her. Either way, when Anne raised her money concerns Ann was already well aware of her circumstances, a fact that left Miss Lister rather embarrassed. The idea, therefore, that Ann was an 'innocent', or ignorant of the idea that Anne might be looking for money, simply does not hold up to scrutiny. Ann knew and chose, deliberately, to pursue their friendship regardless. Ann was both generous and encouraging that afternoon, seeking to put her guest at her ease. When Anne inadvertently broke her ivory book knife which had been a gift from Catherine Rawson, in a turn of phrase that perhaps suggests that Ann understood more about Anne's intentions than even Ann herself realised, she made it clear that she would value any gift from Anne offered as a replacement above any other.[15] She could scarcely have given Miss Lister any more of a clear indication of her regard. Ann also went to the trouble of giving Anne a copy of the *Penny Magazine*, a newly launched publication from the Society for the Diffusion of Useful Knowledge. It proved to be popular and this particular issue covered such topics as the history and form of the olive tree, the importance of the role of mother in educating her children and the life of a Buffalo. Upon leaving Ann that day, Anne wrote that she had 'amused and interested' her.[16] Anne also took Ann's concerns seriously, when she called at Pye Nest in the future she found herself mistrusting everything that Mr Edwards said.

Ann continued with her rounds of social calls and shopping trips over the next few weeks increasingly interspersed with visits from Anne. She also had the company of Catherine Rawson with whom she was planning to go to the Lake District for three weeks at the beginning of September. Ann was looking forward to a change of scenery, but she also told Anne that she would miss her company and not forget her. [17]

The day before Ann's departure she made plans to go into Halifax with Anne, and both women were at pains to make sure that their trip out was in every way respectable. Ann was not used to pushing boundaries and Anne was exercising extreme caution in respect of their burgeoning relationship despite Ann's encouragement, having been burnt so many times before. Anne had meticulously planned her outfit, she was to wear 'a new pelisse sewing on a watch pocket [and] putting strings to [her] petticoat and getting all ready for tomorrow'.[18] Miss Walker called for Miss Lister at Shibden Hall on the morning of 3 September and spent several minutes talking to Aunt Lister, while waiting for Anne to finish getting ready. Another thing that Ann had in common with her new friend was that she was extremely close to her aunt, and she was keen to make a good impression. Ann had brought her smartest carriage – and they set off at 11.50 for Halifax. They planned to make as many social calls as possible and to be seen together. They first paid a visit to the widow of Mr Briggs, then paid a call on Mrs Dyson at Willowfield in Sowerby Bridge. Shopping was next on the list and they went to Throps, a gardening centre to purchase shrubs and flowers, before calling on the Saltmarshes who were not home.

They then called on Mrs Edwards. Ann had to be persuaded to visit her aunt who had sent her what she termed a 'huffy letter' earlier that week. She did, however, bow to persuasion from Anne who was gratified to find that Ann 'seems inclined to consult me and tell me all'.[19] Mrs Priestley and Mrs Edwards were becoming increasingly concerned about external influences on Ann and even at this early stage were cautioning her about the amount of time she was spending with the strong-minded Miss Lister, but Ann was no longer content with keeping her distance. By allowing Anne to accompany her that day she was effectively bringing their relationship to wider attention.

The following day Ann departed with Catherine for the Lake District, but her mind, if not yet her heart, was very much back in Halifax.

Chapter 7

To the Lakes (and back again)

Earlier in 1832 Ann had been invited by her Rawson relatives to join Catherine Rawson on a trip to the Lakes and to stay at Wastdale Hall there, which was owned by the Rawson family. Catherine was the same age as Ann, 'a pretty, elegant girl', and as we have seen the two were good friends.[1] It was a trip Ann had initially been looking forward to, but when she was quizzed by Anne about the places that she would most like to see, Ann said that she would love to go to Ireland to see the Giant's Causeway or Lake of Killarney. Anne asserted that she would have taken her there if she had not been 'promised to Wastwater'.[2]

Did Ann feel a pang at losing such an opportunity? It seems so and she certainly left Anne only reluctantly on the morning of her departure, but by 12 noon on 8 September Ann and Catherine were off on their travels. Before going to Wastwater, they headed for Bowness, near Windermere, having first stopped at Huddersfield.

A guidebook had been published in 1810 that was to ultimately determine the Lake District's future as a tourist destination. William Wordsworth's *Guide to the Lakes* told eager readers not only about points of significance and natural beauty in the Lake District, but also how the individual should view certain points to achieve the feeling known then as 'the sublime'.[3] Wordsworth's poetry was extremely popular and consequently the publication of his guidebook had people flocking to the Lake District, eager to view the sights and experience the clean air of which Wordsworth spoke so dearly.[4] To deal with this influx of tourists Grand Mansions were built alongside the great lakes in popular areas such as Bowness, Coniston and Ambleside. These mansion hotels were designed specifically for tourists such as Ann Walker: Wealthy women with money to spend and a level of education that meant they were quite prepared to be enraptured by the Lakes, which 'never did betray the heart that loved' them.[5] Ann was also walking in the footsteps of many authors that would have been familiar to her; names such as Walter Scott, Thomas Carlyle and Lord Tennyson.[6]

Ann saw '7 lakes before getting to Wastdale', and she and Catherine travelled around for several days, no doubt taking in the majestic splendour of Coniston with its islands that would later inspire Swallows and Amazons, before ending up in Keswick.[7]

The town of Keswick had been established thirty years before as a centre of tourism in the Lakes and by 1810 it had many avenues of entertainment available including, according to Charlotte Deans, a new theatre.[8] It was also famous for the manufacture of textiles, especially cotton, and its great cotton mills were powered by the river Greta. While there Ann visited the marble works, and bought Anne a present – a presse-papier, irrefutable proof that Anne was very much on her mind.

From Keswick Anne travelled to Wastwater where they stayed two weeks with Catherine's family. Wastwater at just under three miles long is England's deepest lake and is generally regarded as the one of the most beautiful and dramatic settings in the Lake District. In 1829 Stansfield Rawson had built Wasdale Hall, having purchased the land in 1811, with money largely drawn from concerns in the East India Company. It encompassed two estates: Crook Head and Low Crook.[9] He had begun almost immediately to plant a huge variety of trees on his new estate, including 180,000 trees in Birch How and the Leys. Rawson kept detailed records and the year before Ann's visit he wrote that the ornamental trees he had planted, including lilian, berberis and stagshorn were 'all doing very well'.[10] Stansfield took many years to perfect the design of his new home which has large barge-boarded gables, exposed timbers and the Rawson Arms mounted over the front door, beneath which Ann would have entered.[11]

The Wastdale Hall in which Ann stayed was very near completion in 1832, although the family would not move there permanently until 1843. Given her keen interest in horticulture, it is not much of a leap to imagine Ann admiring the ornamental hedges, majestic alders and scotch firs. Despite the scenery though, Ann would later state that she had spent all day, every day, at Wastwater thinking of Anne and that she had had a 'very great anxiety to get home again'.[12] Travelling, it seemed, did not agree with her.

Ann returned to Lidgate on the evening of 25 September, tired from the journey, but not too tired to receive Anne early the next morning. The latter had learnt from the servants at Lidgate that Ann was home. Ann was 'very civil' in her conversation and they sat down to discuss both Ann's trip and business while having breakfast.[13] Ann had been giving some thought to travelling with Anne while she had been away and told her immediately that she felt she could not travel to Italy with her, at least not anytime soon, she wished to be at home. A few weeks away in the company of the Rawsons had not dampened Ann's enthusiasm for her new friend though, nor was Anne discouraged by Ann's views on travelling and their confidential conversations continued as they discussed everything from local goings on to the wages that Ann paid Washington. Both women enjoyed themselves very much and they made plans to take breakfast together the next day.

Rather strangely, Ann's man servant James MacKenzie arrived at Shibden Hall just ten minutes after Anne returned home to ask her to send back some books that Ann had lent her from her collection. Given that Ann would see her the next day, the only reasonable explanation seems to be that Ann dispatched James in haste as she wanted to communicate with Anne before morning. I suggest that she in fact wanted to give Anne further encouragement. If so, Anne willingly responded. She dashed off a note to Ann full of florid apologies – 'do pray forgive me before morning' – and told her that she had given her much to think of. Anne signed off the note 'very truly yours'.[14]

The next day Ann rose early, as was her custom. She broke her fast early in general but that morning she was determined to make an effort and Anne described the breakfast Ann ordered as being 'quite a spread'.[15] Typically, breakfast at the time was an opportunity for those with money to display their wealth through produce from their estates and would have included dishes of meat, eggs and fruit. They chatted over breakfast for an hour before they went to another room where they continued to be 'very cosy and confidential'. Ann's day was interrupted just after noon by the arrival of Mrs Stansfield and Delia Rawson, who had come to call upon her and who seemed rather affronted that Anne did not depart on their arrival. Indeed they seemed quite surprised to find Anne there in the first place. Ann however made it clear that she wished Anne to stay. Never one to be intimidated herself, Anne was impressed by Ann's resolution.[16] It is clear that Ann had no intention of giving up her new friendship.

Was Ann aware of the gossip and suspicions that were beginning to stir in her family? The simple answer is yes, but she very deliberately chose to ignore them. Her family eventually gave up and left for Huddersfield when it was clear that Anne would not be leaving.

Once they had gone Ann listened carefully and more seriously than before to Anne's proposal that they travel together. Ann seems to have believed in part that Anne was joking when she had talked of their making plans before but she realised now that Anne was serious.[17]

The two women spoke openly, they talked about tree planting and 'what [Anne] should do about a French maid'.[18] It seemed to Anne that Ann was 'taking all I say for gospel', but she was also listening to Ann, and in particular she thanked her for warning her about Dr Kenny; on the basis of Ann's advice, she had discouraged her sister Marian from consulting him so frequently. In turn, Anne advised that Ann should 'fight shy of the Harveys when they come to Crow Nest', advice that Ann seemed inclined to follow.[19]

After lunch they went for a walk, Anne wished to show her the area that she had developed at Shibden and her new Moss Hut. They 'walked slowly by the new road and Lower Brea, and sauntered to nearly Hall Wood gate in my walk ... on returning [we] rested in the hut and must have sat a couple of hours'.[20] Since her return to Yorkshire Anne had worked tirelessly on making improvements to her estate and had built a Moss Hut (that Anne termed her Chaumiere) which she situated 'near Lily Bank or rather at the entrance of Lower Brook Ing Wood'.[21] It was secluded, cosy and surrounded by trees, being made of oak beams, a thatched roof and with hollies opposite. If Anne had any worries that such a deliberately intimate setting – it was after all designed to be a discreet place in which she could entertain and seduce women – would give Ann pause for thought she was mistaken. Ann enjoyed her afternoon stating that 'she knew not when she had spent so pleasant a day', Anne adds in her diary that she got the impression that Ann liked her more than even she realised.[22] Ann is clearly very happy to be home, and as well as spending time with Anne she met with Washington to discuss estate matters and went into Halifax frequently to shop.

It is difficult to know how far the idea of physical love or same-sex attraction had entered into Ann's mind by now. She certainly liked Anne but so far their interactions had all been bound by the framework of 'courtly love', and confined to romantic language and the giving of gifts, not dissimilar to that used by her in letters to other friends. Though knowing as she did of Anne's reputation, Ann surely cannot have been ignorant of how Miss Lister was hoping that their friendship would progress. The question is, what did Ann want? And the answer seems clear: she wanted Miss Lister in whatever form that might entail. Her eagerness to pursue their relationship can be seen the next day when, despite having said that she would call on Anne and Mrs Lister, the following Monday Ann went to Shibden Hall, after dispatching a note of her intention that failed to beat her there. That morning she had heard that a tenant of hers, Collins, had forced open the barn doors that led into one of her courtyards and she wanted to ask Anne's advice as to how best to deal with it.

Ann could deal with such instances herself, the difference now is that she felt she had a friend with whom she could discuss such things and on whom she could rely. Ann was shown into Shibden's drawing room, and talked the matter over with Anne and her aunt. In the afternoon she and Anne went to the hut and their affection there 'bordered on lovemaking', although it does not yet appear to have crossed into the realms of the physical.[23] They talked of their relationship that afternoon as 'being a thing settled'.[24] Ann was still decided against travelling, though this was a sticking point that both women chose to ignore.

To surprise Anne, Ann sent a parcel ahead to Shibden so that when she got home Anne found 'the press-papier and note from Miss Walker', on her desk. Anne wrote touchingly in the margin of her journal that it was the 'first thing [Ann] ever gave me'.[25] More calls followed and the next day Ann and Anne went to Cliff Hill to call on Ann's aunt, who was very pleased to see them and persuaded them to stay for tea at which Ann waited formally for Anne to take her cream before taking any herself. When Anne teased her about it she smiled and replied that 'at home [I] would not do so but her aunt would have been astonished if she had not done as she did'. Aunt Ann's good opinion mattered to her niece and Ann would always care about her opinion.[26]

Ann seems to have been convinced by now that Anne's companionship was a viable option for her future and that evening she was all smiles. We get a clear glimpse of the loneliness that Ann had been feeling at Lidgate when Ann said that 'she had often looked at all her things and said what was the use of having them with nobody to enjoy them with her'. Now though she felt that her future was once again full of promise.[27] Eager to reassure Ann further, Anne pressed upon her that:

> I had made up my mind in May, the moment I was at liberty to do so, so that it had been well enough digested by me however sudden it might seem to her, and that I gave my happiness into her keeping in perfect security. Said I had built the hut on purpose for her.[28]

The last bit was a lie, but as Ann was the first and last woman she would entertain there it was not too far from the truth.

Ann also accepted that Anne's plan for them to travel was very real, and she agreed although she did request a delay. She had promised to 'have Mr and Mrs Ainsworth in February, they cannot come before', and therefore wished to wait until the end of the month.[29] In another matter though, she did misunderstand Anne's intentions; Anne suggested to her that she should let Lidgate to Washington and his family as 'she would never want it again as long as there was a room for us at Shibden'.[30] It was a suggestion that Ann laughed at, but again Anne was serious.

Ann would have been gratified to know that Aunt Lister and Anne talked of her that night and that the elder Miss Lister 'seemed very well pleased' with Anne's choice of her. The fact that Anne was able to tell her that Ann had 'three thousand a year' did not hurt, nor did the fact that unlike some of Anne's other lovers Ann was both highly respectable and kind.[31] Aunt Lister, however, was far less pleased by the fact Anne was so late home, and Marian shouted at her and had a 'nervous fit'. They had dispatched two servants to try to find Anne when she did not send word, and she was so late that by the time she had returned the whole house was in uproar.[32]

Back at Lidgate alone, that evening Ann's doubts began to creep in. Would she really be enough for a woman like Miss Lister? It seems likely that she also began to seriously consider the physical aspects of their relationship possibly for the first time. There is no reason to suppose that

Ann had any experience in female physical love at all. Plagued by such anxiety and sleeping poorly, Ann was not feeling at all well that week, and she was 'obliged to go out of afternoon church ... in the middle of the service'.[33] In a return to the pattern of previous years, Ann's worries seem to have manifested themselves in physical symptoms. The next day when she met Anne at the end of Hipperholme Lane, Ann was still not feeling well and Anne was worried enough to advise that they should return to Lidgate so that she could rest rather than call upon her aunt. Anxious to make a good impression on Aunt Lister, Ann only gave up the scheme after Anne told her of the talk she had had with her aunt last evening and assured her 'how kind my aunt would be to her, how pleased she was etc.'[34] This was the first time that Ann had appeared unwell before Anne, who was shocked by her lack of energy.

At home and comfortable, Ann felt that she needed to make clear to Anne her deep attachment to Cliff Hill and that she would not consider letting it or Lidgate at this time. They did, however, discuss their possible future finances, with Anne appealing to Ann's sense of economy by pointing out that Shibden was comparatively cheap to run and Ann was surprised to hear that Anne hoped the Shibden estate might eventually yield as much as £2,000 a year.[35] It was Anne's turn then to be both insecure and press for commitment. She asked Ann if 'she thought she could be happy enough with me to give up all thoughts of ever leaving me'.[36] Anne stopped just short of making a full proposal of marriage, but Ann understood nonetheless that this is what she was in effect offering. Both women were viewing their relationship within the heterosexual framework of Georgian society, but Anne resolutely believed that her same-sex desire was a dictate of her God and saw no reason why the commitment to each other should not be solemnised before God. It was a view that Ann struggled to accept.

In response to Anne, Ann passionately explained that 'she had said that she would never marry but that as she had once felt an inclination not to keep to this ... she should not like to deceive me and begged not to answer just now'.[37] Ann clearly wanted to be certain that marriage to a man was something that she did not want. Her previous inclination for marriage had centred around her desire for children and she wanted to be sure that a commitment to Anne, with all it implied, would make them both happy. Anne gave Ann six months, until 3 April the following year, to think before she would ask again and Ann was both surprised and relieved to have bought herself so much time. More immediately though, Ann let Anne keep hold of her hand when she took it, not shying away from the first real physical affection that Anne offered to her. Ann was also delighted with a present of a little gold gondola brooch from Venice by Anne.[38] Ann was promised to her aunt at Cliff Hill that evening and she allowed Anne to walk with her to the gate. Tellingly though, Anne deliberately avoided being seen by Ann's family on this occasion. Both women were aware that they were beginning to walk a fine line in terms of social acceptance.

Chapter 8

Lovers (or how to shock Mrs Priestley)

Ann was giving a lot of thought to her future and when Anne called the next morning she quickly raised the discussion of where they might live again. Anne herself had resolved to leave the matter be for now but Ann wanted to get things clear in her mind. She reiterated her attachment to Cliff Hill, and the hope she had of living there one day, but she did not dismiss the idea of letting it, if she were to move to Shibden. When Anne first raised the idea she had been surprised, now she thought she might see the merit of the plan. Ann also voiced her concerns regarding Anne's intimacy with the Priestley family. She was well aware that Anne was a regular caller on her uncle and aunt at New House, and that they were growing concerned about Anne's closeness with her. She wanted Anne to distance herself from them and Anne assured her she would easily give up her friendship with them.

The afternoon was to be a turning point in their relationship, brought about by Ann's surprising sexual confidence that rather caught Anne unawares. While sitting together, Anne put her arm around Ann in an attempt to be both affectionate and casual enough that she could pass it off as friendly affection if Ann took offence or panicked. However, Ann had made up her mind and laid on Anne's arm while they talked. When Anne finally kissed her she 'return[ed] it with such a long, passionate or nervous mumbling kiss' that Anne was shocked, 'this is rather more than I expected', she confided in her diary.[1] Ann proved to be unrestrained and enthusiastic in her desire for Anne. Ironically, her enthusiasm gave Anne pause. Part of Anne's romantic identity was that she presented herself as the 'male' lead in relationships, Ann's eagerness and sexual confidence threw her momentarily, it was not a trait that she had expected her to exhibit.[2]

So far, Anne's courtship of Ann had very much followed the accepted social norm. Passionate friendships between women in the nineteenth century were not uncommon. However, if they did develop into a physically sexual relationship, then it was not committed to paper. Such passionate friendships were accepted as an aspect of feminine weakness and as being symptomatic of their more emotional nature. Many such friendships were actually encouraged as the means by which women could 'talk house' together, leaving men to rule the universe in peace. Women in such friendships 'embraced, and exchanged intensely romantic love letters ... yet society regarded these friendships as entirely acceptable'.[3]

Ann, however, was evidently enough of a woman of the world to know that by kissing Anne she had crossed a line. While Anne was somewhat discombobulated by the afternoon's events, Ann for her part had no such doubts; she wanted more and asked Anne to come back to Lidgate and 'dine with her at 5 [and then] stay the night'.[4] Despite this bold invitation Ann was nervous, and grew more so as the afternoon wore on. Kissing Anne meant she had, in all conscience, to share a few things that she had so far kept concealed and she spent the rest of the afternoon preparing for the evening. Ann had decided that, unlike on former occasions, tonight they would dine formally and she dressed likewise in an evening dress. In accordance with fashions at the time, Ann's dress would likely have had a scooped neck, with a centre front bodice that was gathered into a narrow waistband emphasising her slender form. It would have had large gigot sleeves and would most likely have been made in silk, trimmed with lace of piping and matched by the silk slippers on her feet. She also briefed her servant James, who would be waiting upon them at table, to ensure the evening ran smoothly.

With the scene set for seduction, Anne arrived at 5 pm and after a dinner at which they exchanged polite conversation about Scotland and its landscape, they withdrew to a less formal setting and James left them alone. After discussing Ann's feelings on Eugenie (Anne's possible new maid) they were soon back in each other's arms. Ann whispered that Anne would soon forget her in between their 'kissing and pressing', and in the style of a gallant suitor Anne dismissed these fears. As darkness fell the atmosphere became heavy and they both became bolder. Ann did not resist Anne's wandering hands. – 'I prest her bosom. Then finding no resistance and the lamp being out let my hand wander lower down gently getting to queer. Still no resistance.' It was at this point, however, that Ann – remembering that she had not made her confession to Anne – began to cry as the words poured out.[5] She said to Anne between sobs, 'that her affections had been engaged to one of the best men', and that they could not be transferred so soon for he had only been dead three months.[6] Ann was clearly not over her Andrew Fraser quite as much as she had thought. Anne reacted with gallantry; she apologised for having been so forward and said that she knew her 'conduct was madness'. Ann seems to have suddenly been overcome by shame at the idea that she could forget Mr Fraser so quickly. Her shame and lack of self-esteem manifested itself more directly when Anne complimented her on her evening dress, Ann's response was to consider this as 'proof that love it blind'.[7]

This was not Ann's only confession of the evening, she also revealed to Anne that recently she had been receiving anonymous letters that troubled her. For the first time the glow and happiness that Ann had felt in Anne's company was giving way to something more real and frightening. Almost certainly these letters had to do with her friendship with Anne. If this was the case then Ann evidently now trusted that Anne would not abandon her, because until now she had concealed them from her. Anne was herself no stranger to 'nasty' letters and usually dismissed them as childish nonsense, but she also recognised that for Ann they threatened her position, reputation and sense of self. The two women had by now been viewed often enough in each other's company to draw attention, and Ann may have suspected (as Anne did) that her own family were behind the letters. Ann was deeply troubled by them but not enough to deter her from spending time with Anne; when Anne tried to tactfully withdraw, Ann would not give an inch and after nearly two centuries we can sympathise with Anne when she writes 'Hang it! This queer girl puzzles me.' Ann maintained that Anne made her happy and despite everything, it was this she held on to.[8] Ironically, Anne tried to counsel her to take her time and be sure, suddenly very nervous of the previous engagement that Ann had made. Ann meanwhile maintained that she 'got rid of all troubles of cousins or letters when with' Anne.[9]

It is hard to escape the conclusion that Ann knew what she wanted, but she was confused about it. The joy she felt with Anne competed with her anxiety, grief and deep religiosity and it was a heady mixture of all four that drove her actions over the next few weeks. The next day she was happy to see Anne and once again gave her physical encouragement. They shared further kisses and gradually they were at ease again together. Ann's insecurities came to the fore again though, when Anne went to leave at 4 pm and hesitated when Ann asked her to stay. Disappointed, Ann said she felt Catherine Rawson might suit Anne better as a companion, a suggestion which made Anne baulk, stating baldly that she 'could not sufficiently respect her common sense'.[10] Searching for a way to prolong the visit Ann agreed she would take Anne's advice and seek Dr Belcombe's opinion on her health, though she laughed, saying he would only say as others had, that all she needed was a good husband, which appears to have been pretty standard advice to 'delicate' women at the time. No sooner had the topic of a doctor been exhausted, Ann then began to discuss poetry. She and Catherine had read Crabbe's poems and though Catherine 'maintained they were not fit to be read'; Ann thought they were fine for women, but perhaps not impressionable young girls.[11]

Ann then flirted and 'pressed herself' to Anne, but in the midst of all this mentioned to Anne that she had a potential suitor in the Highlands and hinted that she was still considering Alexander McKenzie as a husband. It was certainly the stance that she was maintaining in her communications with her sister. Anne responded by calling her 'man-keen', and doubting once again that Ann would be happy with her. That evening, although Ann did not know it, Anne had resolved to 'give her up'.[12]

When not flirting with Anne, Ann was busy with estate business, her drawing lessons and keeping up with her extensive correspondence. On 7 October Anne went to church only to find Ann was conspicuously absent, for her to miss church was concerning enough for Mrs Priestley to insist upon going to Lidgate with Anne. Mrs Priestley did not stay long, but Ann ordered a lunch of 'cold tongue, bread, butter and wine' for her and Anne.[13] She told Anne her absence was due to her mental anguish and that she did not wish to let her down; among other things she was still worried about her 'coldness' of manner. Anne replied in a way that she hoped was reassuring, that she 'had given up all thought of the thing [their marriage] had positively no hope at all,' which was not really what Ann wanted to hear and she reiterated again that she was as yet undecided. To make her point she kissed Anne and lay in her arms, offering Anne encouragement to 'press[…] very tenderly', and Anne got her 'right hand up her petticoats to queer, but not to skin'. Ann did not push her away but her 'thick knitted drawers' proved not to be the most practical of garments.[14]

When in Anne's company Ann's spirits rose and she flirtatiously told Anne she need not be so straight-laced in her conversation with her. Anne took her at her word and regaled Ann with tales regarding the joys of 'pocket holes' – used in Paris for public masturbation.[15] Ann might have thought that such flirtation would impress and appeal to Anne, but the truth was rather more complicated; Anne suspected now that Ann was rather more worldly that she let on. She had not been as shocked by anything the two women had shared so far, as the oddly conservative at times Miss Lister might have supposed; Ann had laughed rather than blushed at her bawdy tales and Anne was plagued by the thought that Ann had learnt to kiss under the tutelage of Andrew Fraser rather than her – Ann was not the only one with insecurities.

Their romantic evening was interrupted when Anne's manservant John, who had been dispatched by Aunt Lister to escort her niece home, unfortunately knocked on the Priestley's door by mistake which had the awkward consequence of revealing to Mr and Mrs Priestley that the two women were spending a cosy, late night together at Lidgate. Both women realised that Mrs Priestley would 'talk us over and think something is in the wind', they were right.[16] Ann cared less for many of her relatives' opinions than we might suppose, but she did fear that rumours would reach – and worry – Elizabeth, and she wrote seeking to reassure her.

Family matters in general were on Ann's mind and she wanted to talk them through with Anne. Her brother's widow, Fanny Walker, had assured Christopher Rawson when she accepted her widow's share that she had no intention of marrying again; it was however a declaration made by a grieving young woman. At some point following her widowhood, Fanny had returned to Halifax and the previous month, on 12 September 1832, she married Courtney Kenny Clarke. Ann kept in touch with her sister-in-law but Anne now told Ann that there had been some issue with the Rawsons over the shares sold to fund Fanny's entitlement and the issue had not been let go by the Rawson family.[17]

Ann was determined to keep Anne with her that day, and despite the latter's initial reluctance, Ann managed to keep her with the prospect of a delicious lunch. While eating the conversation flowed, Ann discussed more of her doubts, the lack of children being top of the list, and debated how important they were to her, Anne told her tales of having been 'a good deal humbugged by a French countess' when she had been travelling. Anne also told Ann that happiness to her 'was in well bred minds more mental than in others'.[18] Ann was flattered that Anne thought she possessed such a mind, heady praise for a woman who had had her fragility of mind confirmed by her family throughout most of her life.

They soon abandoned their conversation, Ann drew the blinds and they lay down 'kissing and pressing'. The blinds however were not enough. They were in each other's arms when, just after 4 pm, Mrs Priestley walked in on them. Ann went both 'red and pale' while Anne had 'jumped [up] ... and was standing by the fire'. Mrs Priestley saw everything in a single glance. She was 'vexed, jealous and annoyed'. It seems as if James's call the previous evening had aroused her suspicions, she asked 'in bitter satire' if Anne had bothered to go home. Ann appears to have been rather speechless, leaving Anne to try to cover by referring to, and joking about, her aunt's anxiety about her travelling abroad so late. Rather recklessly, she then went on to suggest that the best way to sooth her aunt might be to stay at Lidgate; Mrs Priestley's shock quickly morphed into fury and she left immediately in a 'suppressed rage'.[19]

Ann's shock quickly gave away to laughter; if Anne had been expecting her to be upset she was quickly proved wrong. Ann 'laughed and said we were well matched', before pulling Anne down for more kissing.[20] This time she had worn more conducive clothing and she made no objections when Anne put her hands inside her drawers and 'touched first time the hair and skin of [her] queer'. Surprisingly, it was Anne who put an end to the encounter. Her own doubts crashed through her and she put her head down on Ann's shoulder until she was composed once more. Ann was all concern, and waved off her apologies before gently apologising for 'leading [Anne] on'. When Anne had recovered Ann gently probed, asking her about her romantic history. Anne decided not to tell her about her numerous affairs with women ranging from her long-term lover Mariana Lawton to Maria Barlow. She said instead that 'nature' had taught her to kiss; Ann was not naive enough to believe Anne sexually inexperienced, but she was satisfied with the pretty answer for now although 'she should like to know better' in future.[21] The weather was foul that evening and Ann sent her lover home wrapped in her own thick tartan cloak to protect her from the worst of the 'driving wind', which by the time Anne had reached Shibden was in such a fury that she could barely wrestle open the gate. Ann had also made a point of sending grapes with her for Aunt Lister.

Ann seized on the first possible excuse for contacting Anne the next day and sent a note to Shibden to ask advice on the matter of one of her tenants, a Mr Collins, who had taken cows from her land without permission. Her words were intimate and friendly, leaving no room for doubt in the receiver's mind as to her regard: 'How little did I imagine when we parted last night that I should so soon have had the pleasure of addressing you my dear friend ... the plea of soliciting your advice seems at least a tolerably fair excuse.'[22] It's easy to picture Ann eagerly awaiting the reply, which when it came was all gallantry: 'Your note my love surprises me but surprise is not the only or uppermost feeling which engrosses me – I leave you to imagine what I mean ... I can hardly regret even your vexation about Collins. Remember it is to him that I owe your note.' This was nineteenth-century chivalric language at its most powerful, and Ann practically swooned as Anne hoped she would.[23]

Outside of her relationship with Anne, Ann had many matters of family and estate on her mind. The Collins incident had to be dealt with – he was told to return the livestock – and her cousin Edward Aitkinson had been asking for money; she had offered him the generous sum of £500, but he had countered and asked her for £3,000. Ann wanted to refuse him, her relationship with her cousin was not particularly close, and this time she had Anne to look to for help in responding. Ann wrote down Anne's response 'verbatim' and reiterated that she would lend him £500 but no more.[24] Suffice to say, Anne's assistance was not welcomed by the wider Walker family. For her part, Ann was delighted that she now had someone in her corner upon whose judgement she could rely, and increasingly over the next few weeks we hear Anne's voice in her letters as she dealt with estate matters.

Ann had long struggled with the burden of her wealth, when Anne told her that she 'wished she had a third of what she [Ann] had ... we might have managed without difficulty', Ann rather bitterly replied 'Oh no, the difficulty would have been far greater'.[25] Money, she knew, did not buy happiness.

What was making her happy were Anne's visits, that week there was more 'lovemaking and kissing' alongside talk of their future. One evening Ann allowed further intimacies and Anne 'got right middle finger up her queer at three seperate times.' Ann was aroused and she whispered to Anne in bed that she loved her for the first time.[26] Once again though it all became too much for Ann and she burst into tears, saying that she simply could not make up her mind what it was she wanted. Ann now revealed to Anne that she and Catherine Rawson had once thought they would live together and Anne's suspicions were raised, was it Miss Rawson that had 'initiated' Ann to female desire?

The possibility is an intriguing one, but given that language between two women at the time was often flowery and romantic in nature, there doesn't appear to be anything in the two women's communications that specifically suggests physical intimacy. This doesn't of course mean it did not happen. Lesbian relationships, such as that between between Eleanor Butler and Sarah Ponsonby who lived together for forty-three years as the Ladies of Llangollen, did exist, but by far the majority of lesbians lived their lives in silence. Ann admitted she 'always sleeps with Catherine', but again in an age when women sharing a bed was not uncommon this does not necessarily imply anything other than practicality. If Ann and Catherine had been lovers, then they knew not to confide the details to paper and Ann never declared as much outright to Anne.[27]

All the uncertainty and family pressure was beginning to tell on Ann, and she spent a lot of her time lying on the sofa, experiencing back pain, and waiting for Anne to arrive. Ann was tired and languid, and as it always did during such 'episodes' her appetite vanished, leaving Anne to nurse her, feeding her gruel and trying to tempt her with small morsels of sandwich.[28] Ann was moved by Anne's kindness and began to talk again 'as if there was no chance of her eventually refusing' her. Anne was genuinely sympathetic but also urged Ann to see her friend Dr Stephen Belcombe.

The next day it was resolved they would go to York the following Monday, and with this settled she discussed her horticultural plans with Anne.[29] She had resolved to have a wing at Crow Nest 'glazed so as to form a greenhouse'.[30] This would enable her to grow more fruit; perhaps she was tempted by the possibility of being able to grow lemons or pineapples on a regular basis. Growing pineapples in England had been a popular occupation of the wealthy classes for fifty years but older structures often could not cope with the furnaces placed in them as 'the fumes damaged or killed the plants'. Ann's new glasshouse would be adapted to take this into consideration and she wanted to save the money she spent every week buying lemons at Gregory's. As they walked to Cliff Hill the two women discussed the fact that the tree guards along Stony Lane were not 'sufficient protection against the cattle'. Ann wanted to spend time with her aunt alone that afternoon and so Anne left her at the gate.[31]

The next day Ann's plans for her greenhouse began to take shape, 'Hepworth the joiner came before we had done breakfast about the framework for the greenhouse to be made.' Washington had been told of the plan and he now estimated that £11 16s might be a reasonable price for the work which included '60 feet glazing at ¼ 4 pounds masons work 10 shillings wood 40 shillings the rest of the joiner work ... the panes were to be bigger 3 in a row of 14 by 10 inches instead of 4 in a row of 14 by 7 ½.'

Anne helped with the ordering of the supplies, but it was very much Ann's idea. She wanted the greenhouse as a symbol of the 'first thing [she and Anne] had a common interest in'.[32]

Ann went to Cliff Hill to see her aunt the following Friday, Anne had gone to Lidgate to look for her but headed to meet her at Cliff Hill when told where she was. It is noticeable that Ann is far less worried about her aunt seeing her with Anne than with the rest of the family and after half an hour's visit they walked back to Lidgate together.

Ann's visit to York took place on 22 October and they booked into the Black Swan Inn on Coney Street, 'a good dark specimen of the old English inn, sombre, quiet with dark staircases, tidy rooms, curtained beds – all the possibilities of a comfortable life and good English fare'.[33] Ann was anxious and her anxiety was not helped by a visit they paid to Mariana's sister Harriet Milne, with whom Anne had had a previous flirtation and now 'made foot love' with beneath the table. Rather crossly, Ann asked that Anne run her errands for her, which included trips to Myers to see about carriage repairs and the Will Office where Ann wanted to obtain a 'copy of the Will of the late Mrs Priestley of Keybroyde'.[34]

Dr Belcombe had arranged to attend Ann at the Black Swan rather than have her walk to his practice, he spent a little time with her and then Ann left the room while he told Anne all he thought. His assessment was straightforward and delivered with the ease of a man confident in his abilities. There was, he said:

nothing the matter with [Ann] but her nervousness. If all her fortune could fly away and she had to work for her living she would be well. A case of nervousness and hysteria. No organic disease. Though I should be sadly bothered with her abroad unless I had the upper hand and ought not to pet her too much. But going abroad would do her good.[35]

She simply had too much money, he concluded, and nothing to do except in the time-honoured tradition of all idle ladies 'imagine herself unwell'. It was not a diagnosis a million miles from what Ann herself had thought previously when she had sought both company and employment. He prescribed tincture of henbane, which was a popular nineteenth-century remedy known for its stimulant effect which could lead to hallucinations, restlessness and flushed skin. Dr Belcombe's conclusions were very much in keeping with thinking at the time, which relied on preconceived ideas of gender 'hysteria' to explain mental health. There is nothing in Ann's symptoms of low self-esteem, indecisiveness, 'excessive worry and fear about situations' and 'periods of depressive lethargy', that would possibly fit in with a diagnosis today of clinical depression.[36] The physical symptoms, she mentioned to Dr Belcombe, a painful back due to muscle tension, bowel issues, fatigue and headaches are all considered symptomatic of a generalised anxiety condition.

Dr Stephen Belcombe was both prejudiced by prevalent gender-biased thinking and practising 150 years too early to understand the complex nature of mental health. Ann did not record what she made of his diagnosis, but she clearly was not unduly upset and before heading home the two women shopped before breaking up the boredom of the journey home by 'kissing and grubbing' in the carriage.[37]

Chapter 9

Man Troubles

On 26 October Ann sat down to breakfast with Anne and shocked her by telling her that her cousin, Henry Edwards, had once proposed. After dropping this bombshell Ann walked with Anne to Cliff Hill to visit her aunt. While she was there Aunt Walker handed Ann a 'letter with black edging and a black seal'. In it, Miss Bentley informed her that her friend Mrs Ainsworth had been killed after 'being thrown out of an open carriage'. Ann was 'very much affected', and a worried Anne suggested that they return to Lidgate and dispatched a note to Aunt Lister to tell her that she would not be home that day.[1]

Ann was glad for Anne's company but she was not completely open with her either, and tried to make light of her feelings saying rather calmly that 'well now there is no obstacle to our getting off in January'.[2] In reality things were rather more complicated, and the letter she knew would come from Reverend Ainsworth arrived on 1 November. It addressed her in the friendliest terms and hoped that she would 'not forsake him as a friend and begged her to write to him'. The tone of the letter was such that he was clearly laying the groundwork for future more romantic intentions. Ann knew this and admitted that 'she could not misunderstand him.'[3] The deep sense of shame and guilt she felt at having had physical relations her friend's husband now bubbled up within her unchecked.[4] They had committed adultery, was she now morally obligated to accept him should he offer? Ann's mind was whirling; here was a man with whom she had had previous physical intimacy, and the Bible told her that it was her duty to now accept him. If that was so, was her same-sex attraction towards Anne contrary to the will of God? All these thoughts were in her mind as the news sunk in. There was also once again the prospect of children being held out to her; for Ann this was a serious consideration. Her appetite promptly vanished and she spent the evening with 'silent tears trickling down [her] cheeks' as she confronted the reality of her situation.[5]

In a phrase that is rather telling about her true sexuality she told Anne that she 'felt repugnance to forming any connection with the opposite sex', but she struggled to marry her desires with her faith. Although her sexual attraction to Anne was very real, Ann remained undecided about just about everything, yet at the same time promised Anne a lock of hair in the morning – and not one from her head.[6] Tearfully, Ann begged to be left alone until the following Monday but promised to send word to Anne through James of her decision as soon as she had made it. Both women were pale and weepy. Searching for something to do, Ann mended Anne's gloves before she was quite overcome by weeping.[7]

Ann was unable to eat, her stomach thick with tension, but she tried to keep busy. She was interrupted by a parcel that evening from Anne. The enclosed letter was full of business advice but Anne also put a note under the letter's seals which said: 'I am anxious to hear you are better than when I left you. A verbal answer will be quite enough to tell.' Ann was touched and replied that:

> she could not resist the temptation of writing a line or two for I so truly feel with you *il reste un siècle de trois jours* (there remains a century of three days). Waste not one regret on the cutting of the seal. It is more precious to me that you have an idea of. Words are powerless to express my thanks. Suffice that is your gift.

Ann signed the letter 'gratefully and affectionately yours'. She dispatched her note quickly and it was with Anne by 9 pm that night.[8]

Yet despite her words Ann was still undecided. The more she thought about things the more she realised exactly how much she stood to lose; finally, unable to decide, she dispatched a fruit basket containing some grapes to Anne with her answer of further indecision. The fruit basket contained two notes, one saying yes, the other no, and she asked Anne to either choose at random herself, or to ask her aunt to. She wanted to place the decision in Anne's hands writing, 'I have implicit confidence in your judgement … forgive me.' Ann must have known that such an action would bring the straight-talking Miss Lister straight to her door and when she duly appeared through the rain, Ann was waiting for her.[9] They had little time to talk before Mr Outram, Ann's cloth merchant, arrived to discuss some 'lama-hair cloaks at 20 shillings a yard, narrow board cloth width'. When they were finally rid of him, Mrs Dyson called and stayed a quarter of an hour. Tension was high, and when alone Anne told Ann in no uncertain terms that she 'had not been prepared for her note [that] morning ... said she had misled me...[and] ... there had been too many endearments and too great a tie between [them] for [Anne] to go back to what I had been.' Ann listened in shock as Anne declared that they 'should give no more thought to travelling together'.[10] Ann did not know what to think and felt the force of Anne's words keenly. She had not expected that Anne would threaten to withdraw her affection. Very quickly Ann backpedalled and asked for forgiveness. As a peace offering she asked Anne to look over the letter she had drafted to Mr Ainsworth and made the alterations Anne suggested – that she wished from now only to hear news of him via Miss Bentley. There is a definite sense that Ann was feeling shocked by this influx of events and the decision that she was now expected to make. With Anne gone, Ann sought to control the controllable and turned to practical matters; she gave instructions regarding her coal and began to make preparations for the arrival of Harriet Parkhill who was coming to stay.

Word of Ann's low mood had reached Washington's ears and he was pleased to find her 'much better and in good spirits,' when he called. After leaving, Washington encountered Anne, who was coming to call at Lidgate despite what they had agreed. Ann was pleased to see her a day earlier than expected but spoke of business not love, and Anne for her part was almost put out to find her so self-possessed.[11]

The next day Ann received another letter from Mr Ainsworth and this one left no room for ambiguity, he addressed her as 'his affectionate Annie' and made clear that his intent was marriage. Ann had not yet told Anne of the full reasoning behind her indecisiveness, but by Thursday Anne was back at Lidgate where Ann welcomed her and put her to work assisting her with a parcel that she wished to send to Miss Bentley 'containing the books etc for Mr Ainsworth'. Ann was tired, nervous and perpetually tearful as she wrestled with how much of an explanation to give Anne. Her feelings of unworthiness were once again coming to the fore and she used them as an opening to tell Anne of her full history with Mr Ainsworth. Anne was furious on her behalf, uttering that he was a 'scoundrel' many times, while pressing Ann's hands in comfort and agitation. Ann, however, was distraught, telling Anne that she felt morally obligated to accept Mr Ainsworth given what had passed between them. Anne tried to reason 'her out of all feeling of duty of obligation towards a man who had taken such base advantage'.[12]

With Anne's fury Ann's mind cleared, and she declared she would accept Anne's proposal and told her there was 'now no other obstacle between between us and she would be happier with me … I asked if she was sure of this "Yes quite," she asked if I would take her and gave me her word … hoped I should find her faithful and constant to me.' Ann was resolved and quite decided.[13]

Later that night, however, Anne's words were no longer enough and Ann took to her bed. She could not quite shake the fear that she was committing some sort of moral outrage. With no desire to move she was in need of a wash when Anne called the next day. Miss Parkhill arrived and Anne read to both women from the Bible in an attempt to raise Ann's spirits.[14]

To us, living in a secular age, Ann's fears are hard to understand; back then they would have been entirely understandable to most of the population. Religion was both a personal force and a social organisation – and it was heterosexual. For a woman such as Ann, her lesbian desires threatened her entire world; lesbianism and religion were irreconcilable.

It did not take long for these issues to cause a return to her indecisiveness. Ann wavered; she had 'done wrong' and said that God had meant her to marry Mr Ainsworth.

Ann visited her aunt at Cliff Hill and her aunt was alarmed by the change in her. A few days without proper food and sleep had taken their toll and she was now suffering from stomach cramps and chills. Anne and Harriet were very concerned and joined forces to try to make sure that Ann ate and kept her spirits up. On 8 November Anne wrote anxiously in her diary that 'I must be there before she is up in the morning'.

Ann was now technically engaged, but when Anne suggested that she would buy her a turquoise ring she was horrified and answered that she could not wear it 'while still in mourning'. She lay in bed clutching a 'stomach tin' to her middle and suffered 'torments of conscience'. The damp weather did not help and Ann was still in bed at 11 am one day when Anne brought up a note and letter from her brother-in-law that was guaranteed not to improve her spirits, but that evening she felt well enough to come down and play some backgammon with Anne and laughed, winning four hits to Anne's one.[15]

As is typical of those suffering from depression and anxiety, Ann's improvement in spirits did not last the night and the next morning she was in tears at the prospect of travelling with Anne or of making plans. She cried that she still felt 'bound to Mr Ainsworth' by her conscience one minute, and then the next made Anne a present of a nice edition of the Bible. Anne, meanwhile, was seriously considering whether or not it might actually be better for Ann to marry Mr Ainsworth despite his rather unsavoury character, at least to do so might end Ann's fears of damnation. Mr Ainsworth continued to exert pressure and sent Ann more letters.[16] Her family felt that it would be a suitable match and a visit to church that afternoon didn't help her, nor did calling on her aunt at Cliff Hill, and she left there in tears. Perhaps Aunt Walker had impressed upon Ann all that she had to lose if she did not marry – or worse, if she pursued her relationship with Anne Lister to the detriment of her future. Aunt Walker did not discourage Ann's friendship with Anne, but the idea that Ann would give up a husband for her sake was insupportable.

Despite all this Ann couldn't do it, she did not love Mr Ainsworth, 'no it was all her conscience'. She had 'felt affection for him', but she also knew that he was not the sort of man that she wished to marry. To this end she, with Anne's help, wrote conclusively to Mr Ainsworth to say as much. Ann asserted that even without Anne to help her she would have 'gone to London and brought the Chapmans with her ... kept out of the way and done the best she could' to extricate herself.[17]

As her mood stabilised she wanted to thank Anne and decided to send her a copy of *London's Encyclopaedia of Gardening* and two volumes of *Plutarch's Lives*, inside which she placed a note stating that 'if I do recover my health I shall ascribe [it] to you'.[18] She also called Anne 'my love' and made it clear that she would like to see her. With this sent, she dressed and sat down with Harriet for lunch, which she ate from with more appetite than for several days. Ann and Harriet were chatting away like old times when Anne called and interrupted.

It is interesting that Harriet chose later that day to ask Anne if she was aware of Ann's previous engagement to Mr Fraser. Paranoia is a charge later levelled at Ann but it is also certain that, as Anne puts it, 'her secrets were not well kept' by those she trusted.[19]

As Ann's spirits improved so did her physical strength and the next day she managed a four mile walk to Stump Cross Inn. She and Anne then retired to the Moss Inn where they talked sensibly and Ann said that she would 'let [Anne] decide all things for her', while she recovered her health. It was not an idle agreement either, when a letter came that evening to Miss Lister from Mr Ainsworth begging to be allowed to 'send Miss Walker a box that his wife would have left her had she lived to add a codicil to her will', and he excused his previous letters as having 'been written under the effects of opium'.[20] Far from being distressed Ann simply stated that she would do whatever Anne wished. It seems unlikely that Ann was really as sanguine as she stated to Anne, but there is no doubt that having someone to make decisions for her, at least in the short term, was a great comfort to her. A visit from the Miss Wilkinsons also raised her spirits, Lydia Wilksinson was by now engaged to marry the Reverend George Fenton. Earlier in the year Ann had agreed to lend him the not insubstantial amount of £200, which one afternoon Lydia destroyed the bond for.[21] Ann cared deeply about Lydia and was very supportive both emotionally and practically in the run up to her marriage. She also spent more time with Anne out in the fresh air, and they could be found walking in the Cliff Hill fields strewn with wild flowers and inspecting carriages in Ann's stables. Ann nervously approached the subject of foreign travel with Anne and spoke of her fear that going abroad would lead to death, an association it is impossible to think did not come from the death of her brother. Anne soothed her fears but they would not go away entirely, and were fuelled by her Aunt Ann who had similar fears herself and wished to keep Ann close. Ann wrote to her sister Elizabeth to find out her opinion on the matter.[22]

With Ann seemingly better, Mrs Priestley's concerns about her relationship with Anne now came back to the fore. She was surprised that Ann had seen Dr Belcombe instead of Dr Kenny and felt that Ann would not wish to see him again. Mrs Priestley was mistaken however, Ann truly wished to regain her strength and gave Anne permission to 'talk over any plan most likely to reestablish [her] health'. Anne wrote to Dr Belcombe and his response was that:

> The mind is worse than the body, and in this respect I confess I find a nervous young lady much more difficult to manage than I expected. We have relapses which I can neither understand nor guard against.

There is some grinding trouble in the heart, some aching void or something or other that neither medicine nor I can reach.

Dr Belcombe was operating at the very limits of the knowledge of his time in treating Ann, and he knew it.[23]

Even in her 'weakened' state Ann continued to run the estate; she put men to work in the gardens at Lidgate, spoke with Washington and also discussed finances with Anne, offering to loan whatever portion of £2,000 she required to purchase some land near the New Road. She was also well enough to make a trip to Huddersfield in order to shop with Harriet and the two women spent a pleasant afternoon, no doubt visiting shops such as Lancashire's booksellers in Kirkgate which had a good reputation for holding recent titles. Ann was troubled in the carriage when Harriet reiterated her concerns regarding Ann's relationship with Anne, who was waiting for them at Lidgate. Ann wanted her to stay but admitted that 'it was not liked' by Harriet, but first thing the next day she dashed off a note asking Anne to dine and then stay the night. Ann was very glad to see her and was very affectionate to Anne away from the prying eyes of Harriet, but she was in effect reduced to sneaking around in her own home.

Anne's enforced absence quickly took its toll on Ann's health, and doubts began to creep alongside a sickening certainty that she had lost Anne for good with this indecision. Harriet also kept up a constant stream of insults and insinuations regarding 'Miss Lister'. She hoped to discredit her and ensured that Ann was fully aware of the rumours in Halifax at the time. It was an unfortunate coincidence that at around this time Ann likely began to experience physical side effects due to the remedies that Dr Belcombe had prescribed – headaches, visual disturbances and a fever. By 30 November the servants at Lidgate were so concerned that Dr Sunderland was sent for and a note was dispatched with James to Shibden telling Anne to come at once as Ann had fallen ill.[24]

Dr Sunderland arrived and was shown to Ann at around 11 am and was still there when Anne got there at 12. Ann was extremely pleased to see her and her fears came tumbling out. She had thought that the simple absence of 'faithfully' in Anne's last letter had meant that she would abandon her.

The rows with Harriet marked a stiffening of Ann's resolve. Fiercely loyal, despite her own anxieties, she would not allow Anne to be disparaged by her friends and family. Anne was the one who had given her the help she had needed and if her family had hoped to drive a wedge between them it backfired. Harriet's attitude towards Anne simply alienated her further and over the next few weeks Ann became more and more protective. Hand in hand with this came her increased dependence on Anne; Anne was all her happiness and whenever she was left without her at Lidgate, Ann often struggled even to get off the sofa. Ann desperately wanted to get better and Anne was the only one whose approach was actually helping. She increasingly prayed that they 'would be happy together', and took concrete action in the form of writing once again to her sister to ask her advice. Elizabeth Sutherland was concerned by family reports of Ann's 'relapse', fearing that it might signal a return to the worst of her illness. She was not necessarily opposed to Anne as a companion for her sister, however. In fact, she advised Ann that a change of air would be beneficial. She also argued that Anne could introduce her sister to 'acquaintances of high order', and help her expand her social circle.[25] Ann listened to what her sister had to say but it was still not quite enough to convince her to finally make up her mind. Regular visits to church reinforced for her the subversive nature of her desire, whether intentionally or not, and as December approached she remained paralysed by indecision.

Harriet's continued presence was also wearing on her and on 1 December she was so worried that Harriet should find Anne at Lidgate that Anne left early. In complete contradiction to this, three days later Ann stated firmly that Harriet was to go, as 'she is not to dictate to me who I am not to receive'.[26] With Harriet gone Ann invited Anne to stay the night once again, but she knew that Anne was losing patience with her and 'burst into tears' when Anne once again declared that she would take herself off the table as an option so she might be spared 'the agony of indecision'. In response, Ann threw herself into her physical relationship with Anne, in what today might be termed 'hysterical bonding'. She also rather frantically suggested that they might plan to go to Paris together. Anne gently told her that she could not now trust her word as she changed her mind so frequently. In response Ann became distraught, thinking 'it all at an end' between them. On 13 December she was so upset that Anne

1. Cliff Hill, Lightcliffe. (*Image courtesy of Colin Hinson*)

2. Crow Nest, Lightcliffe. (*Image courtesy of Crow Nest Golf Course*)

3. Entrance to Crow Nest, Lightcliffe. (*Image courtesy of Lightcliffe & District Local History Society*)

4. Echoes of the demolished Crow Nest today. (*Image courtesy of Crow Nest Golf Course*)

5. Greenhouses at Crow Nest. (*Image courtesy of Crow Nest Golf Course*)

6. St Matthew's Churchyard as it appears today. (*Image courtesy of Alexa Tansley*)

7. Lidgate, where Ann Walker was living when she and Anne Lister began their courtship. (*Image courtesy of Lightcliffe & District Local History Society*)

8. Anne Lister, Ann's wife.
(*Image courtesy of Wikicommons*)

9. Page from the diary of Ann Walker (*Image courtesy of West Yorkshire Archive Service, Calderdale* reference *WYC:1525/7/1/5/1*)

10. Shibden Hall. Ann's home during, and at points after, her marriage. (*Image courtesy of Shibden Hall*)

Anne   Ann

11. The Lister and Walker Coat of Arms. (*Image by and courtesy of Biljana Popovic*)

12. An artistic impression of the combined Lister and Walker Coat of arms. There were no standard rules at the time regarding same sex unions so this is based on the heterosexual protocol. (*Image courtesy of Biljana Popovic*)

JUSTUS · PROPOSITI · TENAX
PER · ARDUA · VIRTUS

13. John Snaith Rymer, Ann's lawyer at the time of her Lunacy Commission. (*Image created by John H Hansen 1894. Courtesy of the State Library Victoria, Australia, Victorian Patents Office Copyright Collection*)

A List of patients (as required by the 5th and 6th Victoria chapter 87 section 22) now detained in the licensed House for the reception of insane persons of me the undersigned Elizabeth Tose of Osbaldwick in the North Riding of the County of York.

Surname, Christian Name, sex and age of patient, and whether married or Single.	Occupation or profession	Place of residence	Date of Admission of patient, and by whose authority sent, and by whom such patient was brought	Date of Medical Certificate, and by whom signed.	Why Hereinafter found Lunatic by Inquisition.
1. Hannah Gordon. female. 44. single.	Spinster	Overton, Bawtry	1821. and before the passing of the 9th George 4th chapter	1821. William Belcombe. M.C.	no.
2. Mary Nugent. female. 56. single.	Spinster.	York	1823. and Do. sent by Major R. Dunbar, patients Brother.	1823. Do.	no.
3. Sarah Pilling. female. 44. married.	"	Rochdale.	17th May 1831. William Pilling, patient's Husband	18th and 19th May 1831. a Baldwin Wake. M.D. and George Goldie M.D. both of York.	no.
4. Jane Skellow. female. 30. single.	Spinster.	Night House, Doncaster	19th August 1841. Elizabeth Skellow, patients Mother.	12th and 19th August 1841. Robert Storrs of Doncaster and Thomas Stanley Barber of York, Surgeons.	no.
5. Ann Barstow. female. 66. single.	Spinster.	Acomb.	30th March 1843. John Barstow of Temple Thorpe patients Brother.	25th March 1843. M.D. Wilson Hodgson and Samuel Nelson both of Acomb, Surgeons	no.
6. Ann Walker. female. 40. single.	Spinster.	Shibden Hall Halifax.	12th Sept 1843. Elizabeth Sutherland of Udale Fortrose. M.D. patient's Sister.	9th and 12th Sept 1843. Wm Shaw, Surgeon and George Goldie, M.D. both of York.	no.

Elizabeth Tose

Osbaldwick 30th September 1843.

14. Ann Walker listed on the Returns of Private lunatic asylums 1832–1887 QAL. (*MIC 1757/158*) *(Image reproduced by permission of North Yorkshire County Record Office)*

15. Abbey Lodge, Merton. Ann lived here with her sister Elizabeth and brother in law following her Lunacy Commission. (*Photo reproduced by permission of London Borough of Merton*)

16. Ann and her wife continue to inspire artists today. Drawing of Ann and Anne gardening. (*Image by and courtesy of Biljana Popovic*)

Anne Lister
1791 – 1840
of Shibden Hall, Halifax
Lesbian and Diarist;
took sacrament here to seal her
union with Ann Walker
Easter 1834

17. Plaque honoring Anne Lister and Ann Walker's marriage at Holy Trinity Church in York.

sat with her all afternoon consoling her and was quite overcome herself.[27] Ann was relieved when her lover assured her that if she would only be consistent their relationship would be back on. The prospect of losing Anne was too much for Ann and sitting in the moss hut she told Anne that if 'she said yes it would be binding', and that she would 'declare it on the Bible' and take the sacrament with her as well. Ann was still only saying 'if', but she had bought herself some time. In what was becoming an established pattern Ann's mental health improved when she was not faced with a decision. She now felt up to attending to business again and under Anne's guidance responded to her Aunt Plowes, whereby she did not advance a loan request but advised her to improve her situation through the trade of reversionary shares.

Ann now determined to write to Elizabeth again, if Elizabeth agreed with her and Anne's plan to be together and travel, then she would marry Anne. This letter, however, played on Ann's mind. She lingered so long in sending it that by the 19 December Anne considered all things to be off between them once again.[28] They argued and Ann cried and spent a miserable few days alone. There was little Christmas cheer at Lidgate. When Anne did visit they only continued their quarrels, about Mr Ainsworth, Cliff Hill, travel … 'all the usual things', Anne noted with bitterness. Elizabeth advised Ann that the two women should take 'lodgings in York for winter' and then visit her in Scotland the following summer. She said that if Ann still felt it to be the right course then they could 'make a tour of the continent next year'. Crucially, Elizabeth also said that she felt Ann would not marry at the present, and that Ann wasn't ready. When she wrote that, Elizabeth was of course envisioning marriage to a man. It was the answer Ann was expecting and she told Anne as much. Ann had decided for now and her answer was no. It was an emotional day, Ann 'fretted and cried and sighed and said she would not live long', while Anne was disappointed; they were both in tears when they parted.[29]

With things with Anne apparently at an end, Ann's mental health now deteriorated rapidly, so rapidly that all those who knew her became increasingly alarmed. Ann could neither eat nor sleep and without Anne beside her she suffered from night terrors. Before mid-January 1833 she could barely leave Lidgate, she also began to exhibit periods of 'hysteria' where she was giggly and dramatic; Dr Sunderland was called and he diagnosed 'some little excitement of the mind'. Ann was tortured by her lack of 'confidence in God's Will'; in her mind her sins had mounted up, would God forgive her? For what exactly is unclear, it is not certain whether Ann believed her love for Anne was a sin, or that she had sinned in doubting that God had intended her for Anne, or even if Mr Ainsworth was still on her mind. Everyone was now very worried. Anne visited often and sometimes stayed, recording Ann's episodes of what she called 'melodramatic mania'. One day Ann begged Anne to pray for her, pleading that 'it is not only death in this world but a fate worse than death I fear'.[30] Ann was taking very little nourishment and various methods were employed to tempt her to eat more, including keeping a bowl of hot gruel by her bed at all times. As the situation worsened Anne remained at her side.

On 11 January Ann lay in bed, in a room that smelt of Mr Day's turpentine ointment.[31] Turpentine has a long history of medical use, the Romans used it to treat depression, sailors to stop heavy bleeding, and in the 1800s a turpentine rub was considered good for improving the health of the lungs among other things. Unfortunately, it also has a strong smell known to induce headaches and today is considered toxic. Applying turpentine often, even if just to the skin, is considered dangerous. It is safe to say that lying in a room filled with turpentine fumes would not have helped, and likely given Ann a shocking headache. She also had Anne incessantly recite the Lord's Prayer as she tried to rest, leading Anne to write that, 'I think her bedside herself'. Catherine Rawson was now sent for and she was 'frightened' to see Ann's deterioration, it 'disturbed [her] shockingly'. Captain Sutherland and Elizabeth were written to and told of the alarming state of Ann's health. Every night now, Ann was imagining – in addition to the rest – that thieves were trying to break into Lidgate.[32]

Ann also wrote herself to her brother-in-law at this time, a letter that made both him and Elizabeth very concerned. He asked Anne to send him more particulars of Ann's health and her thoughts as to its cause. Captain Sutherland thought that Ann wished for Elizabeth to visit, an action that Anne advised against. Elizabeth had just been delivered of another child and her son also had measles at the time. Anne did however feel that Ann would be happy enough to return with him to Scotland, but thought it would be better that she was not forewarned of this plan. At some point Ann expressed a wish to consult Dr Belcombe's opinion and

Anne certainly felt that he had 'more influence than any other medical man she at present knows'. Dr Belcombe was worried about Ann's rapid decline and prescribed a sleeping draught whose ingredients included 'tincture of henbane – 40 drps laudanum – 6 drops syrop of white poppies – 1 drachm cinnamon or nutmeg water ... these proportions may be increased to 1 drachm of tincture henbane and 12 drops laudanum.'[33]

Captain Sutherland and Anne between them formalised by letter a plan for Ann to be removed to Scotland, where it was hoped that a combination of a change of scene and her sister would restore her to health. Ann was not initially keen when told of the plan, but Anne carefully sold the idea to her with gentle persuasion and Ann's genuine desire to see Elizabeth played a part in her compliance. Elizabeth, Ann knew, loved her dearly and without reservation. She also saw the wisdom of a plan which would put the evil spirits that lived in Lidgate behind her. Catherine Rawson also threw her weight behind the plan.[34] She had come to admire the way in which Anne cared for her cousin and respected her opinion. Catherine also colluded in keeping the plan, and the true nature of Ann's mental collapse, from the wider family. She knew well enough that they would all attempt to scupper the plan and keep Ann in Yorkshire; it is testament to how sincerely she trusted Anne's judgement that she concealed the plan from her mother, aunts and uncles. To this end, Ann was also kept away from church lest her appearance provoke remarks, or worse, the sermon should provoke a crisis.

Yet despite all this persuasion her impending separation from Anne was something that distressed her greatly, she begged that she be allowed to write to Anne saying that 'she would rather write to [Anne] than anyone'. This was discouraged by all, who assured her that Elizabeth would send word to Anne of her health. Preparations continued at a pace while Anne and Catherine kept their vigil at Ann's side. When she was well enough Ann joined them in playing backgammon, gentle walks and prayer, but these instances were rare.

Snow blanketed Yorkshire and made travel difficult; on more than one occasion Anne was trapped and Shibden and unable, despite Ann's pleading, to get back to Lidgate before nightfall.[35] Up in Scotland Elizabeth was frustrated by the weather and wanted both her sister and husband with her. She asked Anne to accompany Ann to Scotland, a proposal it seems that Ann was not aware of: Anne firmly refused.

Chapter 10

Scotland

Captain Sutherland arrived at Lidgate, with his formidable mother in tow, in February 1833 and wasted no time in offering his opinion, saying that the complaint was chiefly in Ann's mind. He suggested that she see Dr Hamilton when they were in Edinburgh. Dr Hamilton, he assured Anne, although elderly was very experienced.[1]

Ann was never very fond of her brother-in-law and, having endured coach journeys with him before, maybe she felt sorry for herself in the same way Anne now pitied her at having to spend time in his 'vulgarish' society. The night before her departure Ann fell asleep in Anne's arms and could hardly bear to let her go, kissing her repeatedly.[2]

Anne's intentions in sending Ann away were good – though she also rejoiced at the prospect of being free of her – but the two visitors that arrived to collect Ann had ulterior motives. Mrs Sutherland quizzed Anne as to whether Ann had ever mentioned Alexander McKenzie, and admitted quite openly that a match between them would clear the man's debts. She referred to Ann purely in terms of her material wealth, calling her 'rated [now] at 2000 pounds per annum', and intended to press her to marry her debt-ridden nephew.[3] Though this marriage plan was not new, Ann was now shockingly vulnerable; she was being sent north in the company of relatives who 'want her (and her fortune) for some of their kin if they can get her'. The Sutherlands were practically rubbing their hands in glee at the prospect of having custody of rich and vulnerable Ann for months on end. Surely, Mrs Sutherland mused, she would not be hard to persuade.

The Edinburgh in which Ann arrived a few days later was gloomy, it had been two years since she was last there and it seems likely they stayed once again at MacKenzie's Hotel. Edinburgh was now a city on the brink of bankruptcy, and riddled with its first major cholera epidemic, the disease ripping through the overcrowded streets.[4] Despite this it remained a popular destination for travellers and was famed for its medical men. While she was there Ann was well enough to go on shopping trips and she sent to Anne, via Aunt Lister at Shibden Hall, a box containing a beautiful rosewood table which she hoped 'may prove [a] useful appendage for her work'.[5] From his letters we know that Captain Sutherland was anticipating a difficult journey with Ann but in reality she travelled well. She declined to seek medical attention from the doctor recommended by Sutherland and instead said that she would trust her recovery to more of the same.[6] From Edinburgh they travelled north from Dunkeld to Inverness, a journey of nearly 100 miles through some of the most magnificent scenery in Scotland. They were heading for the parish of Resolis on the Black Isle peninsula in the district of Ross and Cromarty. At the time, Captain Sutherland and Elizabeth were living there at Braelangwell House.[7] By 24 July 1833 the family would be living at 'Udale in the parish of Cromarty', but when Ann visited the house was undergoing renovations, so it was to Braelangwell she first went, and her niece Elizabeth was born there on 21 October 1832. The family must have moved at some point between October 1832 and July 1833. It was a relieved and somewhat harried Elizabeth that greeted Ann upon her arrival. Ann's nephew George was less than a year old, and her niece Mary had only just recovered from measles.

Braelangwell was a magnificent late eighteenth-century mansion in the classical style, and it boasted ten bedrooms, a magnificent dining room, cosy living room, extensive lawns and a walled garden.[8] Captain Sutherland wrote to Miss Lister and assured her that Ann had arrived safely and that she was well. Ann was indeed feeling better, she and Elizabeth were genuinely pleased to be back together again. She quickly engaged in a programme of light walking and riding to recover her physical strength. The children also proved to be a great distraction and she loved to fuss over her niece and nephew, and helped her sister, although Elizabeth was always anxious that Ann should not over-tax herself. Ann was uneasy in one aspect however, she wanted to hear from Anne and feared – correctly as it turned out – that any letters for her would be intercepted by Captain Sutherland. The same thought had occurred to Anne and when she did write, her letter was kind but extremely proper.

Scotland was no miracle cure though, and Ann soon felt that 'any progress I make one day I lose the next and my fears accumulate upon me'. She was increasingly feeling guilty that she had hurt Anne through her inaction. Despite her sister's company and the hints from both Sutherlands regarding her forming an attachment to Mr McKenzie, Ann found herself quite unable to forget her life back in Halifax and wrote to Anne that 'I cannot forget you or can a few weeks or months obliterate remembrance of the past'.[9]

When not with her sister or the children Ann resumed her botanical drawing and playing the piano. All the exercise she took increased her appetite and she began to put on weight. It is therefore a fair haired, and slender young woman that we must picture when imagining Ann staring out over the Scottish landscape that summer. As May turned into June, Ann found herself applied to for money by her family and she gave Captain Sutherland the enormous sum of £1,000, which we can deduce from later letters she was rather reluctant to do. Ann's thoughts often turned to Anne, and when they did she grew melancholy. Elizabeth was confused by her sister's moods and wrote to Anne that Ann was 'in no better spirits' consistently. Still, it was a vast improvement on those hellish few weeks at Lidgate at the beginning of the year. Anne replied to Elizabeth's letter and sent a stream of advice regarding Ann's care and asked her to show what she had written to Ann herself. In this letter she urged Ann to consult a doctor immediately, preferably Dr Belcombe, and to allow herself to be taken into his care. She assured both women that he would provide Ann with a comfortable setting and 'proper person' to care for her while she recovered her health. Anne must have realised that Ann would have reservations and added an addendum to assure her that this was her personal recommendation and that 'removal and skillful medical treatment are in the first instances absolutely necessary. Half measures never answer and feeble ones but seldom.'[10]

The pattern of her days in Scotland were also interrupted by letters from the persistent Mr Ainsworth, who still wished to address her; he persisted until Captain Sutherland intervened.

By now it was nearing August, Elizabeth's confinement drew near and with Elizabeth incapacitated, Ann grew increasingly uneasy in Scotland. She wrote of her discomfort, and she felt she had to escape Scotland sooner rather than later. Without Elizabeth there to act as a buffer, Captain Sutherland's pressure on her, both for money and on her to marry his cousin, grew stronger. Ann was uncomfortable and she began to plan for her return to Halifax while keeping it secret from her sister and brother-in-law. She knew that they would not approve, Captain Sutherland having made no bones of the fact he hoped to keep her permanently in Scotland. It took some planning, but Ann left suddenly and unexpectedly, without notifying anyone back in Yorkshire of her plans.

Ann returned to Lidgate on Christmas Eve and almost certainly spent Christmas at Cliff Hill with her aunt. Given the speed with which Ann paid a call on the Listers at Shibden Hall it is safe to assume that Anne was foremost in her mind. Aunt Lister told her that Anne had returned to England but was from home and staying with the Norcliffes. Ann immediately wrote to Anne there and expressed once again her gratitude for Anne's care; Anne replied immediately.

Ann settled back down to life at Lidgate with a sense of relief, she paid the required social calls, walked the lanes and spent time with her aunt, all the while counting down the days and hours until Anne returned and she did not have long to wait, Anne was at her door on 4 January. Ann was 'delighted to see [her]' and Anne was thrilled to see Ann and found her 'looking certainly in better spirits than when I saw her last'.[11] Ann had not seen Anne for ten months and now all her feelings and news poured forth. Ann ordered tea and food and the two women sat up talking until 4 am.[12] Ann declared that she regretted going to Scotland and that she wanted to be with Anne, that she wanted to marry her. She told her that she understood this would mean that they would take the sacrament together and exchange rings before God. It was a bold declaration, Ann had not yet transgressed society to the point at which there would be no return. She could have come back to Yorkshire, kept Anne as a friend and sought instead a husband, but she was determined. Scotland had clarified her thoughts, she loved Anne and she wanted to be her wife. For a woman in the early 1800s this was nothing short of remarkable, and it is impossible to overestimate the sheer courage that it took Ann to make such a decision. She risked losing her family, her position in society, her home, her chance of children and turning herself into the subject of gossip by tying herself forever to Halifax's notorious Gentleman Jack. For a woman such as Ann any one of these consequences was no small thing, all together they must have felt almost insurmountable. Ann though had made up her mind; it was worth all this and more to have Anne at her side.

Ann did not consider herself recovered though; she had seen no doctor while in Scotland and she still felt in low spirits. As estate matters began to press once more and family obligations again increased, she felt overwhelmed and asked Anne to take charge of her recovery. One of Ann's primary concerns was that she 'felt so oddly afraid of not caring for anyone', a feeling of numbness that often characterises depression.[13] On 13 January she saw Dr Belcombe, and they discussed her treatment plan. Anne had already spoken to him earlier in the month to 'talk to him about organising lodgings for [Ann] and myself,' in York.[14]

Ann now felt that all was fixed irrevocably between her and Anne. To this end, on 7 January she decided that she would 'employ Mr Grey in York' and that she would make Anne and Captain Sutherland the executors of her new will.[15] She intended to 'secure all to the children', but leave Anne 'all for life'. As her mood fluctuated she opened up to Anne over her distrust of Captain Sutherland, feeling herself hard done by in matters of money and aggrieved he had not thanked her for her help as she felt he ought. Ann was generous, but she did not like feeling as though she had been taken for granted. She wanted to press on with their plans and to this end began to set in motion the process of letting Lidgate, and she spoke to Washington and instructed him to settle the matter.

Secrecy regarding her plans was vital to Ann and Dr Belcombe was to tell no one but his wife about the true nature of her stay; she feared both local gossip and her family's interference. Finally she was satisfied with the arrangements made for her accommodation which comprised '3 rooms and people at 2 guineas a week'. Her new maids were Lucy Smith and Sarah, both of whom she liked very much. Before she moved to Heworth Grange she and Anne took a small trip to Selby and Goole, then on 23 January Ann entered Heworth Grange to recover under the care of Dr Belcombe.[16] Heworth Grange was chosen not only because of Dr Belcombe, but it was also within travelling distance of Shibden Hall. Ann's family were informed that she was staying in York, but not of the true nature of her sojourn there. Ann had told Anne that the key to her family was the support of Aunt Ann and to this end Anne made several visits to Cliff Hill to try to assure her of Ann's health. Her efforts were not entirely successful. Aunt Anne did not approve and knew that she was being kept in the dark, she was very suspicious regarding what matters could keep Ann in York for so long. These suspicions boiled over when Ann visited Cliff Hill on 9 February and she was so cross with her aunt's impertinence that she vehemently instructed Anne not to tell her aunt anything ever again.[17] The whole Walker clan suspected that her health was at the bottom of this odd stay, but an information-seeking visit paid by Mr Edwards of Pye Nest to Dr Belcombe was not fruitful.

Ann ignored letters from her aunt to come home and instead concentrated on her recovery, she had few visitors on Dr Belcombe's recommendation, but instead threw herself into learning French and improving her drawing. The rudimentary nature of her French is revealed in her letters to Anne, in which she asks for her help and correction, but so too is her determination to improve before she went travelling. She did allow one other friend to visit. A newly married Lydia Fenton (née Wilkinson) called upon her as she 'could not sleep till she knew how and where her friend Miss Walker was'.[18] It is testament to their friendship that Ann did not conceal her location nor the purpose of it from Lydia, who was relieved to find Ann much improved. It is easy to imagine that Ann was very isolated during this time, but she did have true and loyal friends independent of Anne that she could have called on if she needed to.

February was a stormy month and by the middle of it Ann felt well enough to issue Washington with a stream of orders regarding the estate and she frequently wrote tightly crossed letters to Anne full of advice and practical opinions. She remained anxious that she and Anne should not betray the true, explicit nature of their relationship in letters that might be intercepted and read, and so these were chatty letters revealing little of either woman's feelings. They do, however, reveal tantalising personal details such as the fact that Ann owned a velvet bonnet that she loved and wished to be stored properly.

Ann's thoughts increasingly turned to her and Anne's future plans. She ordered a Paris guide and requested that Anne order her a copy of *Paxton's Magazine of Botany* Issue 1. Ann was particularly interested in his views on conservatory design given her own plans for Crow Nest and the gardens at Shibden. Ann's future was no longer abstract; when she had agreed to marry Anne she had also agreed to her vision for the future.

Chapter 11

Marriage

On the morning of 27 February 1834 Ann and Anne visited the Norcliffes at Langton. It was not the first time they had called there together, but this visit would be different for as they travelled in the carriage Ann and Anne finally exchanged rings to solemnise their marriage. Anne asked Ann to 'cut the gold wedding ring I wore and [I] lent her the sixpence to pay me for it'. Ann did not give her the ring back immediately but rather 'wore it until we entered the village of Langton', when she put it on Anne's 'third finger in token of our union which is now confirmed forever though little to nothing was said.'[1] In return, Anne placed on Ann's finger an onyx ring that she had bought for the purpose in York. This was to be no symbolic marriage, from this moment on both women considered themselves bound to each other, in every possible way in sickness and in health, until death parted them.

Ann was nervous but she needn't have worried. Only Mr Norcliffe and Charlotte were at home and the visit went very well with Ann growing in confidence as the afternoon wore on. She admired some drawings there and generally made a good impression, leaving happy to be on friendly terms with people of importance to Anne. Ann had also been gratified to hear that Anne's sister Marian had thought that she was more likely to suit Anne 'in every respect' better than Mrs Lawton, and that Mr Lister and Aunt Lister had agreed.[2] That Anne's family approved of her meant a great deal, the more so because Ann could not share even the sanitised version of her marriage with her own family, who she knew would object to her union with Anne in the strongest terms.

For the moment Ann remained at Heworth Grange while Anne returned to Shibden and the two women wrote to each other constantly, Anne offered Ann her opinion in these letters on just about everything but Ann did not always take her advice. She would not, in one instance, 'have Anne paint the carriage' because she wanted to wait, nor would she give consent for the letting of Lidgate until she was quite certain that Washington had arranged things as she wished. Ann also wished to delay the renovations at Shibden, questioning the extent of them. Anne interpreted this as more evidence of Ann's indecision but, as Ann argued, she wanted to spend more time at Shibden before she offered her opinion as to what ought to be done. A glimpse into Ann's character and management style, as well as the way she was viewed by her employees, can be found in part of a letter sent to Anne on 13 March but written to Washington. Ann wrote at least 'one sentence [that was] much too sharp' as she issued her orders. Anne rather resignedly recorded in her diary that Washington would blame her for Ann's sharp tone when really it was her who had urged Ann to use a softer one. Few, including Washington, seemed to realise that Ann's shyness and anxious nature concealed a very sharp, forthright mind.[3]

When writing to her aunt and sister, Ann revealed enough to rouse their suspicions regarding her future plans. She spoke of Anne warmly and hinted at her moving to Shibden, all of which did nothing to calm her family's fears. Nor did her writing to Captain Sutherland wishing to discuss the division of joint Walker family property. They feared what a confident Ann, under Anne's guidance, might do with family money if left to her own devices.[4] Their disapproval was no longer going to prevent Ann from acting as she wished though, and she happily agreed to the second part of their marriage taking place.

The 30th of March dawned very fine and the two women, after sharing 'three kisses' and having breakfast at 8.30 went to the church of the Holy Trinity in York where they took communion together, signifying the solemnization of their union. It was the first time that Anne had 'ever joined [Ann] in my prayers, I prayed that our union might be happy'. Both women believed that their union was now valid in the eyes of God. Ann would always struggle with her sexuality in relation to her faith, but she would never waver in the belief that she was from this moment on truly married to Anne.[5] Ann Walker and her wife had made history.

They spent the afternoon paying calls, then walked to Heworth before going to a service at Monk-Bar church at which, given that Anne fell asleep, we can safely say Ann paid more attention. They sat up talking until after midnight and Anne notes in the margin of her diary that they also had very enjoyable sex. In the morning they went to the Register Office to enquire about getting a new manservant, as Thomas was leaving to be married, and Ann bought some 'silver forks at Cottle and Barbers'. After which Ann had her drawing lesson, the subject of which was perspective, before walking down the Stockton Road to get some fresh air before dinner.[6] After spending the night kissing, Ann was not ready the next morning when Washington called and he was forced to wait while she dressed and had her breakfast. One has to wonder if Washington, while he waited, was at last beginning to appreciate Ann's true character, rather than blame her foibles on Anne. When she finally came down they discussed business matters before Mr Brown arrived to give her a further drawing lesson, at which she admired an 'interesting diagram illustrative of his new system of perspective'. Anne was also impressed and the two women kept him there until 1 pm talking. They also 'went [to] pay Wolstenholme for his designs of Oak chimney piece and doors for the north room' at Shibden.[7] This was just one part of the renovations planned which were all part of Anne's plan to transform Shibden into a true family seat, now she had access to Ann's money.

Determined not to be caught out again, Ann was up early the following day anticipating Washington's early visit. She instructed him to 'let Manningham have the toll' and to pay the mason she had employed '68 pounds for the whole job'. It is often assumed that Anne took over the whole of the estate management after the two women married but it is very clear that this was not the case, Anne indeed takes pains to note once again in her journal that it was Ann who met and dealt with Washington, not herself.[8]

Ann had long wished to visit Duncombe Park and once Washington was dealt with they decided to set off. It was a journey of about thirty minutes by carriage and they 'alighted near Crayke castle', where they admired the fine and extensive views. Ann spent the evening knitting and mending while Anne planned their next day's adventures – a walk to Rievaulx Abbey – and the sky burned red.[9] This division of labour was a pattern that would continue throughout their marriage.

Both women were keen to see Rievaulx and made a point of walking up the 'steep cawse road to the far terrace'. Despite all this walking Ann was not at all tired and so they chose to walk to Wass themselves to meet with the carriage rather than send for it. Such frequent episodes of physical activity belie her doctors' observations that Ann was physically frail. That evening they stopped off at Langton where Charlotte Norcliffe rather bluntly asked why Anne had brought Ann with her, for Miss Walker she had heard was 'crazy'. Anne set her straight on this matter and said that Ann was just shy. Charlotte was not convinced and spent most of the evening trying to convince Anne that she was doing Ann a disservice by 'taking up with her'. Ann had retired upstairs by this time but it couldn't have been a very comfortable evening for her, she was quite deliberately excluded. Bored and annoyed Ann dozed off before she meant to, but Anne woke her when she came to bed and they sat up late talking.[10]

Charlotte Norcliffe seems to have realised that she had erred and the following day she kept silent on the subject of Ann and only noted rather wryly that her fortune was considerable. Ann was back at Heworth Grange by 9 pm, and they had spent such a pleasant few days together that rather than returning to Shibden that night, Anne dispatched a note to her aunt to inform her that she would be staying with Ann for another few days.[11] The note dispatched Ann ordered coffee and they sat talking over it until well after midnight, their future travel plans featuring at the top of the bill and after her initial reluctance Ann was now keen to get away. All in all Ann's married life had got off to a much better start than seemed possible a year earlier.

As Ann's health continued to improve over the next few weeks she rode out more often and letters flew between Heworth and Shibden frequently as together Ann and Anne discussed everything from business, and the improvements at Shibden, to Eugenie's thoughts on the location of a misplaced cloak. The only blip healthwise for Ann came in mid-April when she suspected that Dr Belcombe would want to alter her medication as she was sore in her intimate area. Anne, upon being told this, immediately feared that she had given Ann a sexually transmitted infection, as she had done to Isabella years earlier. She felt terrible but luckily the issue turned out to be something else.[12] Possibly Ann was suffering from a UTI.

Ann felt able by now to resume paying social calls and on 15 April she went to stay at Shibden. Ann was nervous, this was a precursor to her moving in permanently and she feared that now things were more certain they would be awkward. She was, however, welcomed warmly by Marian and Anne's father and it took only ten minutes for her shyness to fall away. After speaking to them for a few minutes Ann was taken upstairs to see Aunt Lister, whose leg prevented her from moving around. Ann had been particularly worried about Aunt Lister's health and took pains to enquire about it in her letters to Anne. She found Aunt Lister in a lot of pain, but she was 'really glad to welcome [her]'.[13] From Shibden she paid a call on her aunt at Cliff Hill, who despite her misgivings regarding Ann's actions welcomed her gracefully, and she also oversaw some business at Lidgate afterwards before returning to play backgammon.[14] Ann also heard from Elizabeth whose letter enclosed one from Mr McKenzie in which he renewed his addresses. She returned this unopened along with a letter that Anne helped her to write, categorically refusing him.

Ann was often left alone during the evenings at Shibden and her relationship with Marian became a friendship as the two women spoke together. Marian at this time was seriously considering marriage to Mr Abbott and Ann was probably a more sympathetic listener than Anne, who was always rather black and white in such situations.[15] On 20 April Ann made her first appearance at church with Anne by her side, after which she inspected '30 of the Sunday school boys', and 'examined them in their catechism'. Lightcliffe was Ann's preferred church, not least because of her involvement in the Sunday school there and it was a conscious decision, and a brave one, for her to appear there with Anne at her side. Rather inconveniently Ann also began to bleed that day, the first time she had done so properly in over a year. Good food, gentle exercise and far less stress was beginning to pay dividends on her physical health. With the first church visit over with Ann was now determined to get on with visiting the family tribe. On just one day in April she visited Blake Hall to call on Mr Joshua Ingram in Huddersfield called on Mr Aitkinson, and went to Gledholt to call on the Rawsons. Then it was on to Mr Wilkinson's before heading home to Shibden where she still had energy for 'pretty good' sex.[16]

It was not all plain sailing though, a visit to Cliff Hill on 24 April left her 'tired and cross'. Given the frequency with which visits to Cliff Hill leave Ann out of sorts it seems reasonable to suppose that her aunt persisted in her disapproval of Ann's life choices. Aunt Anne's disapprobation was the one Ann found most difficult by far to bear. She was not, however, willing to give up on her family or friends and was as generous as ever. On 29 April she bought Mr Bewley's niece a handsome tea service costing 21 shillings as a wedding present, lent her family various amounts of money and renewed her local philanthropic concerns alongside activities at the

Sunday school.[17] This kept her busy while Anne went away for a few days. She also kept a close eye on Aunt Anne's health and sent for Dr Sunderland in Anne's absence when she grew concerned about her one evening, but all was well she assured Anne in one of several letters. She had everything under control.

With Anne's encouragement Ann wrote to her sister and brother-in-law wishing to discuss their views on dividing up the Walker estate. She wanted to clarify exactly what income she could expect in the future as Anne had big plans, which included buying Staups and the imminent sinking of a coal pit as well as the expansion of the Shibden estate.

Ann returned to Heworth Grange at the beginning of May but began to plan for her leaving permanently. Upon her return she was pleased to see Sarah, her maid, whose company was a 'great comfort to her'. She also planned a drawing trip with Mr Brown as a birthday treat and they set off on Ann's 31st birthday. Ann, with her wife and Mr Brown, travelled through Boroughbridge to Richmond where she spent three days sketching during the day and learning to improve her Worsted work in the evening. Under Anne's guidance she finished off a stag design footstool and read *Clarkson's History of Richmond*. She also sketched both Barnard Castle and the mighty rock formations at Brimham. This was good preparation for their honeymoon journey, the organisation of which Anne had well in hand and on 30 May, Ann had her hair cut by Parsons, to ensure that she would look suitably fashionable upon their arrival in Paris. All Ann's plans were now focused on her forthcoming honeymoon journey and at some point she packed a slim notebook with a marbled cover; it was to become her travel journal.

Chapter 12

Diarist

Ann Walker began her journal on 4 June 1834, the day she and Anne Lister set off on their honeymoon journey.[1] She had spent the previous day, like travellers everywhere, in a flurry of last minute preparations taking charge of the packing while Anne dashed about running errands. It opens with the inauspicious words, 'dearest very poorly', but despite this the two women set out from Heworth Grange. The weather was good, and making good time they headed for Barnby Moor where the inn they stayed at was very comfortable but Ann was worried about her wife who was 'very much tired and knocked up'. Ann stayed downstairs while Eugenie helped Anne to change, but she became worried and ventured upstairs to find that Anne had fallen asleep.[2] Rather clumsily Ann helped Anne to bed, a process that apparently went less than smoothly given that Anne writes that Ann 'got [me] into bed as best she could.'[3]

The next morning Ann went downstairs and took her breakfast alone as 'dearest [was] so ill [she] did not rise till 12 o'clock in the afternoon', with a 'pain in her back and a terrible bilious headache'.[4] At a loose end, Ann walked about and noted that 'Mr and Mrs Canning/brother to Sir Stratford Canning and three ladies arrived.'[5] The Canning family was a well known one, and Sir Stratford would serve on and off throughout his life as the British Ambassador to the Ottoman Empire. Later she sat at Anne's bedside, talking and watching Anne take a little sago. She ate her dinner there before going to speak to Eugenie to request arrowroot for Anne to take. The irony of this role reversal cannot have been lost on Ann, who, although worried, relished the chance to cosset her wife for a change.

The next day Anne was able to take some boiled milk and bread, a standard invalid dish of the time described as an 'instinctive palliative'.[6] With something in her stomach Anne felt better and although she was still 'weak and burnt up with fever', she dressed. They were heading to

Grantham and by the time they arrived Anne was feeling well enough to take more bread and milk. They were staying at the George Inn, a smart, brick building that had been constructed in 1789 Ann though was not impressed, the 'smell [of the] paint – very disagreeable'.[7] Keen to get away and after a 'disagreeable breakfast' the next morning they continued their journey south. Ann was relieved that 'dearest was rather better' and they visited Burghley House, where the housekeeper showed them around. Ann was particularly pleased to have seen Carlo Dolce's *Saviour Blessing the Elements*, and other 'good paintings'.[8] She seems to have determined that she would note all the art she saw. From Burghley they travelled south towards Stevenage, sharing some cold ham together in the carriage.[9]

It is clear that Anne still wasn't feeling very well, and the next morning she was 'overcome by fatigue' as she tried to read to Ann and so she rested on a sofa until 1 pm while Ann again observed other travellers. At 1 pm they set off for London and upon reaching it took rooms at 13 Albemarle Street, as the Hawkins' Hotel at 29 Albemarle Street, where Anne had lodged previously, was regrettably full. Constructed in the 1690s, Albemarle Street was an extremely fashionable location; it was London's first one way street and was famous as the location of the offices of Lord Byron's publisher John Murray. Their rooms at number 13 were rather disagreeably up three flights of stairs, and 'bad stairs' at that. They ate dinner at 7 pm, which consisted of 'veal cutlets, green pea soup and good gooseberry tart', and Anne sent a note to Mrs Hutton, asking her to come at 9 in the morning.[10] Thanks to Anne Lister's scientific mind, we know that the room Ann slept in that night was precisely 68 degrees Fahrenheit/20 degrees Celsius.[11]

The following morning was a fine one, and they had breakfast at 10 am, after which Mrs Hutton dutifully arrived and measured Ann for a new habit. Women's habits at the time were standard travelling wear and would have consisted of a high necked, tight waisted jacket, with fashionable dropped shoulders and gigot sleeves that would have been worn over a shirt and long matching skirt. Ann then paid a visit to Dumergue's (24 Albemarle Street) where she had a tooth extracted and filed. Despite the rather gruesome reputation of nineteenth-century dentists, Ann's ordeal could not have been too bad as by the afternoon she was 'very well'.[12] Probably at Ann's suggestion they then went out shopping – her shopaholic tendencies and status as family present-buyer, by now being well established. Ann shopped at Cornhill's to buy blue spectacles, which she later wrote to encourage her sister to also buy, before returning so that she might try on her habit.[13]

While in London Ann also dealt with other family concerns and went to Acre Lance, in modern-day Brixton, to visit her Aunt Plowes and left a note there for her Uncle Thomas Edwards, another sibling of her mother, who lived in Regents Park.[14] The next morning it was Ann's turn to feel unwell; she woke up at 7 am feeling 'bilious' and went back to bed. Anne was also not feeling good and wrote that 'my head was still not well'. Both women stayed in bed all day, only rising to take some food at about 3 pm. When feeling better Ann tells us affectionately that 'dearest [had been] all attention.'[15]

In London Ann also attended to business and visited Hammersley's bank three times. The bank was a trusted one and before they left London both women dropped off some letters there and a 'brown paper parcel containing Ann's will'.[16] Hammersley had long been Anne's London banker and it was usual for her to leave important documents there before departing on a trip abroad. She advised Ann to do the same.

The start of their journey proved to be rather more eventful than they expected as they headed south. Just before the Greenwich turnpike, which was located at the junction of Greenwich High Road and Blackheath Road, their carriage bumped into another cart which knocked the cap off their back wheel. George had to oversee the repairs, almost certainly undertaken by Gowar and Sons who were based near the toll. Ann had hoped to visit Rochester Cathedral but in the end they stopped in Rochester for only a few minutes to pick up some sandwiches and scones to eat as they drove along.[17] After spending most of the day in the carriage it was a relief to arrive safely at Canterbury. Ann's focus there was Canterbury Cathedral and the delight with which she recounts the details of her visit is clear. She notes, in a manner that it will soon become evident is her habit, the cathedral's key architectural details: 'length of choir 100 feet, height 810 to vaulted roof'. She also notes that Dorothy, a widow, bequeathed the pavement in the cloister, and greatly admired the 'Black Prince's monument, his coat of armour, gauntlet and sword.' Other details such as the fact the steeple was damaged by a storm in 1703 were likewise faithfully noted.[18]

After her visit, Ann went for a walk around the city. Canterbury in the 1830s had a population of around 15,000 people and much of the medieval city was still then intact, streets that would later be destroyed by the Luftwaffe. The city was prosperous and flourishing, on the very cusp of rapid industrial development that was driven in part by the presence of the Canterbury to Whitstable railway which had opened four years before Ann's visit. This increased industry fuelled an expansion in trade and commerce that Ann appreciated as she walked around the town and she was impressed by the range of shops available. She wrote, in a way that would have made Henry Tilney proud, that the shops were 'very good – particularly for Muslins'.[19]

From Canterbury it was on to Dover, they arrived at 4.30 when their carriage clattered into the courtyard of the Ship Inn, on Custom House Quay. In 1834 it was a busy staging post, when Ann stayed there there would have been eight mail coaches leaving every night for London, following the twelve to sixteen that travelled the same road every day. It is therefore safe to assume that the hotel would have been bustling when Ann drew up. Mr and Mrs Worthington were 'very civil' to her and she enjoyed herself thoroughly, playing on the piano before sitting down to a dinner of 'cutlets, plain boiled pudding, claret and strawberries'.[20]

The next morning they 'board[ed] the Furet packet' under Captain Hamilton. They left the shore at 8.30 am and were underway fifteen minutes later. Once again it was Anne's ill health that caused concern; she was copiously seasick on the journey out, Ann herself was 'not sick at all', rather to her surprise.[21] By 11.15 they had crossed and were at anchor. Their carriage could not be taken ashore before 2 pm, so instead Ann got in a small boat with her wife and Eugenie and they were taken to the shore landing 'alongside the pier about 12 ½', George was left to sort out the transport of their carriage. Anne was still not feeling well so they headed straight for the hotel, where Anne slept while Ann, who was more hungry than tired, went in search of Chablis and biscuits.[22] Again Ann seems to have relished the role of caretaker. By mid-afternoon they were both hungry and had a dinner at around 3 pm that consisted of 'sole, veal cutlets, tart, strawberries and cherries'.[23] They were away from Calais just after 5 pm heading to the Hotel de Londres at Boulogne where they were soon in bed sharing kisses and giggling. The bed was so small that Anne kept 'almost tumbling out'.[24]

From Boulogne they travelled to Abbeville, where they stayed at the Hotel d'Europe, a relatively new establishment that had opened about thirty years earlier after Catherine Pierron had bought the building to turn it into a travellers' house. Ann did not wish to go far after their arrival so they only went to the local church to have a quick look around before strolling on the boulevard and through the gardens. At 8.30 they were back at the hotel and Ann carefully recorded that they ate a dinner of 'soup, pike, poulet, pigeon in peas, apple, strawberries, cherries, almonds and biscuits for dessert'.[25] Anne adds that there was also 'potato and cauliflower'.[26] Her journal entry for this day is particularly important because it is the first time that she uses the nickname 'Adny' to refer to Ann, no longer is she the formal Miss Walker or even Ann to her wife.[27]

It was by now nearly midsummer; the weather was very warm, and the markets of France were overflowing with fresh soft fruit and salads. Ann's love of fresh fruit is an intimate detail that becomes increasingly obvious in her journal and she is almost constantly noting that she ate berries of one type or another. Ann also particularly enjoyed a visit to the Tapesserie des Goberlins. The factory had been revived under the Bourbon Restoration having been temporarily closed during the French Revolution. Ann was very interested in the tapestry and the manufacturing processes that they were using, writing that there were '64 persons constantly employed of which ten were pupils, who work only for the royal family'. Perhaps she was thinking of her own endeavours to provide education for those on her estates. As for the tapestries themselves Ann called them 'exquisite and it is almost impossible to distinguish them at a little distance from paintings', she particularly liked 'one of a white dog and hound ... the background was particularly beautiful'.[28] Ann's observations would have pleased the owners, the factory had run from 1663 to 1690 under the supervision of Charles le Buen, court painter to Louis XIV, and the aim had been to make tapestries so fine that they appeared to be paintings.

Ann entered Paris through the barriere de Clichy in the northwest of the city.[29] In 1814, when 800,000 foreign soldiers marched on Paris at the close of the First French Empire, it was at the barriere de Clichy that Marechal de Moncey defended the city with his army of 15,000 students. A force that valiantly resisted the advancing Russians until an armistice could be declared. They were staying at the Hotel de la Terrace where Isabella Norcliffe joined them at dinner. If Ann was irritated she didn't say so, only recording that 'Isabella Norcliffe came into my room and complained excessively of the heat.'[30] Ann retired early leaving Anne and Isabella to chat about her, Isabella expressing her amazement at Anne's choice. Anne robustly defended Ann saying that 'Miss Walker had more in her than people thought'.

Shopping was on Ann's mind the next morning and she went out to order gloves and shoes, before they called on Madame Figuerol, the dressmaker, who arranged to call the next evening and measure Ann for stays before heading out to dinner at the opera, but Ann was not feeling well. Her period had arrived while they were out and she was caught unawares, like many women before and since. Ann was tired but was delighted to find a letter at the hotel from Miss Lister, which was written to both women alongside two from her Aunt Aitkinson.[31]

The next day for Ann brought a visit to the Louvre with its '20 halls of statuary, saw the celebrated statue of Diana a la Biche in Parisian marble … holding in her left hand the bow bent down while in thought', as was her custom, Ann records the particulars of the art she sees. Ann walked the 'gallery of paintings [it] is a quarter of a mile long, we walked to the end and back again. The only picture we had time to really stop and look at was a Madonna, saviour and St John by Raphael.'[32] This is not the first nor the last time that Ann would subtly record that she felt rushed by their travel schedule and it seems likely that she had wanted to spend more time looking at the paintings. In contrast, Anne writes in explanation that she felt they should not 'strain our eyes over things of less value'.[33]

They then went to the Palais Royale, the huge and impressive palace that had been built for Cardinal Richelieu in the 1630s, although by the time Ann was seeing it the architecture had been extensively modified. The courtyard Ann writes was 'surrounded by shops of every description [and] one side of the court is now the residence of the Duke of Orleans, oldest son of King Louis Philippe'.[34] Prince Ferdinand Philippe, Duke of Orleans, had been born in 1810, when his father was in exile in Sicily. King Louis Philippe had ruled France since 1830, proclaimed king after his distant cousin Charles X had been forced to abdicate following the July Revolution. For the first ten years of his reign he was very popular, with many Frenchmen believing that he offered France the best chance of peace and stability. The Paris that Ann was walking around was very much his city. She walked along the Galerie d'Orleans, one of Paris's most famous covered arcades and part of the duke's artistic redevelopment. It had been completed only four years previously, the light stone would have shone bright in the summer sunlight. While there they 'ordered plate and 100 cards' for Ann before buying gateaux and cakes from a patisserie which they washed down with lemonade. In the late afternoon they went to visit the 'exposition de l'industrie française', which consisted of '4 very long buildings, containing everything one could possibly think of'. There were fabric, carpets and chimes, but what really caught Ann's eye 'was a model of the interior of a watch constructed for the professors of the arts of the trades to give lectures upon. The price is 5,000 francs but Mr Perrelet [the maker] says that after so much time and labour he shall lose by it.' Her eye was also drawn by 'a footstool with velvet cover' and an innovative wine bottle rack whose unusual form she sketched, somewhat oddly, in her journal. She ordered a bonnet from Madame Thomas and she was 'tempted with [a] cashmere shawl at De Lisles'.[35]

Friday 20 June was a lovely hot, sunny day. While Anne was out dealing with the passport issues Ann wrote letters to her aunt and to Miss Lister, then when Anne returned they went back to the exposition. Upon their return they found that Miss Berry had left them a ticket for a box at the Theatre Francois Palais Royal that evening, at which Ann thought that 'Madame Mante performed the part of the princip admirable and in a very ladylike manner.' It was not good enough though to prevent her practically falling asleep during the break in between the pieces. There was one more stop to make that evening, and they sat for half an hour with the Norcliffes, both to take their leave and to give Isabella a 'snuff box that I [Anne] had bought for her but inadvertently left at the engravers 3 years ago'.[36] Whether or not Ann had any objection to Anne giving this gift to her former lover we don't know. We do know that she was relieved to get back to the hotel though, suggesting that the evening had been rather trying.

Chapter 13

Into the Mountains

Before she left Paris Ann wrote to her aunt that she was 'delighted with all and very happy'.[1] Rather to her surprise, travel was suiting her and she was revelling in seeing new sites, in exploring new technologies, and in shopping. She also 'finished letters to Mrs Lister and my aunt, marked 4 petticoats and wrote to my sister – told her all we had seen and done'.[2] While Ann was back at the hotel, 'dearest went to take coffee with Lady Charlotte Lindsay and [the] Miss Berrys, who were very civil', and she talked about travel costs with other explorers such as Colonel Moore, 'who in a tour of 4 years had been all over Greece and Asia Minor and Syria', and he gave Anne 'some useful information'.[3] Ann was very much excluded from these practical discussions; something that was later to cause conflict when the issue of expenses arose. Ann was finishing her sewing having made a pair of calico drawers, when Anne returned and the two women shared some wine and strawberries, taking advantage of the cooler air to sit up into the early hours. By morning the weather had broken and it was raining when Ann put on her hat and headed to church, where she enjoyed the sermon that was preached from Luke, recording in her journal that it lasted for twenty-four minutes and concerned virtue and the punishment of vice. In contrast, Anne was 'half asleep the whole time'. After church Ann shopped, purchasing more gloves including '6 from Peivat Rue de la Paix', and some for Miss Lister. In a very human detail, Ann notes that 'mine from Prevait far better than those from – but from both the fingers are too long'; Ann had small hands.[4]

The next stage of their journey was to Geneva, and when they returned to the hotel they found their passports and visas were waiting for them. After an afternoon spent in having her hair dressed so that Eugenie might learn the *mode actuelle*, food was once again on Ann's mind and she ate a dinner of 'Beef, Volu vont and rice pudding', before they 'drove to Bois de Boulogne [and] walked there 40 minutes'. On the way home Ann saw the carriage men of Paris light their lamps and it's easy to picture her looking out and watching as passing lamps helped to illuminate, for a moment, the dark corners of the city.[5] Ann was up early the next day at 6.30, and she 'marked two pairs of gloves' and had breakfast before they drove to the bank Lafittes to get money and then on to Madame de Bourkes and the Miss Berrys. It is noticeable that these social calls are the subject of far more ink in Anne's journal than in Ann's. While Anne records details of people and conversation, Ann was far more inspired to write by the Tuileries Garden, which she walked through later in the day noting wistfully 'almost all the trees [had been] destroyed by the allies.'[6]

From Paris they travelled to Essonne – 'stopped ten minutes George fastening nuts of screws' – and drove 'through the forest de Fontainebleau' to the Hotel de la Ville de Lyon. After checking in they headed out to view the Palace.[7] Ann was delighted to be shown 'the table on which he [Napoleon] signed his abdication April 5th 1814'. Her interest in the Palace is clear, as is her enthusiasm for the gardens where she 'saw the tulip tree flourishing plentifully and growing much higher than I ever saw in England.' Anne tells us that Ann, 'tired could walk no further', but Ann herself says nothing of the sort.[8] She was, however, hungry and back at the hotels she ate 'soup, mutton cutlets, veal cutlets poulet, souffles, cream, strawberries and biscuits'.[9]

At Sens Ann and Anne 'stopt at the cafe … Adny had cafe au lait which warmed her and took off her sensation of faintness'. Again Ann herself doesn't mention feeling ill and it is notable how often these feelings of illness in Ann coincide with her being hungry. It is something that Anne also notices and she wrote in a letter to her aunt that Ann 'requires to eat oftener than I do: but we manage very well about this'.[10] Their differing appetites, as well as the referral to hunger as sickness, definitely becomes a recurring theme in both women's accounts. After having coffee they went to view Sens cathedral and there Ann saw 'a very fine monument of the Dauphin, son of Louis 15th by Couston' that served as his tomb after he died of tuberculosis, aged 36. Although he died before he could inherit the crown, he was the father of three French kings and Ann thought the 'figure(s) full of imagery'. Reading this diary page brings one so close to Ann that you can almost touch her; half way through writing about the church her pen either breaks or runs out of ink and she must have got up at that moment to change her pen or fetch more ink before continuing.[11]

That evening Ann and Anne shared a bottle of champagne that Anne had bought over from 'my cave at rue st vincent', alongside their kisses and Ann rather overdid it, for the next morning she was 'on the pot all the time', which delayed their departure. Anne feared that this was the beginning of a decline in Ann's spirits, but given that she was fine the next day it seems more likely that Ann was just hungover, tired and hungry. The weather did not help and 'black clouds, winds and thunder' were rumbling about them.[12]

They arrived at the Hotel de la Cloche at 4.30. Today the hotel occupies a different spot having moved location in 1880 when the Place Dracy was being constructed, but the Hotel that Ann stayed at would have been found on the Rue Guilliama. Ann lay down for a few minutes before going to the museum. Neither woman was overly impressed with the paintings, but Ann admired the 'beautiful tombs of Duke of Burgundy and Philip de Hardi [that were] removed from the Chartreuse at the Revolution'. They were, she recalled, 'beautiful sculptured on top and at the sides most beautiful tabernacle lock'. As seems to have been their custom by now they went for a walk in the evening, 'getting some orange syrup at the confectioners by the way'.[13]

Not far from the hotel are the Jardin botanique de l'Arquebuse that Ann called the 'Jardin de Plants', when she wrote about her visit there that afternoon. It was then 'just lately begun', the plants having been moved there in 1833 from Dijon's first botanical garden. Here Ann was in her element as she walked around, examining the plants. She was delighted to discover 'the name of the plant whose leaves are quite white, that was in the greenhouse at Crow Nest – Cinesacia'; Ann writes the plant name twice, clearly unsure as to how to spell it. There were also 'acacia trees, Magnolias, Oleanders, Marigolds – of which the French are particularly fond, dahlia poppies and carnations' to be seen.[14]

The next day, 29 June, was to be another day of travelling. This time Ann 'ate biscuits in the carriage' and Anne notes with satisfaction that this 'seems to have suited her very well'.[15] Anne is at last realising that Ann needs food! They were heading into the mountains and here we get a clear glimpse of both Ann's sense of humour and the camaraderie that she shared with her travelling companions. Anne records that there was a row that day:

with the Postillion – very impertinent – so would only give him 15 sols per poste, because 1 ½ came to 22 ½ sols he would not take the 23 sols would have liards because he thought I said I had none – would not take the money at first – had the maitre de poste up, very civil but got out of the way – threatened to send for one of the police … Ann laughing, George trembling like an aspen leaf she said.[16]

The image of Ann breathless with laughter while teasing George as the others look on in amusement is a vivid one.

The next day they set off early, leaving Morey and travelled 'along a beautiful narrow gorge … from Morey to Rousses'. They walked up a hill for twenty minutes and then breakfasted. As they drove off, heading for Switzerland, Anne grumbled that Ann was 'all the while on the pot – has very often two motions a day – she was sickish and peevee as usual but noyau afterwards in the carriage did her good'. The idea of Ann settling her stomach with liquor seems rather counterproductive but it apparently helped.[17] Ann herself makes no mention of ill health and they were both delighted with an inn they saw when they stopped in Gex, 'we thought we could well spend a few days there'. Ann ate trout for lunch before they headed to Ferney and Voltaire's chateau. Sadly Ann left half a page of her journal black, clearly intending to fill in her observations at a later date, but she never got around to doing so. We know however from Anne's journal that they were shown Voltaire's chamber and *salle à manger* before going around the gardens with their magnification view of Mont Blanc. Anne gushes about her visit and it seems likely, given her interest and education, that Ann shared her feelings. The fact that in the village afterwards Ann bought a little bust of Voltaire and lithograph of his chamber and chateau furthers this assumption.

Mont Blanc was on Ann's mind as now they were heading to the mountains proper, she thought that Anne was likely to go to the top and said 'she would certainly go too',[18] despite recording rather ghoulishly that she had heard of two Englishmen who had died making a similar attempt the previous year. They arrived at Geneva that evening at 5.30 and 'engaged 4 very comfortable apartments at Hotel de Bergues'. Ann became interested there in the construction of a 'sort of suspension [bridge] which has been completed and opened in 6 weeks'. They went to the Post Box to collect their mail and Ann found that she had several letters including '2 letters from my sister forwarded from Paris, one of which first went to Heworth Grange'.[19] That evening we get the first hint of discord between Ann and her wife when they had some sort of bedroom disagreement which culminated in Ann, according to Anne's journal, saying that 'I [Anne] was long about it that I gave her no dinky dinky that is seminal flow and I excused myself and came away'.[20] Her precise meaning is unclear but both women were upset by the argument.

Despite her pleasure in receiving her letters Ann was upset by their content. Her aunt, she was told 'was very much hurt that she did not know sooner I was travelling abroad though it had been talked of by all the world for some months'. Ann was 'sorry to hear this, it was out of my powers to tell her sooner as I did not know myself ... it had never been intentionally uncommunicated'.[21] Business affairs had also followed her abroad and she wasn't happy with some of the proposals put forward in a letter from Washington. Ann wished to decline his proposal to rent Lidgate to Mr Hird for '60 pounds a year and furniture on a value of 5% for 3 years wanting several alterations'. Anne wrote Ann's letter but there is no indication that the decision wasn't Ann's own, in her own journal she expands on her thoughts; that she 'would rather wait and let the house and lands undivided even if I got less'. Ann kept a copy of the letters and 'sent [her] signature and date for Washington to file up'.[22]

Most of Ann's day was taken up replying to these letters. The issue of her aunt's hurt feelings was clearly playing on her mind, as she wrote again about it at the end of the day's journal entry. Ann's diary entries for the next few days are very short, she writes down the minimum of information. It seems things were still not quite right between her and Anne. Anne had told her that 'she had rather affected me on Monday night', the evening of their disagreement. Whether this was due to lack of sex or from the comment Ann made is unclear, but it seems likely that the discord between them is behind Ann's brevity in her journal – we find no account of what 'dearest' was doing and Anne lets us know that there were no kisses again that night.

Ann's brevity means we have to rely on Anne for an account of the next day's events, as they left Geneva and headed for Bonneville. The weather had been stormy for days, and they were entering that part of the Alps prone to the sort of storms that Mary Shelley describes as 'grander and more terrific than I have ever seen before ... observing lightning play among the clouds in various arts of the heavens and dart in jagged figures upon the piny heights'.[23] Thirty minutes from Bonneville 'the thunderstorm was so near and so loud and the lightning so frequent and vivid Ann's lips turned pale and she was a good deal frightened', perhaps Ann's fear or her courage in facing it, led to an end of the tension between them for that night they had a 'good kiss'.[24]

The two women were now preparing for the 'mountain wanderings' section of their honeymoon. Bonneville, situated in the confluence of the Arve and Borne and at the foot of the Mole was the perfect place from which to explore the Alps. Ann and Anne both took their time sorting the clothing they would need, before setting off the next day for Montavert. Glacier Montavert was the eighteenth-century name for a section of the Alps glacier on the northern slopes of Mont Blanc. Well known and famous as a travelling destination, it was mentioned in work such as Ann Radcliffe's 1791 noble *The Romance of the Forest* in which the heroine visits the glacier; and in *Frankenstein*, Victor Frankenstein ascends Montavert to meet his creation and 'refresh his tortured soul.'[25] Ann 'walked about ½ way and rode about ½ the way up letting George ride while I [Anne] walked'. They ascended and 'went up about 100 yards on the mer de glace, Ann between 2 guides'. At the top they 'picked up a little rain' and because of this they were back by 2 pm, having walked down very quickly. They then headed out again to visit the church, where Ann 'had a long conversation with the priest about England and the Protestant religion'.[26] As a memento of her morning excursion she purchased a small model of the mountain in the town. Good relations were fully restored and Ann had a 'good long kiss' that night with her wife. However Ann 'could not sleep, got up and was very sick'. Such a physical reaction would have been familiar to those living in the Alps among travellers, who were unused to exerting themselves at altitude, but there was no time to feel unwell. The next day they set off again, Ann wearing her 'old outram cloak', with two guides, three mules and George. Ann started the day by riding but dismounted after a while and walked the last half hour into les Oches alongside Anne. Near the top Ann felt sick and 'could ride no further', she sat down and cried, then, determined not to be defeated, she got back up 'mounted and went to the top'.[27] Anne clarifies that at 3 pm 'we reached the top of Vauzaz'. It was a truly remarkable feat and what a sense of achievement Ann must have felt, as the expansive view opened up around her. It was a very happy Ann that walked back down; they were staying that night at a 'auberge du glacier a trois tetes at contamine', which was basic but comfortable. Ann writes modestly that they 'had wine', Anne rather expands and says that between them they drank two bottles of vin d'asti blanc and that she had to help Ann 'get her things off and put her to bed she was literally tipsy'. It seems, however, to have been a case of the blind leading the blind as Anne herself was not entirely sober, her first words the next day being 'not better for my bottle of vin d'asti last night' – both women were hungover.[28]

Chapter 14

Rather Primitive Accommodation

For someone who was hungover Ann did very well the next day; she was up early and had a much needed cup of coffee before going to Nant Borrant then, as now, one of the few places in the area to stop and get refreshment.[1] After breakfast they set off up Col de Bonhomme, a mountain pass that ascends a total of 13.7 miles. The route involved a steep ascent in the snow. Ann was 'frightened at first', but she persevered and they traversed twenty-one small snow-filled valleys reaching the top of Col du Fours. Ann's nerves were not helped by the fact that she heard a story of two Englishmen, Mr Campbell and Mr Rowley, who starved to death there. Ann devotes half a page to recalling how the poor men's 'vital spark [had] fled the flesh before the return of the guide'. On the way back down on an area of descent George slipped and 'honey potted down 20 or 30 yards', luckily he was fine and managed to stop himself against a rock. Ann, in a letter to her aunt about the incident writes that:

> she would have been very amused if you could see us in our mountain scrambling trudging sometimes almost up to our knees in snow … George who was shewing off his agility in getting over the snow unfortunately slipped and down he went for a considerable distance, and must have gone to the bottom but for a piece of rock against which he contrived to stop himself.[2]

The auberge they stayed at that night was 'a mere chalet, but comfortable apartment between cows', but despite its limitations, Ann was pleased with the 'excellent mutton' and she chatted to the owners about their living arrangements.[3] Ann was up early the next day ready for another steep ascent to cross the Alle Blanche and Lake Combai. Their route took them up the Col de la Seigne, and it became apparent that, rather alarmingly, their guide had little real idea about the mountains. They saw an avalanche on glacier de Motets, and there was a lot of snow and

ice about. The ground was 'hard and slippery', but they made reasonable
progress and by 9 am they were safely at the Chalet l'allee blanch where
Ann ate some poulet and drank more Asti, fortifying herself for the day
ahead.[4] They trekked on, arriving at Courmayeur – an area famous for its
range of alpine flora, some of which the two women recorded. From such
a location Ann would have been treated to spectacular views, whichever
way she turned, of the Matterhorn and Mont Blanc.

For the next few days Anne does not write in her journal, as a result it
is Ann's voice alone we hear as they continue their travels.

'One of the prettiest villages' she had ever seen greeted her as they made
their way from Courmayeur via Pre St Didier to Arrier, where they had
lunch. A temporary triumphal arch had been erected there to 'celebrate
the arrival of [the] two Sardinian princes' who were expected the next
day.[5] As a consequence, the hotel where they had planned to stay was
full. Instead they went to the Hotel de la Poste and took a comfortable
apartment before walking out into the town where Ann bought ribbon
and soap and ate her first apricot of the year. It was then on to St Remy, in
a region that would later become famous for inspiring Van Gogh. When
they got to their apartment there was:

> a Lady and Gentleman from Chamouni who had passed us on our
> way to Aosta, very civilly begged us to enter. Lady was English … a
> widow with good fortune … she told us she was related to the Duke
> of Argyll and acquainted with Mrs and Miss Campbell who were
> waiting at Geneva til weather was favourable for ascending Mont
> Blanc … Gentleman was Russian.[6]

They all dined together and Ann heard and recorded more stories of more
people who had been lost in the snow and whose bodies had not been
recovered until the spring. From St Remy they headed to St Bernard,
which had been famous since 1800 when it had been used by Napoleon to
traverse the mountains with 40,000 men in order to surprise the Austrians.
Previously, during the reign of Augustus, the Romans had taken the area
from hostile local gallic tribes and under the Emperor Claudius, a Roman
road had been built through the area, at the top of which was a temple
dedicated to Jupiter, described by Ann as 'cold, bleak and snow clad'.[7]
They stayed at the Hospice which was rather busy and Ann did not find

the company to be congenial, the choice of an awkward-looking man, an army officer and his sons, or a young man in poor health did not appeal to her, and she and Anne went to bed as soon as they could.

The following day Ann was also taken to see the Morgues, where the bodies of those who died in the mountains were placed for identification. It was rather a morbid way to spend the morning, but Ann seems to have been intrigued.[8] They left St Bernard at 12 noon, ate at Liddes and arrived at Village du Ferrer at 10 pm, where once again the accommodation was not to their liking, There were 'only two rooms for us guides George and widow with eight children, two children slept in our room that cried half the night, did not undress'. Ann met this situation with practical good humour writing to her aunt that 'I assure you these little adventures not only served us to laugh at the time but afterwards they made us feel the comfort and value afterwards of a good hotel.'[9]

Col du Ferret was their route the next day, and they climbed the mountain there – 'ascent of mountain very steep, got a third guide to the top, beautiful view' – female hikers and mountaineers in the Alps were not unheard of at the time, but their exploits were rarely widely reported. In fact the achievements of female mountaineers were so overlooked that when in 1808 Marie Paradis had climbed Mont Blanc, no one was aware of it – the credit being given to aristocrat Henriette D'Angeville thirty years later.[10] Ann and Anne on their honeymoon really were trailblazing.

It was by now almost midsummer and they travelled on 'through Pre St Didier – a town still in the Aosta valley at over 1,000 metres above sea level – Goletta, Pont to petit St Bernard', embarking on '2 leagues of descent to Bourg St Maurice'. A town which nestles in the heart of the Alps and is known for its stormy weather, lying as it does on the boundary between the warm continental climate and the oceanic one. Variations in air pressure there are extremely common. They experienced the area's infamous climate in action the next day when rain came down as they headed towards Les Chapieux. They were now doubling back on themselves and Ann writes that the 'snow on Col de Bonhomme [was] considerably less' than when she had passed it the previous week. There had also been some damage to the road and Ann 'saw nearly 100 peasants who had been ordered by the king to mend the roads'. She also tells us that Anne chatted with two young women who admired the quality of Ann's habit. The weather continued to be problematic and great thunderstorms rolled in.[11] Ann writes with relief that a Frenchman they had encountered chose to ascend Mont Blanc only as far as the Grand Plateau rather than attempting the summit as the storms would have made it too dangerous. A few days earlier she had put stones on a monument to three women who had been lost in the area, but she does not seem overwhelmed by fear. Her tone is factual, not frantic, showing a human concern for those she had met on her travels. They stayed at Belle Vue for only half an hour and then descended to Chamouni, where they stayed in rooms opposite those they had stayed in before. Ann was pleased to find that these rooms were much nicer and that there were views of Mont Blanc.

Yet another mountain awaited them the next day and Ann 'ascended Mont Brevent' that lies 2,525 metres above sea level and is noted for the cliffs near its summit. Ann 'walked 3 parts of the way to the chalet to lie down there while dearest went to Cheminee'.[12] The next day was one of more travelling, this time to Martigny heading through Argentiere, le tour and over Col de Balme where at the temple of Belle Vue they stopped for lunch. The scenery Ann writes was 'beautiful' and she again underlines the word, but she was less happy to note that she had been bitten by the mosquitoes that plague the area in summer. They passed the cascade at Pissevache the following day arriving at Bex by about 2 pm where she listened to a thunderstorm rolling about. After a lunch of '4 dishes of fruit' she, perhaps to drown out the sound of the thunder, sat down to play at the piano. It was a pleasant afternoon and Ann was so pleased with her dinner that she declared it the best that she had 'had on the continent'. They left Bex as there was 'not a bed to be had in [the] town' – the rain had flooded the paths and the men who were working at clearing it carried Ann and Anne 'over on their backs' and then drove the mule and dragged their carriage through.[13] They travelled on to Martigney as the thunder roared and the lightning flashed all around them, perhaps she had grown used to it by now as Ann makes no mention of being afraid.

We know Ann ascended another mountain the next day, unfortunately it is not clear which one, before she went back to Chamouni. Back in the town Anne went out to 'order a complete collection of plants', while Ann stayed indoors and washed Anne's gloves which we can only assume had got muddy and damaged on their day's scrambles. The weather continued to cause them issues the next day when, after church, they went up Fieger, on which Ann saw a 'very fine view [of] five glaciers all at once', they then 'went to chalet where cows are kept 80 in number – drank some milk'.[14] They were just heading down when a huge thunderstorm rolled in and the heavens opened. Anne had not worn her cloak so she raced ahead while Ann followed her wife as fast as she could, noting rather proudly that she got there only eight minutes after Anne. Wet and cool, they stayed in that evening as the rain continued to pour down all night and well into the next day, the weather meant that they were forced to abandon any hopes they had of ascending Mont Blanc.

Given this, they spent the evening discussing their plans, and by the next morning they had determined that they would leave for Geneva and they were there two days later. They went straight to get money and to collect their letters before shopping. There were letters waiting for them from Mrs Lister, Mrs Lawton and Elizabeth. In the same way Anne had previously copied letters for her, Ann now did the same for Anne and they wrote together and 'between [us] copied my letters to Pi [Mariana]'.[15] The next day saw Ann shopping again, she went to the booksellers to buy more mineral samples as well as prints of places they had seen on their travels. The next day in her journal is confused, Ann was evidently writing it in retrospect and got the dates on which she attended certain events muddled. She wrote about a music concert only to cross it out before writing about it again the next day. However, we know from Anne's journal that it was on the next day, 24 July, that they went to a concert 'of the Helvetic victory of musee at the cathedral', one that Ann deemed 'excellent but singing was inferior'.[16] That evening Ann rebuffed Anne's advances, something that the latter records twice, somewhat put out.

Geneva was bustling, and when on 25th they went to a performance at the theatre, it was so popular that even arriving two hours early they only 'got in with considerable difficulty, took the last bench in the pit'. Despite the crowds Ann was very impressed, she thought it 'very prettily decorated 3 tiers of boxes being covered with white calico and wreaths of roses and leaves round the top and bottom of each tier'. Ann also thought the singing was far better than that of the previous day 'Monsieur Drouet's performance on flute in the Overture de Der Freischutz – perfect.' Ann's enjoyment and love of the music is palpable.

When they went to leave they found that it had once again begun to pour with rain and so they were forced to linger until the weather eased. With an almost audible sigh Anne writes that Ann was hungry again, she was 'obliged to take her to a cafe for a bun and lemonade'. Obviously still hungry, Ann took her dinner a couple of hours later back at the hotel and then spent the evening sketching the screen and sofa. When she had finished the two women went to bed, but they found to their embarrassment that the bed creaked when they moved and so the ever practical Anne put 'Ann's bedding on the floor [instead] and we had a good long kiss'.[17]

Ann wasn't happy with a sketch she had taken and redrew it then went to another bookshop where she bought some books on history, purchases which Anne suggested and approved of. At 12.45 they were were 'off to Feigere – then to Cruseilles – beautiful view of Lake Geneva ... an amphitheatre of mountains'.[18]

While there Ann and Anne took a charabanc – a usually open-topped type of horse-drawn carriage – to the lake and then along to the 'foot of the mountain Dere'. At Aix there were again no beds to be had but they went to view the Roman baths frequented as 'by the invalids'. The L'Enfer both women found particularly hot and suffocating, Ann 'could not even put her head into it'.[19]

Both women lamented that darkness fell and they could not see much on the road as they went to Chambery, where they arrived at La Parfait Union, near the cathedral. It was now uncomfortably warm, and it was 21 degrees Celsius by 10 am when they left the hotel to explore the town. They stumbled on a bookshop and spent some time inside, Ann 'bought prints of Savoy and read part of a book giving advice to young ladies to always seek friends and company of 'their own sex', it is easy to picture Ann and Anne exchanging wry smiles as they read that.[20] A woman that they met out shopping was extremely helpful and gave them advice on, and directions for, how they could best visit Aix. Anne as usual took charge of the arrangements and negotiated at the Hotel de la Poste that they would take a 'char to go this afternoon to Bout de Monde and a phaeton for tomorrow to Aix'. Having sorted these arrangements they walked to Les Charmetts, which Rousseau and Madame de Waren had used as a retreat. It had quickly become Rousseau's favourite residence and is mentioned in several of his works. We know that Anne was an admirer and follower of his, in her diary entry for 20 August 1823 she quoted Rousseau writing, 'I know my own heart ... But I am made unlike anyone I have ever met.'[21] To Rousseau human desire was part of nature, and God created all nature. To remain true to yourself was therefore the ultimate human goal. It was one Ann was trying to embrace.

Chapter 15

Greengages and Strawberries

After a morning of Rosseau they followed in the great man's footsteps back into town, buying greengages to snack on.[1] They went to the hotel so that Ann might 'have her cold fowl' before going out in the charabanc to La Bout du Monde. On the way they passed Doria falls and stopped to see a paper mill. Ann was intrigued by the paper manufacture process and devotes half a page to describing it. On the return journey they stopped at a nursery garden and ordered some roses. The 'herbiary [was] above 6,000 plants', famous for its roses, dahlias, peonies and camellias. After spending so long admiring the flowers, they only just got back to the hotel ahead of a violent thunderstorm.[2]

The waterfall near Gressy was their destination the next day and Ann morbidly writes that Madame la Baronne 'met her death [there] by falling into one of the crevices. In the endeavour to extricate her, her gown gave way which made her head bound against the side of the rock.'[3] Afterwards Ann took a boat to the monastery at Heutcombe where at 4.35 pm they 'went to the house of the concierge de palace and begged the favour of being able to take our luncheon there', after which Anne writes that she visited the fountain 'dragging Ann after me'.[4] This implies reluctance from Ann, yet we know from her journal that the fountain was empty at the time which perhaps was the reason why she did not wish to walk out to it, or the fact that she knew the boat was waiting – it did indeed have to wait forty-five minutes for them. On the boat on the way back Ann struck up a conversation about the Grande Chartreuse, to which she was told ladies were never admitted, and fanned herself as they sailed back across smooth water.[5]

The heat continued and Ann fretted at Monsieur Burdin Botanical gardens about how the roses would cope in the heat. She needn't have worried; just as they were leaving the rain came down and they only just made it back to the hotel before a full-on storm rolled in which continued all evening and prevented them from going out. Neither woman minded as they went to bed early and 'had a good long kiss' instead.[6]

The next day was the last in July and both women were up early on account of the rain which forced them to abandon their plan of going out in an open carriage to the Grande Chartreuse. There were, however, other distractions, Ann went 'to [Anne] at eight and ten minutes had shewed me her bosom and on my asking took off her night things and stood naked, so then got into bed and had a kiss'.[7] This was not an action that the Ann of three years earlier would have contemplated. This was an Ann confident in her sexual appeal. Due to the rain there was no hurry and they took their breakfast late, before ordering from Mr Burdin 'a complete collection of alpine plants to be sewed on to white paper and bound and classed and ticketed in families and species according to the system of Linneaus at 200 per thousand to be 5,000 or thereabouts'; the plants would not be ready before their departure so he was given the address of Shibden Hall. Sorting out their plans meant that they were not able to head out until 3 pm for a drive. They travelled 'three postes to Les Echelles, derived its name from a torrent having anciently worn a hole through the rock which was the only road to Chambery til Charles Emmanuel made another'. As always, Ann was keenly interested in everything going on around her, and made several other notes on the road's development and rebuilding. They were at Les Echelles by 6 pm and ate a dinner of 'potage, trout, chicken, roast mutton riz au lait', followed by strawberries.[8] Eager to be off they took breakfast early and engaged a chair to Pont St Laurent, they were stopped at the French border by guards who wished to search them until Anne, rather forcefully, objected and showed their passports.

They engaged mules and a guide and rode to Grand Chartreuse which Ann found to be 'particularly fine, high mountains, and ravine and gorge finest I ever saw', she also observed that the road was 'very good for mountains'; Ann clearly felt qualified to pass her own judgement on such matters by this time.[9] Once again they were chased by the weather and only arrived at an auberge half an hour before yet another violent thunderstorm rolled in. Anne had requested a bed so that Ann might lie down, but none was forthcoming. In a moment of tenderness Anne was 'cross to see poor Ann so comfortless', and Ann gently reassured her that she was fine.[10]

They left at 3.40 pm travelling by mule, though it quickly became apparent that Ann's mule was lame; when it stumbled, Anne put her onto her own mule. A few minutes later though and the guide's mule was lame; after some juggling about, Anne finally lost patience and 'mounted George's mule and let the guide have the stumbler and made George mount behind Ann', with that sorted they continued as best they could. Luckily the rain held off and they were able to take a charabanc to the Inn at Les Echelles. They had planned to go out again to see the Chapel of St Bruno, but as it 'would take us an hour to go and return'. They decided that they best not risk it as it looked like rain. Ann ate strawberries for breakfast and dinner with which she was 'very well satisfied' – until that is they got the bill, which Ann records was charged at 8 francs, which was more than they had paid in Geneva.[11] Irritated, they set off on the old road and explored some caverns. They 'went on half an hour into it, sometimes on hands and knees, into a lake at the far end', before travelling on to Parfaite Union.[12] It was Anne's turn to be tired that afternoon and she fell asleep in a chair for half an hour. Ann probably put the finishing touches to her letter while Anne slept. When she woke they posted letters to Aunt Lister back at Shibden, after which they again went to a bookshop and then saw the 'preparation for taking suckers of rose trees and plants' at Monsieur Barin's garden. A gardener, Frederick Burnier spoke to them about the specimens there, where they had been taken from and what care they would need back in Yorkshire. Ann was in good spirits the next day and very pleased with the beautiful countryside 'particularly all the valley down to Bourg Maurice'. They had to stop for a few minutes while their passports were examined upon entering France, but by 3.30 pm they were at Les Ambassador Hotel.[13]

Despite the comfort of the room Ann did not sleep well and was woken with a bowel complaint at 5 am; she continued to feel unwell the next day. They had breakfast at 9.30 but Ann was back and forth to the privy. Ann went out with her wife and George after lunch but she was tired and they didn't stay out long. Once again, however, food seems to have been the cure; back at the hotel Ann had 'a biscuit and brandy and water … and was better'. Revived, Ann headed back out at about 5 pm and 'went to M Fournier' in order that she and Anne could look over the mineral specimens he was selling in his shop 'Horologer'. Ann thought they were 'beautiful specimens' and was feeling well enough to climb six flights of stairs so that she could view some more. She was also fascinated by a lock which 'no one could open unless the person recollected the way he had last turned it'. After leaving, Ann's shopaholic tendencies struck again and she bought yet another '3 pairs of dark coloured gloves'.[14]

At the village of Sassenage they got out of the carriage and walked up the hill to admire 'a beautiful view of Grenoble'. Ann walked half of the way to the top but then was tired and so Anne continued to the top alone. It was boiling hot and they walked back down rather quicker than was comfortable on account of Ann's bowels. She could not have been feeling too unwell for she had a picnic lunch, sitting on one stone and balancing her usual cold chicken on another. After taking refreshment they went to visit Sassenage's grottos, cascade and a 'singular rise of water that cannot be seen without a candle'. She and Ann joked about buying a 'peeping out old tower [of the] ancien château de Sassenage'. They were in good spirits and got out their parasols to use for measuring some large populars they saw.[15] Anne and Ann discussed land management with their guide as they travelled around and heard about cotton manufacture in the area. The road back – 'the great high road to le Croise haute' was shockingly poor and Ann got sick in the carriage. Not too sick to appreciate a Roman bridge they encountered, of which she writes, 'two of its best characteristics being Roman as it is put together with mortar which is not usually used in Roman bridges or buildings'.[16]

The following day Ann tried to take coffee at breakfast but was forced to leave the table feeling unwell. While resting, she demonstrated her excellent needlework skills and showed George how he should mend his stockings. Anne ordered her some broth and fricandeau before she went out. Ann rested all afternoon and wrote in her journal and then '2 ½ pages to my sister'. She then took out her inks and worked on some of the sketches she had previously taken.[17] That evening they travelled to Voreppe where Ann seems to have put her foot down over the accommodation; it had fleas and, more importantly, there was no dinner available so despite Anne wishing to stay they moved on to Voiron, where they stayed at the Hotel du Cours. To Ann's relief there was a dinner of fricandeau and potage. Ann's bowels woke her again at 5 am the next day, and finding herself cold she went into Anne's bed hoping she would 'warm her stomach'. It did so and the two women began the day with a 'long good kiss' that improved Ann's mood and she was delighted with an 'excellent breakfast' that she enjoyed more than any other on their travels. Anne also made her tea for the first time in their Jones's hot water boiler. Ann was delighted with it, and enjoyed a 'large plate of strawberries' alongside. They went to Pont St Laurent to view the new road and then on to Saint Etienne where they saw women sitting in their doorways, spinning.[18] Ann's pain continued as she notes with uncharacteristic emotion that she was 'very down for a little while'. The country they were travelling through was 'very pretty', but on one occasion they had to stop and Ann was obliged to go behind a barn with her 'disturbed bowels' as there was 'neither pot nor necessary available' – no small feat in her travelling dress.[19] They were treated to a lovely view of Lyon as they approached the city and that night they arrived at the Hotel d'Europe. Ann was very pleased with the price of 18 francs per day with breakfast at 2 francs and dinner at 8 pm.

Lyon is considered to be the capital of the Auvergne-Rhone-Alpes region and at the time Ann visited was the scene of rapid industrial expansion after the devastation of the French Revolution during which, in 1793, the city was besieged by the Republican forces of the Montagnards which had led to a localised devastation and the decline of the city's trade and industry for a time.

After an early breakfast Ann headed to the shops and this time she bought a 'black satin shawl for 80 francs and dearest a white one for 140'. Ann liked Lyon and bought a plan of the city that afternoon, but she also noted the presence of 'ten thousand military still in Lyons' following violence that had erupted there on 15 April during which 1,000 people had lost their lives.'[20]

The next page of Ann's journal is devoted to discussing the manufacture of velvet, the process of which they viewed that afternoon and the details of which she noted carefully. Ann was impressed by a piece she saw being made in 'beautiful green 1 ½ ell wide and to be 45 ells in length and before embroidered with gold according to order was to cost 250 francs of 10 English pounds an ell – the order was from the king of England and would be completed in 8 months'. She was pleased to note that trade in the city was recovering and that there were fresh peaches for dinner – less pleasing was the fact that when the black shawl she had purchased earlier had arrived damaged.[21] This meant that they were obliged to go out, on 11 August, to return it. The 11 August also saw Ann and Anne quarrel. Ann, it seems, had secrets; frustratingly, we don't know what this particular secret was but neither did Anne, who was cross that she 'could not get her to tell'. As a result Anne was 'not inclined to talk to Miss Walker'; Ann knew that Anne was 'displeased' by her reticence and wrote that 'dearest was in low spirits'.[22] If Ann had wanted to keep her secrets, her resolution gave way in the face of Anne's displeasure and she ended their quarrel 'by explanation, all made up', and wrote with relief that 'dearest quite as fond and as kind to me as ever'.[23]

Coal pits were next on their itinerary and, given her ambition for the Walker pit, Anne wanted to see the Comagnie de cate Thoilliere; Ann travelled a third of the way down the mine before turning back while Anne went to the bottom. Interestingly, Anne writes that it was she who sent Ann back to the top as she became 'afraid for her and sent her back'. While happy to get wet shoes herself, she did not want Ann to suffer any discomfort. Ann was all smiles at such tender care and Anne – rather to her own surprise – found that she did not wish to leave Ann too long and so cut short her visit. Their quarrel, the first for several weeks, seems to have shaken both women.[24] In a similar vein, Anne made tea for Ann, while Ann carefully kept back a bunch of grapes from her breakfast for Anne to eat.[25]

Travel issues plagued the next few days; horses could not be found at La Bergere, while no accommodation could be found at Lezoux. The accommodation they did find had no satisfactory lock and so it was left to Anne to 'fasten [their] door with handle of our tea apparus.' Although they found humour in the situation, both women were beginning to tire. Ann ached and Anne 'rubbed her all over with Brandy' to help her sleep, and would have done the same herself but for the fact she 'did not like the smell or feel of it'. The weather wasn't helping either, Anne had 'never known it so hot', and one night Ann was 'quite overcome', much to the alarm of both Anne and their hostess, who moved them quickly to a 'smaller but cooler room'.[26] Despite all this, Ann enjoyed seeing the petroleum spring at Puy de la Poix where they 'walked all over the rock and tho the sun was broiling found no danger of leaving our shoes stuck fast', which relieved them both. On 16 August, while Anne and George went off to explore a silver mine, she enjoyed a leisurely day of 'picking strawberries for dearest', writing letters, and drawing. In particular, she 'copied one of Mr Browne's drawings – then read a description of geological society at Clermont.'[27]

Despite her happiness, marriage was not a magic 'cure' for Ann and there are little hints in her journal that her anxiety and depression was beginning to creep back in. Ann woke at 2 am one morning 'quite frightened, fancying someone in the room who had opened the window'.[28]

Anne reassured her and lit a candle, and no more was said about the incident, but both women were relieved that Ann was well the following day and able to rationalise her fears. Ann was also beginning to miss her family and when they arrived back in Paris on 21 August, she was very disappointed to have no letters waiting for her and not even a comfortable room and a visit to the Church of St Roch could quite stave off Ann's disappointment. She consoled herself by buying yet more presents:

> bought grey ribbon for Mrs Lister and my bonnet and went into toy shop ... bought shawl for my aunt at La Page's and one for dearest and one for me ... went to Giroux dearest bought scent bottle with pin cushion [for Aunt Walker] then back to toy shop in Panorama Alley bought a figure of a large man sort of tumbler on table.[29]

They left Paris at 5.30 pm on 24 August, and travelled north wrapped up against the 'very cold' night. They did not stop until Abbeville for some breakfast, where George reported that the carriage required repairs, and Eugenie, that she was feeling unwell. After getting the carriage repaired they pressed on towards Dover, and 'entered Calais and at Quillacqs at 5.30 heard English packet would start for Dover at 6 – breakfasted on board and weighed anchor at 6.30 wind and sea in our favour'. Like many a traveller before and since, Ann leaned out eager to catch the first glimpse of the white cliffs of Dover.[30]

Perhaps Ann had always intended that her journal primarily to be a travelling one, for she stops writing initially when she got back to England. We know from Anne's journal though that the two women slept together for the 'first time since Paris' and that they then travelled to Wright's Hotel in Rochester before moving on to London where they stayed at 26 Dover Street. In London Ann had her hair cut 'by a man from Trufitts, Bond Street', and dispatched letters to Yorkshire. While in London she also subscribed '1 guinea for a finely illuminated black letter copy of a poem of the Middle Ages', and purchased an estate plan case at Peacocks, Salisbury Square, alongside numerous books.[31] They left London on 29 August, they were at 'St Albans at 2.30 ... at 4.30 left the great road ... and turned right to Northampton'. It rained all the way to Newport Pagnell, where they stayed overnight. Well rested, they travelled north the next day, and they reached Shibden by 9 pm.[32]

Chapter 16

Facing the Music

Ann's return to Shibden marked a new stage in her life. Immediately upon her return she went to call on her aunt at Cliff Hill, but if she was hoping for a warm reception she was to be disappointed. Her aunt 'scolded [her] all the time' and made 'no shew of pleasure to see [her][1].' Privately, Ann was a newly married woman, but outside of the protective sphere of Shibden everyone in Yorkshire wanted to know why the quiet and wealthy Miss Walker had moved into Shibden Hall. It was Ann who bore the brunt of this curiosity, when Mrs Priestley called and spoke with Ann and Marian, she deliberately did not ask for Anne, meaning that Ann was left to answer her bad-tempered questions. The same day, Mrs Rawson and Mr Edwards of Pye Nest also called and left cards prompting Anne to declare that they would see no more visitors that day.[2] Aunt Ann had not been appeased by the letters Ann sent explaining herself and scolded her vehemently, but Ann would not be persuaded to return to her family at Cliff Hill and threw herself into her new life. She ordered that some of her furniture be brought to Shibden, the 'nicest pieces', and within two days of returning she and Anne were also measuring the north parlour for a new carpet.[3] Ann also met with Washington and Mr Hird to resolve the matter of letting Lidgate.

Aunt Ann proved more stubborn than Ann had hoped and when she called at Cliff Hill on 8 September she found her aunt was 'crosser than ever' and refused to shake Anne's hand.[4]

In keeping with their newly married status, Anne now applied to Mr Wilkinson to rent a family pew at Lightcliffe church so that she and Ann might sit and worship together. This was very important to Ann and both were pleased when the reply came back that they could have the Mytholm pew, from next Sunday. It was to be the 'front pew [as befitting Ann's status] in the north gallery, nearest to the west gallery'.[5]

The sinking of a coal pit that had long been her wife's ambition was also taking shape. Demand for coal was rising exponentially and there seemed no reason now to delay. The Rawsons were already leading the charge to keep up with demand, but Anne challenged them by sinking the Walker pit, with Ann's money, near Coney and Brierley Hill on the road down into Halifax. Though it was Anne's project, Ann was far from uninvolved and on 18 September she went with Anne to Brierley Hill to meet with Holt 'about getting waster for John Bottomley and about sinking pit'.[6] This pit would put Ann into direct opposition to her Rawson relations and, unsurprisingly, her Aunt Rawson in particular was horrified. Despite this, Ann had always been keen on the scheme, perhaps there was an element of family competition as well as the fact that a successful joint business venture with Anne would surely help to silence her family on the merits of the alliance.

Mrs Priestley and Mrs Rawson might have remained implacably hostile, but to Ann's relief, as winter approached, her aunt's attitude showed signs of thawing. Ann continued to visit her and before the month was out Aunt Ann had consented to warmly press her hand and even speak civilly to Anne, although shaking her hand was still a step too far.

There was more good news as well in the shape of a letter Ann received on the 21 September which informed her that Elizabeth had been safely delivered of a healthy baby boy on 16th – 'mother and child doing exceedingly well' – Ann immediately sat down and wrote three pages of effusive 'compliments and congratulations', so keen was she to write back that on her first read through of the letter she missed the name of the baby – and laughed that she had to read back to find he had been called John after her brother.[7] Ann received the news on a Sunday and with her letters hastily written and sealed she went to church, giving thanks for her nephew's safe arrival in her prayers. This good news did not, however, negate her increasing impatience with Captain Sutherland. His refusal to decide or act on the division of the joint Walker property meant that Ann feared he still had hopes of being able to draw on her own income. On 27 September she drank '4 glasses of Madeira' as she 'raged against him'. Familial interference was thoroughly getting on her nerves – the more so because locally she was being branded as 'cruel' for having 'abandoned' her aunt in order to travel with Anne. Her aunt now asked Miss Mary Rawson to be her companion at Cliff Hill and on hearing this Ann burst into tears. She was hurt by her aunt's actions but rallied, remarking cynically that 'those who did most for people were not always most thought of'.[8] In contrast to her own family's actions, the Listers rallied around, with Mr Lister and Marian going so far as to call at Cliff Hill. Aunt Lister soon became Ann's beloved 'Aunty'.

When Ann moved into Shibden Hall, running the household became even more complicated. There were now effectively three financial households within one building along with six servants, and the question of exactly who should pay for what was one that fluctuated wildly as everyone adapted to living together. To deal with this new financial reality Ann and Anne both consulted their lawyers Parker and Adams, who were becoming increasingly suspicious of the exact nature of the two women's relationship. Upon their marriage Anne Lister felt that she had a right to Ann's Walker money, as a husband would do. Ann did not object to this but maintained authority over her own affairs, and on 14 October she and her sister reached an agreement under which each received just over £3,000 from their joint Walker inheritance. Ann agreed to give Anne £1,000 of this, but Anne was to offer security against her capital. Anne could spend Ann's income, but for the actual capital Anne provided legal security much like anyone else.[9] While Anne Lister was known for her forthright business dealings, Ann's way of dealing with money matters was rather more subtle. She was happy to be forthright with Washington but when it came to the familial finances she couched her demands in sisterly chit chat. On 15 October she wrote Elizabeth a letter which gives us a clear snapshot of Ann's thoughts at this time. Ann opens her letter with friendly concern, but then makes it clear that she wanted the money owed to her and would no longer wait. Instead she told Elizabeth, 'I have therefore ventured without waiting for the writing to you and your answer to give Mr Adam (Mr Parker being at Harrogate) instructions to settle the business without delay … consider what you would like to be done with your share of the money.' She also told Elizabeth clearly that she planned to 'invest some of my share advantageously and consequently shall not have it paid into Mr Briggs' bank … securing the money from Messrs Rawson' before quickly moving on to discussing the baby's christening.[10] The matter of Mary Rawson and her aunt was on Ann's mind, she tells Elizabeth that she had not been personally told of it, but also that she was 'grateful and thankful that my aunt had at least someone … I have often felt uneasy about her'. Ann tells us that her aunt had indeed turned down her proposal to do the same. It is impossible to not get the impression that Ann here is trying to both express her hurt and justify her actions to the sister whose approval she cared for. She wanted to make sure that the record was set straight. What else could she do, she added, she could hardly 'force herself' upon her aunt and she hoped that Elizabeth would not think 'harshly' of her like many people seemed to do.[11]

Those who were quick to judge Ann might have felt differently if they had seen her that evening. Far from living 'wildly' or an unchristian life at Shibden, Ann sat down to sew 'charity baby clothes'.[12] One other issue came up in Ann's letters to her sister at this time and that was the Sutherland's treatment of their Lidgate tenants. On 30 October 1834 she met with Washington, who was appalled at the Sutherlands' cruel treatment of their tenants. He showed her a letter from Captain Sutherland, which ordered twenty-five distresses, he 'owned he would rather write 20 letters to Scotland than serve the distresses'. Ann herself was upset by Sutherland's attitude and 'annoyed – cried a good deal' before discussing how such actions might be mitigated and the tenants treated more fairly.[13]

Now settled at Shibden, Ann often picked up Anne's daily newspaper *The Morning Herald*, by doing so she would have been reading a Tory newspaper and at this time politics began to play a more important role in her day to day life. Anne Lister was a staunch Conservative/Tory landowner. Ann's own political position prior to her meeting with Anne is difficult to discern, but she soon was influenced by Anne's views. Halifax at the time, like many other industrial towns in the north, was undergoing rapid change. The old water-powered mill industry in which the Walkers had made their fortune was being replaced by larger steam-powered mills. Alongside this came all the associated issues of poverty, working conditions and sanitation. The 1832 Reform Act had created Halifax as a new parliamentary borough, entitled to send two members to Westminster. Anne Lister had campaigned for the Tory candidate, who in 1832 was the vehemently Conservative James Stuart Wortley.[14] It was a position shared by Ann's family; Christopher Rawson and Henry Edwards helped to run his campaign, and Anne and Ann had used 'persuasion' to try to swing the vote in his favour. Rural tenants like Ann and Anne's were in a vulnerable position, there was no secret ballot at this date, so the two women could see exactly who had voted for whom. One such tenant was John Bottomley of Brierley Hill who leased his farm from Anne Lister, he paid rent of £26 and so was entitled to vote in the new Halifax borough. Anne Lister had told him to vote Tory, but the Whigs had told him that they would never employ him again if he did so, which was not an enviable position to be in.[15]

As autumn wore on Ann and Anne continued to work together to sort out their finances. Ann took pains to laboriously copy out her father's will and other family documents to show Anne the full complexities of her estate. Both women consulted a lawyer and came to realise that it was nigh on impossible to break the entail. Ann realised she was, however, able to leave Anne her entailed property which consisted of 'scattered pockets of land, tiny coal mines and industrial properties in central Halifax'.[16]

In October Ann was aggravated to receive a visit from her cousin James Ingham of Blake Hall, who it appears had been persuaded by her family to visit and propose marriage to her. He was politely received but Ann was far from amused by her family's continuing interference.

Outside of all these concerns, Ann consistently wanted Anne to work less and worried for her health. Evidently having abandoned traditional means, on 11 November we find Ann hiding the key to Anne's study to force her to come to bed early. 'Goodish' kisses followed, Ann had achieved her objective.[17] In other domestic news, the saga of Marian's marriage drew on, and Ann found herself in the middle as Marian and Anne annoyed each other equally. Marian felt herself in the way in the new order at Shibden and she yearned for some independence from her family, a position Ann could certainly sympathise with. Marian's relationship with Anne became increasingly fraught as all these issues bubbled to the surface and in December Ann was on hand to comfort Anne after one particularly serious argument. Ann was astonished to find her wife so upset and 'consoled and calmed' her.[18]

By now Ann was clearly struggling to keep up with her journal, her entries after her return to Shibden being very short, but we see in them Marian becoming dearest Miss Marian, trees being planted and wardrobes modified as the year drew to a close. What Ann did not know was that during a visit to Mariana Lawton over the Christmas period Anne was 'caught off her guard' and slept with Mariana. Mariana sent Ann a little pocket book, as a token of her friendship, but Anne admitted to her diary that Mariana would try to lead her astray from Ann if she were to give her a chance.

Chapter 17

Bonnets and Bother

1835 began for Ann with a visit from Miss Ann Plowes, who was not going to let Ann's new living situation prevent her from visiting her cousin. Ann also set about organising a collection of 'shirts etc for the poor people'.[1] Her local reputation for good works and generosity, however, was soon undermined by the growing national campaign for reform.

The beginning of 1835 was dominated by local elections. The vote between the Tory (blue) candidate and the Whig (yellow) one was bitterly fought and anyone who was anyone wore their chosen ribbon pinned to their chest. This election would come to be known as the 'window breaking election' and many Tory supporters found themselves targeted as the working men of the town wanted Whig-led social reform.[2] Violence and bribery were rife and with Anne not above bribing her tenants, neither she nor Ann would escape the election unscathed – and it did not take long for the attacks to become personal. On 10 January, Washington brought to their door a copy of the *Leeds Mercury*, in which it announced the marriage of 'Captain Tom Lister of Shibden Hall to Miss Ann Walker late of Lidgate.'[3] It was clearly an intentional jab at the two women, who both took it in good humour in Washington's presence; privately though 'A [Ann] did not like the joke', it brought to the fore all her old insecurities.[4] Perhaps it was Washington's association with that morning that irritated Ann; by the 17 January she wrote that she had to 'lecture' him on estate matters, and their relationship would become increasingly tense.[5] Their reputation in Halifax was not helped by continuing work on the unpopular Walker pit. Ann and Anne found themselves attracting 'new incivility' when they shopped in Halifax, reinforced when the *Halifax Guardian* reprinted the 'marriage' announcement. It is testament to her strength and her love for Anne that Ann did not consider staying at Cliff Hill to ride out the storm, instead she braved the worst that society could throw at her. This resolution was helped by the fact that her Aunt

Ann was truly beginning to come around. She did not approve of her niece's actions, but she loved her and found she could not hold onto her disapproval in the face of Ann's improved health and happiness.

Ann's days now settled into a familiar pattern, she was frequently out and about paying calls and conducting business with Anne. She also attended lectures by the Philosophical Society and musical recitals. Domestically, she cared for Aunt Lister and helped to navigate the minefield between Anne and Marian. She also wrote frequently to her sister regarding the division of the unentailed Walker property. With Anne behind her, Ann was far more forceful in this regard than she had been and often rewrote her letters often under Anne's guidance. By 13 February Ann had told her solicitor Robert Parker, who was becoming a regular fixture in the women's lives, that she hoped to have the business concluded within six months. To this end Washington was now 'busy about the valuation' of this property.[6] It was an issue that dominated the next year of Ann's life.

The spring of 1835 was cold, and snow was still covering the ground in late March. Ann kept herself occupied with estate plans and in reading extensively, Anne bought her a set of books on ecclesiastical art history, which she enjoyed reading. Aunt Lister's health was a constant concern and they engaged Dr Jubb, to treat her. There had been a fall out with Dr Belcombe who seems to have resented Anne having taken Ann abroad and out of his care so soon, as well as opposing her marriage on his sister's account.[7]

It is clear that Ann was keen to learn more about her estate and responsibilities, and Anne was happy to teach her. In March, Ann made a 'summary on one sheet so as to shew at a glance the relative value and continents of every farm etc', they concluded that her 'rents per annum equalled 407 pounds 12 shillings and 6 pence', her navigation shares £506 and 'lot one [unentailed property] if she gets it 1,527 pounds 7 shillings and 3 pence'. The total of which was a huge £2,774 9s 3d.[8] Such valuations allowed Ann to write again to her sister with clear figures while Robert Parker wrote to Captain Sutherland, and by late March progress was finally being made. Ann though had a decision to make, and the question of just how much her family trusted her in financial matters was about to come to the fore. Elizabeth Walker had been severely criticised by the Walker clan for allowing Captain Sutherland to have the rights over her property in 1831, now Ann Walker it seemed wanted to do the same with

Anne. On Friday 13 April, Ann went to Cliff Hill and spoke with her aunt. Her aunt told her that as Ann seemed determined to leave money to Anne, she had 'cut A [her] out of her will for it. Neither Ann nor Mrs Sutherland to be executors but Mr W. Priestley.' Ann told her aunt that she was mistaken and that she had left everything to Sackville, a fact that pleased her aunt. However, Ann also reiterated her intent to stay with Anne at Shibden and that 'if she did not marry ... we should mutually give each other a life estate in all we could'. Aunt Ann objected to this but she remained open to further negotiations, which was as much as Ann knew she could realistically hope for.[9]

Hostility continued to be felt acutely by Ann as the public and private attacks on them continued. On 15 April she received a letter from a 'well wisher' who wanted to 'save' her from Shibden and who abused Anne. The writer was 'sure that [Ann] is unhappy and will do all to aid her getting away from [Anne]'. The reality was that Ann was in many ways happier than she had ever been, the two women's relationship in private was very happy and with plenty to do her mental health continued to improve.[10] When she did feel unwell Anne cosseted her, feeding her 'light veal broth', and Ann repaid this kindness by mending Anne's clothes and purchasing items to keep her warm on her travels.[11] Whatever the truth of the matter though, no one outside Shibden Hall saw Ann's situation in a positive light – except perhaps Elizabeth, who seems to have been genuinely delighted that Ann was so well, and not terribly bothered about the means by which her health was achieved. Elizabeth, under her husband's close observation, wrote to Ann and told her that they would come to Halifax in July to try to come to an estate settlement once and for all 'when the land will be seen to the best advantage'.[12]

The election of a new schoolmaster for Hipperholme school was also on Ann's mind. Ann supported Mr Warburton, while William Priestley wanted Mr Carter, a dispute that did not help smooth family relations. In the end Ann and Anne got their way, but relations with the Priestley's continued to deteriorate so much that Ann feared 'the breach was now too wide to ever be made up'. This fear of familial estrangement was not enough though to deter her from pushing ahead. She and Anne were in the right and Ann now made Robert Parker aware of the mistreatment she had undergone during her stay in Scotland regarding the financial liberties and pressure Captain Sutherland had put her under. Ann cried when she recounted her escape back down to Yorkshire, and Robert Parker was quite astonished at such an account.[13]

Ironically, given later events, Ann was judged very much 'old enough to judge for herself and that she ought to be independent', as such instructions regarding her finances were left to her to issue. To this end she and Anne travelled to York to meet with Jonathan Gray in the hope he could help further clarify Ann's financial situation. Gray seems to have thought that the Sutherlands were stalling for time, which was what the two women wanted to hear, and he wrote to them.[14] This firmer tact was reiterated by Ann on 15 April, when she signed a codicil to her will, 'authorising and desiring me [Anne] as her trustee to proceed with the division of the joint property if not completed at her death'. Captain Sutherland was furious that Ann was essentially accusing him of behaving badly in the matter of the Walker estate and he sat down immediately to scrawl a response.[15] He assured her that 'we have long been anxious for a division of the property' and that she had not told them of her wishes until the previous December. He then appealed to her sisterly concern, assuring her that Elizabeth was anxious to see her but could not travel before July due to the fact that she was nursing and there was smallpox in the area, which made them both very anxious. It is very difficult to determine whether Sutherland was in fact stalling; he had little reason to in reality, but the depth of Ann's dislike for him was becoming more and more apparent and she was not cowed by his pretty words. All of this talk of inheritance did bring one issue to the forefront of Ann's mind. She continued to lament that she herself would not have children. Ann devoted many hours to making baby clothes for her relatives, and local children, as an outlet for her maternal feelings. Anne was not unfeeling and told Ann gently that she would not wish to be an 'obstacle to anything you have so much at heart'.[16] Ann was still only in her early thirties and children were still a realistic possibility for her, but her desire for children was not enough for her to give up her life with Anne. Childlessness was a price that she was willing to pay, even if it sometimes made her cry.

The election troubles continued to rumble on, and they spilled out into estate matters. With the election looming Samuel Washington found himself in a very difficult position. Anne and Ann both made it clear that they 'should not intend to have a steward who would not give us his vote and interest', but he was also employed by Captain Sutherland, who was not a Tory supporter.[17] Ann was fully in support of her wife in this matter and said 'she would exert her influence as much as [Anne] would', and that it was only due to the delicacy of the situation that she had not spoken to him on this matter before.[18] Despite this, Wortley lost the election. The working people of Halifax had spoken, and their dissatisfaction with local landed families such as Walkers and Listers would later become Chartism.

Ann breathed a sigh of relief when the elections were over and on 13 June at Shibden she wrote a letter to Captain Sutherland and to Mr Gray, under Anne's direction.[19] They had agreed that Ann should take Lot 1 of the property, which included Bouldhsaw Farm and Clough and the coal contained within, valued by Washington at £1,400. Ann was pleased and the letter she sent in response is much more friendly than others she and Anne had sent of late. While the letter was copied from a drafted one by Anne, the last few sentences are all Ann. She expresses her relief that her nephew John was recovering well and referred to her nieces and nephews affectionately as 'my little pets'.[20] In truth though, Ann wanted as little to do with her brother-in-law as possible, a view shared by her aunt who had had quite enough of Captain Sutherland's demands. When Elizabeth wrote to say that they would be visiting in July and staying at Cliff Hill, both Ann and her aunt stated that they would rather they stayed at home.

Despite her relief at its resolution there is some suggestion that Ann was not entirely happy with the settlement that Anne had helped her draft. Nor was she afraid to challenge Anne; on the 6 July she 'snubbed Anne' in front of the servants and later refused to go with her to see her father for coffee.[21] A day that caused Anne to write that 'I must not and will not get the master … her temper wants some management'.[22] There is something refreshing about hearing of Ann's outbursts of temper, too often she is thought of as merely passive, but clearly this was not the case. She cared passionately about things and was not always willing to give way, especially if she felt an injustice had been done.

Unfortunately for everyone involved, the matter of the Walker inheritance was not done and dusted, and Robert Parker found himself increasingly trapped between his Shibden and Sutherland clients. Anne accused him of being too pro-Sutherland, while Ann increasingly did not 'much [like] his manner', and retorted that but for Anne she would not use his services. If Ann was becoming frustrated at Anne's interference so too was Captain Sutherland, who went so far as strongly hint that he did not trust Anne Lister's motives in the matter.[23]

Despite her involvement in the school Ann was beginning to grow bored. In *Jane Eyre*, Charlotte Brontë wrote that 'one must be courted, you must be flattered – you must have music, dancing and society – or you languish, you die away', and Ann was beginning to languish.[24] She had hoped that her marriage would give her access to the upper echelons of society and expand her social circle, but this was not proving to be the case and Ann was growing resentful, declaring that Anne 'should not have claimed powers you did not possess'.[25] When the two women visited London, Ann complained bitterly that Anne went alone to visit Lady Stuart. Why Anne felt the need to deliberately exclude Ann is unclear, but it upset Ann greatly, to the extent that according to Anne's journal she doubted her wife's affection.

These doubts were not calmed by the fact that Anne was also constantly borrowing money from her; Anne's accounts for this year are littered with references to £20 or £40 borrowed from Ann and it was beginning to grate. She was afraid that Anne's spending would ruin her and it didn't seem at the time as if her concerns were unjustified.[26] The construction of the Walker pit was in its final phase, and more cash was needed to deal with all the last minute issues, but as yet it had not made back a single penny. Likewise, Anne's refurbishment of Northgate House was a financial drain. She had resolved to convert it herself, writing that 'I spare no expense in making it as convenient as I can. There will be on the ground floor five sitting rooms, besides the bar and casino: on the first floor two sitting rooms connected with bedrooms, twelve bedrooms, bathrooms and three water closets.' It was estimated that this would eventually return 10 per cent at least on her investment, but for now it was all outlay.

With these concerns on her mind Ann again began to show signs of ill health. She was weepy and 'sickish', feeling herself to be constantly unwell. While in London Ann saw Sir Benjamin Collins Brodie, who concluded that this was simply 'nervous pain … there was no disease. Said she was just the sort of person for nervous pains but there was nothing to fear.' As always when feeling unwell, Ann's thoughts turned to religion and by August she was 'sickish while reading from the psalms'.[27] This wasn't a health crisis on the scale that Ann had experienced before, however.

Matters such as finding the perfect schoolmaster for her Sunday school kept Ann engaged in the world outside Shibden. Ann was determined to find the perfect fit for the children and to this end she visited the British and Foreign Central school to enquire about two teachers.

On the way back to Halifax Ann visited Warwick and Chatsworth, and she took the waters at Buxton which were said to cure all, and there was also a visit from her sister to look forward to.

Aunt Ann had asked Ann to stay at Cliff Hill for the duration of their visit, perhaps anticipating that their stay might be a little fraught given the state of family relations – Ann agreed.[28] Ann and Elizabeth were genuinely delighted to see each other. Elizabeth had brought down her eldest son Sackville, then 4 years old, and Ann doted upon him. Aunt Ann had been right to expect trouble though, the following day Ann was furious that Captain Sutherland wanted to be given half the estate rent books and swore that 'she would not give them up'. In return, Captain Sutherland accused her of wanting to start a quarrel. When Anne came to visit she found Aunt Ann and Ann both sitting in stony silence while she was obliged to 'agreeableize' with the Sutherlands.[29] Ann spent time with her sister while Captain Sutherland travelled to York to speak with Mr Gray, who persuaded him to take a more tactful approach with Ann. It was advice that he took and Ann graciously accepted his apology the next day. A heavily pregnant Elizabeth's nerves were by now stretched to breaking point and an argument between the sisters caused Ann to spend a whole day crying, but this did not prevent her from standing up to her Elizabeth. Ann's backbone was proving a revelation to many. Anne was impressed, but keen that her wife should not overtax herself and insisted that she not stay at Cliff Hill for so long again.[30]

The 26 September was a big day for Ann, who was to lay the foundation stone for Anne's new Northgate casino.[31] This was a bold and brave decision. After such a public act there would no longer be any public ambiguity about the nature of her and Anne's relationship, but despite the public hostility Ann was very well pleased with this honour and had Mr Gray help her write her speech of thanks to the builder, Mr Nelson. She and Anne set off at 10.45 in the morning, decked out in their pelisses. A clear indication of the tensions surrounding the event can be seen by the fact that Marian Lister, who had wanted to attend, was ultimately 'too nervous' to do so.[32] As it turned out the day went without a hitch –

luckily, as over 100 people attended. Ann performed her part very well and in her speech hoped that the hotel would be well received both locally and by travellers from further afield. They buried a time capsule in the form of a 'large open mouthed Greek glass bottle', which contained a message on a lead sheet rolled up tight. It read:

> The first stone of a spacious casino which will be annexed to a handsome hotel to be erected at Halifax was laid on 26 day of September AD 1835 in the sixth year of the reign of King William IV by Miss Ann Walker the younger of Cliff Hill, Yorkshire, in the name and at the request of her particular friend Miss Anne Lister of Shibden Hall Yorkshire, owner of the property.

The bottle was placed beneath the foundation stone that Ann then struck three times 'earnestly' with her mallet. As the two women headed back to their carriage, the crowd gave three cheers. It is easy to imagine Ann breathless with delight, grinning at her wife as they drove off to pay a call at Cliff Hill. Ann's good mood meant that when the Sutherlands enquired about a black tin deed box, they were shown it.[33] Elizabeth was also shown the casino inscription and 'seemed pleased'. All in all, Anne declared that that evening at least, they were 'capital friends'. Ann easily persuaded her sister and brother-in-law to stay and they 'took a glass of wine and biscuit', and she followed this up by staying at Cliff Hill for another day or two to help her aunt, who was finding entertaining tiring. Ann and her aunt were now closer than ever.

All the time she spent at Cliff Hill was making Ann somewhat homesick and even while she was enthused about the Shibden renovations, she also made plans for planting by the gates of Crow Nest. She planned to build a carriage road up to the house, a scheme which Anne met with doubts. Tensions continued to grow between the two women, and increasingly Ann seems to have felt trapped. She wanted to travel to Leeds and Huddersfield to shop, but in October complained that Anne had had the carriage that day and so she could not.[34] She did, however, visit Leeds with Anne to interview a Mr and Mrs Barber for the post of schoolmaster for Knowle-top school on Crow Nest land. Ann's impression of them was favourable but their conflict in religion was a concern, Mr Barber was what Anne termed 'a radical'. Ann was at Cliff Hill when another candidate, a Mr Sharpe, called at Shibden; Anne explained to him that it was Ann with whom he needed to speak and would not make a decision in her absence. He turned out not to be a suitable candidate but Ann gave him £6 to cover his travel expenses anyway.[35]

Ann was passionate about her school and the later part of the year sees her teaching there herself, taking the children through their catechism, and she was annoyed when one Sunday in September the weather prevented her from going. Often she rode there, usually using Anne's pony as her own was 'not manageable enough'.[36]

October at Shibden found her comfortable enough to make preserves, which was a traditional province of the lady of the house.[37] It has often been assumed that Ann was 'looked after' by Anne following their marriage, but their relationship was very much a two way street. Ann's letters and Anne's diary are littered with examples of Ann's day to day care. She often helped to dress Anne and took pains to do her hair for her on many a morning. Ann might have been disappointed that Anne had not introduced her to her high society friends, but she was determined to establish her social life, no matter what gossip was circulating about her at the time. Just a single week in October saw Ann shopping in Halifax and calling 'at Heath on Mrs Fenton then to Cliff Hill' one day, going to Brookes at Hipperholme and Cliff Hill the next, before attending the school and church on Sunday.

On 17 October Ann was once again at Cliff Hill and she was 'much pleased' when she got back to Shibden in time to deal with her tenant Mr Roberts and his wife, who she told must either quit her farm and land or else pay the rent of £28 12s for the land and 5 guineas for the cottage. [38] Her ability to manage her own affairs was not in doubt, and Ann made it clear that Anne's interference would not be welcome. That evening Anne was banished to sit with her father and Marian while Ann conducted her business.[39] That season Ann also gave orders for Washington to buy Home house and the land around it from George Armytage for about £5,000, evidence that like her father and grandfather before her, Ann was determined to add to and develop her family estate. This was considered by Anne to be an excellent decision, something Ann likely remembered when making business decisions later in life.

Another matter in which Ann and her wife were united was in their concern for Aunt Lister's health. In December, Anne wrote that she was not 'not likely to rally much or perhaps continue very long … my aunt so poorly'. It was not a cheerful beginning to the Christmas period. Ann escaped to Cliff Hill, where her own aunt was ill and ensured that Anne, who herself was feeling unwell with headaches and her bowels, ate as the doctor ordered, making her take port and a biscuit at luncheon on his recommendation.[40] She sat with Aunt Lister who confided in her that 'she did not know if [this time] she would recover or not'; she had never spoken to Ann this way and she clearly 'thought herself in danger'.[41] Christmas for Ann passed in a flurry of health worries and philanthropic works; on 23 December she spent the day trimming bonnets for her Sunday school girls.[42] On top of this, petty quarrels were the order of the day; Anne refers to Ann's odd temper when, just after Christmas, she disagreed with Anne and cried over Honley Mill. Ann always hated it when they quarrelled and she felt 'very low and poorly' for days afterwards.[43]

Chapter 18

Burning Ann

The quarrels between Ann and her wife continued and Ann spent most of New Year's Eve in tears, but it was not just Ann who was feeling downcast – the whole mood at Shibden was melancholy. Ann was regularly seeing a doctor and 2 January gives us a tantalising clue as to exactly what Ann was being treated with by Mr Jubb. He had prescribed her a 'blue pill and pill galbanum 2 to be taken every or every other night for a while'.[1] These blue pills were something of a nineteenth-century phenomenon, and each doctor or pharmacist made them to his own prescription but the main ingredients were usually a mixture of mercury, glycerol, honey, liquorice and something called Althaea. They were used to treat almost every condition imaginable, in Ann's case they were probably prescribed to help her with her constipation and generalised pain. Mercury of course is toxic and it has been estimated that two blue pills might have contained as much as 100 times the recommended level of mercury today. They were certainly not the sort of thing that anyone, especially a woman with mental health concerns, should have been taking. Pill galbanum was also prescribed, and this would have been more useful; even today it is used to treat symptoms such as poor appetite. Ann was also being treated for a blister between her shoulder blades. Ann's lack of appetite was concerning her wife and Anne began to write down what and when Ann ate.[2]

Ann seems determined to try to be cheerful though. One day she got up to take coffee in the blue room with Anne and was 'in good spirits, blithe as a bee'.[3] Part of her reluctance to eat downstairs seems to have been that with her blister she could not bear to wear her stays, and was not yet comfortable appearing downstairs in less than proper attire.

Overriding all of this though was her continuing concern about money; she told Anne that she felt she 'had caused all the expense, wished I had told her before etc etc'. She went as far as accusing Anne of misrepresenting her financial situation; she claimed that Anne had told her she would need to pay £50 per horse but now she said she would need £250 a year. Anne explained that the £50 was not including servants' wages, but Ann does not seem to have been convinced. She also wanted to 'sport her own livery' and not Anne's, which seems to have differed in respect of the button used. Ann's dissatisfaction broke out and she and Anne had a row on 4 January.[4] The root of the matter seems to be, as always, that Ann wanted to control her own life, and her own money, something that Anne was not keen for her to do, as the 'man' of the marriage. Anne very much felt that the decision making should be left to her and she became increasingly frustrated and callous towards Ann as she sought to placate her. She did not understand why Ann would not just simply fall into line, but she doesn't seem to have understood that Ann mighthave, if Anne had taken the time to explain things to her properly. Nine times out of ten she acknowledged Anne's superior intellect and judgement, but she would not do so blindly. Nor would she apologise if she did not feel that she was in the wrong.[5]

The coldness between herself and her wife was very troubling to Ann, and though she made no apology she did kiss Anne tearfully and they 'talked kindly' about the school at Lightcliffe. All this tension meant that Ann was not sleeping well. Stuck inside by the cold, Ann spent her time with Mr Lister and Aunt Lister, whose health continued to yo-yo alarmingly. She took to practising French again, but Ann was bored. With Anne out and about dealing with estate matters she was stuck indoors with little to do except worry, and Anne's financial records from the beginning of 1836 illustrate that Ann was right to be concerned. Money was flowing out of Shibden with alarming frequency, with little new income coming in as yet.[6] Soon tension boiled over, this time Ann objected to the carriage Anne had ordered for going to church. Nor did she wish to put on the boots that Anne recommended, it was another row that was, in reality, over very little, but it demonstrates how tense the atmosphere was between Ann and her wife.

Ann had nearly reached her limit at Shibden; she told Anne in January that she had gone so far as to make plans for leaving Anne and going down to London alone, and was thinking of asking Jane Chapman to accompany her. Ann had also thought that she would take art lessons down there; whether this was a pipe dream or something she seriously considered is unclear, but it does offer us a glimpse of the sort of life Ann wanted – and it was one of city dwelling, fashionable society and art. Touchingly, when Ann confessed all this to Anne, her wife assured her that she would help her if that was truly what she wanted.[7] This denouncement seems to have cleared the air, while both women threatened and thought of a life apart in reality they remained deeply committed to their marriage and they began to make more of an effort with each other. They had a 'tolerable kiss' on 8 January and Anne wrote 'we are alright'.[8] An undercurrent of discontent was still bubbling away though, and it took little to bring it to the surface. Ann wanted to travel again she told Anne 'she did not wish to be here and got all wrong', Anne replied that she stayed for her aunt and that she was grateful that Ann had 'kept the peace at Shibden'.[9]

Ann gritted her teeth at Anne's requests for yet more money. Nevertheless, she helped fund Anne's latest enthusiasm, some meer-work, which included a plan to build a reservoir below Shibden to eventually power a waterwheel for the colliery, and on 3 of March, Ann watched Anne proudly show off as they walked to the engine together.[10] Ann was shown the new cascade, and listened to Anne's optimistic financial forecasts, she 'hoped to make from 200–300 pounds by the meer eventually'. Eventually being the key word here, but Ann was really trying and did not want to upset the apple cart. She was not happy though, and began to drink more in the evenings, a fact that she showed awareness of. She feared that her 'illness' was returning and that when people found out it would add even more fire to the gossip about her locally. Thoughts of a possible Paris trip later in the year buoyed her spirits momentarily, and with this prospect dangled in front of her Ann was willing to appease Anne further in the matter of finances. When Anne asked her about going to York and suggested that Ann 'has better give [her] a legal power to manage me and give me a life estate etc', Ann made no objection, wanting to show Anne that she was fully committed to their union.[11] For now, all idea of separation on the part of both women was forgotten.

As Anne Lister's activities in the area continued at a pace, tongues continued to wag about the two women and more specifically about just how much of Ann Walker's money was she spending. With this in mind the two women's business rivalry with the Rawsons worsened. The Rawsons, knowing how unpopular Anne and Ann were locally, went out of their way to stir up reformist resentment against them. Specifically in relation to the 'Caddy Field slums' between Halifax and Southowram.

Ann owned property near the area and at some point damage was done by 'pillagers' to a well there on Water Lane. The precise details of the incident remains unclear, but the issue seems to have been whether Ann owned the well or whether it was a public well with access for all. As towns such as Halifax expanded all over the country the issue of access to clean water became an important one, and one that was often linked to local politics. Ann certainly believed that the well was hers, but when the case came before the magistrates one witness swore that 'he had got water uninterrupted at the well for 60 years'.[12] Anne retorted on her wife's behalf 'that if it is a public well Miss Walker does not know it – but she only wants what is fair. She has no wish or thought to do wrong or hardship to anyone.' Anne and Ann both suspected that the Rawsons were behind the vandalism. Ann sought legal advice on the matter from both Gray and Parker. Gray thought that as the well was 'always within the limits of her private property and if it was made and always repaired and kept in order by her predecessors in the property ... Ann can still maintain her right over the well as her private property'. The situation, however, deteriorated and on 13 March Anne wrote that she and Ann spoke with Mr Parker who told them that there had been 'a mob of about 200 people headed [there] ... paid for by Rawson of Hope-Hall!'[13] He was all for taking legal action against some of these people or 'putting a barrel of tar into the well and spoiling the water for a year'. Ann did not want this, but she was overruled as Parker said that this would put her case on a much stronger footing, and Anne was all for it.

The whole thing left Ann feeling very low. She instructed Washington to do as Anne had agreed, but it went rather against the grain. Perhaps it was the moral implications of the harm that this might do to her poor tenants that troubled Ann, for she spent the afternoon on her knees in prayer. Ann's distaste for the incident seems to have affected her willingness to attend to estate matters and she increasingly gave Anne authority to give orders while she instead focused on her school.

With this all rumbling on, Ann went to York with her wife, staying at the George Inn to rewrite her will under Mr Gray's guidance. She left the bulk of her property as previously to Sackville Sutherland, but Anne Lister was now made sole trustee and a life tenant in Ann's un-entailed property, Anne Lister made a similar arrangement regarding Shibden should Ann outlive her.[14] The making of this will gives us a clear insight

into Ann's train of thought at the time, and she also asked Gray to add
a clause whereby Anne would be given the entire management of her
estate if she should fall ill or feel unable to manage the estate herself.
She said she would much rather such a task be given to Anne than to
Captain Sutherland. Mr Gray hesitated to implement this, he said that it
was 'rather difficult' and that it needed to be given full consideration, at
the moment at least he had no thought that Ann could not manage her
lands and estate herself. He urged Ann to reconsider adding the clause
concerning her health as it would give Anne such power over her life.
Anne wrote that she 'would not take any unfair advantage of her or of
anyone if I knew it', and was satisfied that Ann had no such thoughts
of her seeking to take advantage of her in this way – Ann trusted her
wife absolutely.[15]

Not even a lovely dinner in York of 'mock turtle soup [to modern
ears, a rather unpleasant sounding mix of calf organs and brains] boiled
salmon, roast loin of lamb and pudding and tart nicely cooked' could
raise her spirits, though she did use her time in York to look up some
family wills at the manuscript office and found the one she was looking
for regarding William Walker of Lower Crow Nest. Ann was working
on her family genealogy and the well incident prompted her desire to look
into the history of her family property.[16]

Estate matters reared their ugly head again though and she and Anne
appointed Thomas Adam to defend them when the matter of the well
poisoning came before the magistrates. Mr Rawson was 'furious' and
threatened that he would not grant Anne's Northgate licence and Mr
Adams thought that Ann would be forced to give up the well. Mr Throp,
a nurseryman near Water Lane, condemned the Rawsons' stirring up
of discontent, but despite this Ann lost the case.[17] Washington had the
unenviable task of informing Ann on 25 March that she would have
to give it up and Ann was very angry indeed. She raged at Anne and
'damned [her] off', evidently blaming Anne for making the whole matter
worse.[18] Ann hated injustice and felt that the whole sordid incident
had further sullied what was left of her name in the district. The court
convicted the four men of poisoning the water on Ann's orders, and the
public reporting of the incident annoyed her further. Locally Ann was
now being portrayed as cruel and immoral, something that would not
have been further from the truth, but as access to fresh water was by now

considered a human right, her reputation took a further battering. Ann abhorred the attention and Holt claimed that it was out of spite towards Ann that Rawson had behaved as he did. Why the Rawsons acted in such a way is unclear but it seems likely that it was fuelled by Ann's family's horror at her relationship with Anne and their resentment of her bankrolling her wife with Walker money. There is also the suggestion that he wanted some cottages in Caddy Fields and was using the opportunity to garner support for his venture.[19]

Things came to a head when effigies of Ann and her wife were burnt in the streets of Halifax, by the town's resentful population. Effigy burning was quite common at the time – especially in politics, but Ann was truly horrified.[20] She was miserable and even her aunt's support and personal attacks on Rawson did not help raise her spirits. She began to refuse to take wine as well, fearing that she would be tempted to 'take too much'. Personal tragedy followed and on 30 March Ann received a letter to say that her nephew John was dead; Ann grieved for her 'poor nephew' and prayed every morning for days for his soul.[21]

Another tragedy was also brewing: Mr Lister's health was rapidly failing. Ann spent all day with Anne at his side on 31 March, while Mr Jubb offered murmurs of hope, which surely he knew were unrealistic. Even the Priestlys overcame their scruples regarding Ann's life at Shibden to pay their respects to the dying man. Ann dealt with the whole situation well; she helped to keep the peace between the nervous and bickering sisters, and sat with Mr Lister and prayed, but to no avail. Mr Lister died on 3 April peacefully, and so easily that Anne 'scarce knew when the last breath had passed away'.[22] Ann helped Anne prepare the sheets the next morning and set about writing letters to her aunt and others who had to be informed. Anne was distraught and Ann walked with her wife and read prayers with Aunt Lister. Ann grieved for the man who had been so kind to her. Like many bereaved persons before and since, she also found solace in tasks such as putting away the linen and drafting instructions regarding the coming funeral service which went off without a hitch. Anne writes that she was thankful that once everything was over she could sit quietly by Ann's side, giving us a touchingly intimate picture of two women who, despite everything, could still find peace in each other's company.

Mr Lister's passing marked the end of an era at Shibden and Marian made immediate plans to leave.[23] By now Marian felt Ann to be 'one of the family', and, once she had left, the two women missed each other's company. Ann also badly wanted to escape Halifax and agreed to bear the whole of the expenses for travelling, instructing Washington to pay money into Anne's account for the purpose. When the two women were again in York, Mr Gray quietly took the opportunity to ask Anne about her wife's mental state and Anne, with genuine honesty, replied that she 'has simply been low and nervous but never insane'.

Ann though would not be travelling just yet, estate matters as well as Aunt Lister's health further delayed their plans. She did not fail in her duty to Aunt Lister and Anne's diary entries tell us that Ann often sat with her, talking and reading. With an air of mortality hanging over Shibden Hall, Ann continued to pray frequently and she joined a Society for promoting Christian knowledge.

Ann was at Aunt Lister's side and called her wife to come upstairs 'just in time' to see Aunt Lister breathe her last on 10 October.[24] Ann then sat in silent support while Anne wrote the necessary letters. Aunt Lister's death cast a long shadow over Shibden and lowness of spirits affected both women.

Chapter 19

A New World

Early 1837 saw Ann busier than ever at the school and she went there nearly every day.[1] She also walked and rode regularly, being on 22 February caught in a rain and hailstorm, with wind so strong that she could barely walk.[2] Two days later Ann went to bed very late, and awoke when she heard a knock on the door. She called John, who fired a pistol shot in warning and woke Anne. Ann swore that she had seen a light in the saddle room and Anne went to investigate.[3] Such incidents have long been used to illustrate Ann's increasing paranoia, but Anne found that the door was indeed unlocked and concluded that someone had been in the room. Nor was Ann unnaturally troubled, the next day she was off to the school as usual and that evening wrote to her sister on business matters, she wished to sell some building ground in order to improve her day to day finances. Typically, Anne corrected the letter for her, before it was sent.[4]

Later that month Anne caught a cold and Ann instructed her to rest in bed while she rode her pony to the school and then to Cliff Hill. While out, Ann heard that Jenny Filton was ill and so rode to check on her. Anne was rather put out that Ann had been out so long, only getting back at 5 pm when she had expected her at 12, and had gone out, but upon her return Ann made her come indoors saying that if she must do something, then she could read in the warm. Ann was not above asserting her authority when she felt her wife needed looking after and Anne's illness bred affection for they had a 'good kiss' for the first time in many weeks.[5]

It seems inescapable though, as we follow Ann's day to day activities in early 1837, that she was seeking to forge her own life away outside of Shibden and Anne, who had failed to provide her with the society she promised. She was often out at the school without Anne even seeing her, and 28 February saw her visit Halifax alone with George, returning to Shibden only briefly before riding out to Cliff Hill. She only spared

Anne the time to beat her at backgammon.[6] We also see Ann, following Aunt Lister's death, showing an increased confidence in her dealings at Shibden, perhaps finding it easier to do so now. Ann ordered a new stove from Ropers for the north parlour for more warmth when she attended to business matters. She also had an issue with their servant Cookson, and wished for Anne to dismiss her; the servant troubles had evidently not been solved with Marian's departure. Anne's lack of support in the matter irritated Ann, who felt that as 'mistress' now at Shibden, servants were her domain.[7]

Ann's frustration is palpable and with this in mind it doesn't seem strange that we find her attention increasingly drawn to Cliff Hill. She began to undertake some maintenance tasks there, ordering that William Keighley cut down a large poplar close to the house. Still though she could not quite shake the need to ask Anne's opinion, and sent for her to give it before she made further decisions regarding the gardens. Her philanthropic concerns continued apace, and she continued to sew and knit clothing for the poor of the neighbourhood alongside undertaking visits to the sick; in March, Mrs Dyson at Willow Hall fell seriously ill and Ann visited her, despite the inclement weather.

Travel, though, was never far from Ann's mind; she made it clear that she wished to at least go away for Easter and they agreed on a trip to Bolton Abbey.[8] Before they were off on 17 March however, Ann once again alerted the household at night to the fact that she thought someone had broken in. Anne went to look, armed with her pistols, but wrote that she expected to find no one. The next morning, however, it was proved that there had in fact been a break-in and Ann was understandably insistent that if she had been listened to the night before, the persons could not have spent so long in the building.[9]

Finally, on Maundy Thursday, she and Anne were off towards Skipton where they stayed at the Devonshire Hotel. Ann took her pills and wore a belladonna plaster for the journey, which she felt helped immensely. Belladonna contains chemicals that can block the function of the body's nervous system, and even today belladonna plasters are prescribed for backache and nervous pain. In this case at least, Mr Jubb knew what he was talking about.[10] In Skipton they sat at the castle and walked the gardens quite happily. Snow fell as they travelled to the Devonshire Arms, where they stayed for a night 'too well cloaked up to suffer from the cold'.

Having learnt from their honeymoon journey Ann took the precaution this time of travelling with a provision basket.

The trip away did wonders for Ann's sex life and she and Anne resumed their marital relations enthusiastically and pleasurably. They travelled to Keighley where, at Akeds in Low Street, Ann bought *Easy Lessons in Mechanics*, perhaps wanting to understand more about the work her money was paying for.

When they returned to Shibden Ann declared that the 'change of air and Brodies plaster [had] done her good', and apologised to Anne for having been irritable prior to their departure. She was pleased that the north parlour at Shibden had now been determined as her sitting room, something they seem to have decided upon while away and she braved the 'very snowy afternoon' to travel to the school and then call upon her aunt.[11] While Ann was out and about Anne oversaw the putting up of a bookcase in Ann's new parlour and then watched for Ann's return through the storm before taking her to bed for a 'goodish one'. Ann fully claimed the north parlour as hers the following day by serving Anne coffee there.[12] From her new parlour she wrote to her sister, and discussed the selling of the land at Landsmere. Ann and Anne disagreed on the matter but Ann did not fall in with her wife's wishes and determined that she would consult Gray instead. Ann had caught a cold but she was off to school again within days, though she had to go on foot as the ground was too icy for her to take the pony.

Continuing bad weather and biting cold kept both women close to home as the year moved toward mid-April. One day Anne's eye was cut by a thorn while gardening and Ann cheerfully ignored Anne's instructions not to send for a doctor.[13] Mr Jubb came the next morning and ordered that leeches be applied, Ann remained at her wife's side, forgoing church until Anne said that she might go while she slept.[14] Perhaps Anne feared that Ann herself would doze, as one phrase in particular keeps recurring in her diary at this time: the fact that Ann snored – 'Could not sleep for Ann's snoring all night', and, 'she snored so I could not sleep'.[15,16] This led to Ann and Anne beginning to sleep apart for the first time since Ann's arrival at Shibden, though it was not a solution that either woman welcomed.[17] Feeling guilty, Ann got the kitchen chamber ready for Anne to sleep in, wanting to make sure that she would be comfortable.

Ann's discontent was growing however, and by July she was giving serious consideration to removing to Cliff Hill or Crow Nest, writing to her sister to discuss the matter as Lidgate was still let. She also gave thought to visiting Scotland despite the presence there of Captain Sutherland, but these ideas were ultimately swept away in a tide of tears and recriminations. Aunt Walker's health was now beginning to fail; Ann was often at Cliff Hill and sent many letters to her sister in Scotland to keep her informed of their aunt's condition.[18] By August Ann's days had settled into a pattern whereby she would spend her evenings reading with Anne, before setting off early to go to Cliff Hill every morning. This put her under considerable pressure, and on 2 September Ann fell asleep in the north parlour one morning before waking in a panic and riding quickly to Cliff Hill. Aunt Walker rallied one day and then seemed at death's door the next, it was an exhausting rollercoaster and Ann's health began to suffer. Mr Jubb told her that she 'has a great tendency to inflammation', but her aches and pains hardly seem surprising when you think Ann had ridden or walked between Shibden and Cliff Hill every day for months.[19]

Ann's personal feelings are hard to guess during this time; she is so frequently out of the house that Anne scarcely mentions her except in relation to their reading or sleeping together, and in Ann's letters to her sister she writes almost exclusively about her aunt, the children or the estate.

There is, however plenty, of evidence that Ann was keeping up with the maintenance of her own estate. When she met with Barstow in early 1838, regarding the fact that the waterwheel at her mill had broken, she withstood pressure from him to act and repair it quickly, arguing that it was no good doing so while the water in the brook was still so high. She also insisted that the waterwheel must not be used until the repairs were done. Likewise when Hartley came to see her about building a new power-loom shed, offering her a 7.5 per cent return, and she retorted that she would accept no less than 10 per cent.[20]

Financially, her wife was still borrowing money frequently and Ann cried in frustration and despair when Anne sat her down and told her that it would take a thousand pounds to completely settle all her affairs. Ann did not advance her such a sum but she did still give money frequently, such as on 26 January when she gave Anne £30 to pay her bills. Anne rather patronisingly writes that she 'talked her into a better heart' about it all. Ann's financial fears were somewhat alleviated by her receipt of the rents in January 1838. She gave Anne '500 pounds to put in the bank, one hundred and sixty being her interest to Mr Gray and the rest for [Ann's] own to the Misses Preston. Ann rode to Whitley and Heath and sent by George 300 pounds to Briggs and kept 146 pounds at home.' Ann also knew that she would have another £60 worth of rents in a fortnight. All of this meant that Ann would have £1,300 plus the 'Honley Mill and Hinscliffe coal besides.'[21]

With this in mind, Ann and Anne began to talk about travelling again and discussed destinations, France, Italy, Norway and Russia were all touted options, and Ann noticeably began to increase the time that she spent studying her French. Both women also bought, and borrowed from the library, books on Norway and Russia. It is difficult to get a true impression of Ann's health at this time, Anne frequently writes that Ann is 'cold and poorly', that she ate little and had to be coaxed into taking hot wine and biscuits, something that Anne was at pains to keep track of. On the other hand however, Ann was still well enough to pay visits and frequently ride or trek to Cliff Hill, and Halifax. Nor did her health prevent her from keeping up a correspondence with her family and friends; Lydia wrote to her often and when her father had an issue with his curate, it was to Ann that she turned for reassurance and advice. Ann cared deeply about her friends, and when her acquaintance Mrs Broadbent fell ill she wrote to Mr Lyon at the Manchester infirmary asking him to call and see her. Ann bore both the trouble and the expense herself.

Chapter 20

Ann Saves the Day

Ann's wish to travel finally came to fruition when, in the spring of 1838, she and Anne departed Shibden.[1] The previous day Ann had spoken with Washington and finished her final preparations. The plan was that their journey to Belgium would improve Ann's health and both women also hoped that travelling again would bring them closer together. By 5 May Ann was in London at Crawley's hotel, where she wrote to her aunt to ensure that this time there would be no misunderstanding about her plans.[2] The next day she had her hair done by Mr Faulkner in order that she could present herself smartly in Paris, then that afternoon they journeyed to Iron Wharf to catch their boat.[3] Travelling was already improving Ann's appetite and she ate biscuits, tongue and wine while waiting for Anne to sort out the more practical matters. She stood for a while out on the deck until the strong cold wind forced both women to take shelter in the carriage. The voyage was unusually rough and Anne was very sick; Ann was also unwell but she managed to sleep for most of the journey – snoring loudly. Upon landing in Antwerp both women stumbled to the hotel, feeling rather delicate. Intriguingly, Anne tells us that they brought Ann's journal ashore, but if the journal still exists, sadly it has not yet been found.[4]

Ann was impressed with Antwerp and they stayed there a few days before heading to Malines (Mechelen) where they visited the church before stopping at Vilvoorde to see where Tyndale was martyred.[5] By 9 May Ann was in Brussels, where her happiness was further increased by the eating of three or four fresh oranges. That evening she sat curling Anne's hair while the latter slept, giving us a touching picture of the casual intimacy that existed between the two women. While Anne spent time learning about mining, Ann enjoyed shopping and visiting galleries. On 10 May they strolled in the botanic gardens and Anne joined in the shopping buying Ann 'a pair of thread gloves'. As on their honeymoon the two women kept up a fast pace, and the next day they reached Waterloo.[6]

The monuments Ann saw there made sombre reading and they viewed the grave of Sir Alexander Gordon.[7] The nature of the visit seems to have cast a shadow over the rest of Ann's time in Brussels and neither she nor Anne were sorry to be off, heading for Louvain where another botanic garden awaited them. They were staying at the Hotel de Suede, which was very comfortable and, crucially, had fresh oranges available. While there they had a private tour of the house of Monsieur Vandenschrickx, who was a wealthy art collector. Ann's excitement at seeing such a collection, which included Ruebens and Sneyder, can easily be imagined.[8]

Over the next few weeks they travelled to Saint Trond, Orcy and Liege, where Anne left Ann while she descended into the Saint Marguerite Coal Mine. Little details about Ann's travelling habits litter Anne's journal, giving us fascinating details: Ann liked to have her hot drinks quickly, she took her pills intermittently and ate a ridiculous number of oranges. Frustratingly, we know that she also wrote in her diary on a regular basis. Ann went to the theatre on 16 May where the 'company of ladies made the most head-rending din … ever heard from female voices', it was not the most relaxing evening, but Ann's spirits were buoyed by such outings.[9] The next day, however, she was unwell and her head and neck were aching; Ann lay on the sofa while Anne undressed her and comforted her with cherry brandy. Thanks to Anne we also know that Ann's period had started that day, which is a possible explanation for her pain. There seems to have been a question as to whether or not they should travel on to Spa given Ann's health, but she was determined to go on. They stayed at the Hotel d'orange and Ann felt much better for a large, good dinner and bottle of lundel. The next day she felt well enough to go with Anne to the Waterfalls of Coo. The road there was so bad that Ann gave up on the carriage and got out to walk until the heat proved too much for her and she declared she would rather stay where she was and sketch. Ann insisted that she was quite alright to be left alone; after the chaos of the morning she seems to have enjoyed the peace and solitude, sitting in the sun surrounded by fragrant wild black juniper and bilberries. When Anne encountered some peasants on her walk they told her that they had passed Ann and that she was very happily sketching away. Anne, however, determined that the scenery was too beautiful for Ann to miss and arranged for her to ride one of the carriage horses, much to George's astonishment. In this way Ann finally reached the cascade, she thought it beautiful and was delighted that she had gone to see it after all. All in all, it was one of the best days she could remember.[10]

Poor roads continued to plague their travels, when they travelled to Remouchamps Ann was frightened by the carriage's violent jolting, although she did enjoy viewing the grotto there wearing a straw hat and blue blouse given to them by a woman at a little auberge. By 22 May they were back in Liege where Ann was, in the modern parlance, 'hangry', to Anne's annoyance, and on the 25th they arrived in Charleville-Mezieres.[11] On one memorable occasion Anne fell asleep only to be woken by Ann 'calling out [that] the hat was gone – 2 or 3 times to call to the postillion and [Anne] in taking off [her] velvet travelling cap 2 combs flew out – George had to run back – Ann laughed much and long'. The image of Ann shrieking and helpless with laughter is a touching and vivid one.[12]

The chalk hills of Rethel held less attraction for both women than the pretty valleys they had previously journeyed through and both were pleased to get to Reims on good time. Once settled in the city Ann made it her habit to get up early to sketch in the cathedral, and took a trip to sketch at the Roman ruins. Ann liked Reims and was sorry to leave it, the more so for the fact that the roads were still terrible, in consequence of which at Epernay she drank rather too much champagne and was hungover the next day when they went to see Mr Moet's cellars. Thankfully, the roads improved as they approached Paris and they were able to travel at a 'hard gallop'. Upon entering the city they had trouble finding accommodation, finally taking a little anteroom salon and one bedroom at Le Meurice, and it was a harassed Ann that went to bed that evening.[13]

Again Anne writes that Anne became poorly but this seems (yet again) to have been an issue over food; Ann was hungry and breakfast was very late. Anne writes that Ann was a poor thing not fit for much, but Ann was quite well enough to explore, sketch and shop while in Paris. She also wrote to her aunt and was pleased to receive a letter from her.

From Paris the plan was to head south to the Pyrenees, but June saw tensions rising in Ann's marriage. Part of the issue seems to have been that this trip was less well planned, both in terms of accommodation and expense, than their honeymoon. This uncertainty led to 'harassment' and short tempers all round. Ann was also suffering from a rash on her face, and when visiting Versailles she was overcome by the heat and fainted.

Anne was not amused and called Ann's illness 'humbug'.[14] She consulted a British doctor in Paris, one Dr Double, who advised Ann to take the spa waters of St Sauveur and Bareges in the Pyrenees, which fitted in well with their plans. To help take care of Ann a French maid called Josephine was hired, and by 20 June they were heading south. On 25 June, Ann was happily eating strawberries as she travelled through fine country towards Poitiers, where they stayed at the Hotel de France.[15] Ann visited the cathedral and was well enough to walk for most of the day.

The curse of poor roads struck again the further south they went, but despite this Ann said that she wished to continue. Anne disagreed but Ann was insistent, and Anne spent the journey muttering 'I told you so', as they had 'such a jolting', and ignoring Ann. Ann, meanwhile, sat calmly and was quite well upon their arrival in Curray where she went out to sketch the church. Irritated with her wife, Anne could not resist noting that she felt the church was not worth sketching, but said nothing to Ann.[16] This little incident gives us an insight into how tense things were between the two women, and Anne's journal is littered with such petty quarrels which inevitably end in one or the other of them sulking. The next day saw Ann sketching the cathedral exterior at Angoulême and shopping for books quite happily, but she lost her temper in the evening when she was forced to wait until 11 pm for dinner. Her mood was not improved the next day by very heavy rain and the two women travelled onto Bordeaux in stony silence. Ann was in no mood to be conciliatory either, and she was annoyed when Anne looked at some new books she had bought.[17]

Gradually though the atmosphere thawed; Anne, despite her grumbling, wanted to make the best of things and it is logical to assume that Ann felt the same way. They travelled on through heavily wooded countryside to Ondres where they saw the famously beautiful lake, before driving onto Bayonne from which they could see the 'fine long line of the Pyrenees'.

Despite such beauty, the area to which Ann was travelling was perilously close to the Spanish border. Spain at this time was being ravaged by a civil war being fought over the succession in the House of Bourbon.[18] Prussia and Russia supported the Carlists with money and weapons, while on the other side Britain had sent troops to aid the widowed queen. From St Jean de Luz on 4 July Anne wanted to take a boat trip out to St Sebastian in Spain and engaged what appear to have been smugglers to row them out. This was a step too far for Ann, who, although she bravely got in the small boat tightly clutching Anne's hand, finally determined that the waves were too high and she was dropped off to go back to Saint Jean de Luz while Anne continued on. Ann was not amused at being left alone (with all the luggage!) and did not give Anne a warm reception when she returned the next day having viewed the slaughter ground of Hernani.[19] Ann was much more amused by the beautiful views she saw the following day at Peyrehorade, and by which she was charmed. Peace broke out as the two women sat and enjoyed salmon.

Neither woman was entirely happy though, and it was with some relief that they arrived at Luz-Saint-Sauveur on the 9 July. Once there Anne sent for Mr Faba, the doctor and director of the baths. For Ann to take any of the waters she had to have his permission. He read the report that Dr Double had sent and agreed that Ann could both bathe and take the waters there. He did, however, refuse permission for her to have a douche applied to her face for ten minutes every morning, something it is hard to imagine Ann much regretted.[20] The thermal baths at Luz-Saint-Sauveur were already famous by the time of Ann's visit. The thermal waters there are rich in mineral salts and sulphur and the liquid comes to the surface at a warming 33°C. Thermal baths had been established there as early as the sixteenth century and by the time of Ann's visit the hydrotherapy offered there was at the heart of scientific and medical studies; if she wanted the best up-to-date treatment, Ann had come to the right place. Mr Faba decreed that Ann could bathe on a Thursday morning and begin drinking the waters on Wednesday morning. She was 'to take 2 glasses of the Eaux bonnes water at an hour's interval with 2 spoonfuls of cow's milk and one of sirop de guimauve [marshmallow] in each glass of water'.[21] Luz Saint Sauveur would be Ann's base for the next six weeks, and they used it to explore the local area. Ann particularly liked Grust, where she and Anne rode to look down the valley. Her days consisted of little outings in the morning before she returned to Luz Saint Sauveur to throw herself into the prescribed regime of bathing.

Ann was not solely there for the baths though, she wanted to explore the area alongside Anne. Anne's thoughts were firmly fixed on the mountains and she engaged two guides: Jean-Pierre Charles for herself, with whom she had travelled in 1830, and his friend Jean-Pierre Sanjou for Ann. On 23 July Ann rode with her wife to Gedre from where they intended to climb Pimene and descend to Gavarnie where Ann would sleep while Anne continued up Vignemale.[22] Ann was then to meet her wife at Bujaruelo just across the Spanish border. She was to be accompanied by Bernard Guillebet, brother-in-law of Charles, who was to climb the mountain with Anne. Bad weather, however, forced a change of plan; both Ann and Charles felt that it was too cloudy and the climb was delayed by two weeks, during which time Ann sketched the mountains almost daily. On 5 August the climb was delayed yet again, Ann was 'starved and poorly' – no doubt due to the fact she had been following her wife around all day with little hope of food – and the weather was bad, but the following day there was hope of improvement in the weather.[23] It was determined that Ann would stay where she was, and await the return of Bernard with the horses who would then 'bring Ann … to meet [us] at Bouchero'. Ann was very nervous on her wife's behalf; the weather was still far from ideal, but she knew better than to deter her. She did, however, offer her wife one piece of invaluable advice. She absolutely insisted that Anne take her crampons, nagging until Anne gave way – 'Ann had persisted in my having crampons with me'. It was an insistence that saved the day for Anne, who, as it turned out, would not have been able to complete the ice-drenched climb without them.[24]

Unfortunately we don't know exactly what Ann was doing while her wife ascended the mountain, but we do know that she arrived in Gavarnie at 9 am on the 8 of August, the day after Anne's ascent to meet her, and it was a happier reunion as they basked in Anne's achievement. However, on 14 August Ann was sitting with Anne enjoying some wine at Pierrefitte when Charles made the scandalous accusation that Anne had not completed the ascent, but got 'sick on the glacier'. Anne was furious and clearing up this matter consumed the next few days. Ann was 'as much annoyed' as Anne, she was fully aware that her wife's achievement was truly remarkable. By 16 August they were on their way back to Lourdes, where Anne touchingly ensured that Ann had a place to rest before she went to consult a lawyer.[25] Ann wanted to go with her wife, but ultimately decided to stay at the hotel and rest, because worrying about Anne had meant that she had slept poorly. Ann dozed and upon waking was annoyed that Anne – staring out of the window – did not hear her when she asked what the lawyer had said. She had been eager to hear, but now seems to have felt that Anne had spoiled it and they headed back to Luz, once again barely speaking. At Gedre Anne finally obtained her certificate of proof and was delighted, however she also understood Ann well enough by now to know that any delay to dinner would not be appreciated and so she hurried back to join her. Ann did not appreciate the effort though, and pointedly picked up a book to read rather than converse with Anne. On 26 August Ann finally gave way to Anne's attempts at reconciliation and was 'persuaded to get into [Anne's] bed after a little previous play and then in quarter of an hour had a pretty good kiss.'[26]

Such harmony did not last. On 14 September Ann became irritated when Anne, and then Josephine, tried to help her on with her habit; as a consequence, when Anne wanted to alight she would not, instead taking her horse on ahead.[27] She would, she said, 'choose for herself and God grant that she might choose well.' She also brought up again the issue of money – Ann felt they were being far too extravagant. Once again Ann and her wife were not speaking; this time Ann had had enough and the next day she wrote to her sister, stating that she wished to 'take the part of Crow Nest not occupied by Washington', she could not, she said, 'think of returning to Shibden after what [Anne] had said yesterday'.[28] It is worth noting that Ann was not entirely honest with her sister here; attempting to save face and rather than admit that her marriage was failing, she told Elizabeth that Anne intended to remain abroad and that Ann did not wish to be away from her aunt for so long. She must have given thought to the sneers and chuckles that she could face back home; the excuse was thin and she knew it. Anne blamed her entirely for the situation and told her that she had not been a good companion to her, words that cut Ann to the quick. Ann seems to have thought that Anne would leave her then and there, for the next day she was relieved to see her and they talked until 'all was good humour'. It is almost possible to see Ann's gritted teeth the next morning when Anne was once again late for breakfast, but she submitted to Anne's rather patronising talk with good grace.[29]

With good relations somewhat restored, towards the end of September Ann felt well enough to travel on to the region of Eaux-Bonnes, where a local gendarme mistook Anne Lister for a man, and believed that she was travelling fraudulently under a woman's passport. He withheld the passport and Ann was forced to accompany her wife to the police barracks to sort out the matter. The receipt issued to Anne by the gendarme states that Ann was travelling with her as her niece, for propriety's sake. This made sense but Ann was upset, she saw this as a slight and accused Anne of not acknowledging her. It was a tearful Ann that travelled on when they were finally permitted to continue their journey, to the Hotel de France at Pau. While there they met with the prefect Mr Duchatel to whom they related the whole sorry incident, both women had been very embarrassed and Anne wanted an apology. In Pau we also get a glimpse of what Ann was reading at the time, on 30 September she bought from a bookseller near Collongues a 'little French grammar [book] and a sort of History and 1st Horace', not exactly light reading.[30]

Ann very much kept to herself over the next few weeks; she rose early and Anne was often forced to ask Josephine where she was and when she would be ready. Nevertheless, a sort of truce broke out and on 1 November she sat for twenty minutes on Anne's knee before they quarrelled again.[31] All these arguments badly affected Ann, she was tearful and complained of pain in her neck. Anne's diary increasingly reveals that she wanted to be rid of her wife; on 9 November she called her 'an incubus on me', and Ann no doubt sensed this change in Anne's attitude, but both women seem incapable of actually listening to each other.[32] Ann maintained that she wanted to make her own decisions, she complained bitterly that 'she never has her own way', while Anne insisted that she was being held back by Ann.

Yet another truce was called on 14 November, by which time they were in Paris; they seem to have mutually decided that sex was the answer and fell into bed together with heartfelt apologies.[33] More sex followed over the next few days, and Ann only left their bed to mend some clothing of Anne's. This, however, did little but paper over the cracks in Ann's marriage and when they returned to England both remained deeply unhappy.

Chapter 21

Return to Shibden

Ann arrived back at Shibden Hall on 27 November 1838 to swirling snow. England was in the grip of one of the coldest winters in memory and she was quickly beset by worries over her aunt's health and the state of Cliff Hill, which she feared was going to ruin. She was also worried about Anne, who she begged to cheer up as 'she could not bear to see [her] so unhappy', although she stopped short of promising Anne the money requested for the running of Shibden. The break had done little good – they were right back where they started, arguing over money and fretting over family matters. Jealousy began to rear its ugly head and as Anne sought to re-establish contact with her friends, Ann censored her letters – including one to Mariana which she disapproved of, saying that Anne wrote as if she 'cared too much'.[1]

In search of purpose, Ann's attention turned to her beloved Cliff Hill, and she ordered maintenance and a series of improvements to be carried out there. While Ann's attention was fixed on Cliff Hill, Anne continued to pressure her for money for the Shibden estate, but Ann held firm and Anne's diary entry of 3 December gives us an insight into why. Ann, she writes, felt that it was her duty to take care of and expand her family estates 'as her father had been very kind to her'. Money worries that day led to a full-scale row, and in frustration Ann cried that 'she had no comforts herself', which upset Anne so much she fled upstairs in tears, resisting Ann's attempts to comfort her.[2] Despite Anne's anger and frustration she still wrote that evening that the thought of parting from Ann distressed her, and Ann shared her feelings. Ultimately, Ann loved her wife and did not want to leave her. The next day she gave Anne £300 to pay her bills. In a reversal of their usual roles, this time it was Ann who took charge and set things in order while Anne rested her reddened eyes. Ann told her gently that 'she could not do without [her]', and Anne agreed that 'we [should] be mutually dull without each other'.[3]

The school had been on Ann's mind while she was away and once home she wrote to the Fentons to discuss the schoolmistress. Anne, however, wanted her to give up the school, partly resenting the time it took to deal with, and partly because she felt the strain of it was too much for Ann's health. It was to become yet another source of tension between them until December saw Ann finally give up her activities at the school – it was to be a fateful decision.

Now she was home, Ann wrote more frequently to her sister and was delighted to receive a letter from Elizabeth on 19 December in which she was assured that 'little Ewan talked of Aunty Walker and ditto Lister', often.[4] Ever the dutiful aunt, Ann sent presents and treats north.

Perhaps thinking of Anne's desire for more money, Ann began considering selling her navigation stock. Anne disapproved and the ensuing quarrel left Ann in low spirits and floods of tears, as she felt that Anne did not have 'any confidence' in her. Ann spent New Year's Eve crying and January saw no improvement in her spirits. Anne writes that she spent the month 'either poorly or wrong or both'. Ann was in fact under considerable pressure, as mistakes regarding the estate in her absence had to be corrected and her aunt's bad health continued. On top of this her sister was afflicted by various money and family concerns, about which she frequently wrote to Ann.[5]

Loneliness also began to set in; on 13 January Ann lamented that all 'their' friends were really Anne's.[6] In low spirits Ann's appetite began to fail, her aunt annoyed her by inviting the Miss Rawsons to Cliff Hill and she felt that her aunt was taking her for granted. Aunt Walker seems to have taken some offence that Ann had not visited her at Cliff Hill as soon as she had returned, and Ann blamed Anne for it. In typical fashion, having said as much, Ann then acknowledged that it had in fact been simple mischance and apologised, giving Anne £50 in gold.

Despite everything Ann remained fiercely loyal to her wife. When, on 13 March, Aunt Walker asked Ann if 'she would have been better at her own house at Lidgate [rather] than Shibden', Ann angrily retorted no, and that she had never regretted her decision, and in fact she rather took offence and 'wondered at being asked such a question'.[7] Was this the truth? Or was Ann too proud to admit that she was unhappy? I think the truth probably lies somewhere in the middle; her marriage had not been all she hoped, but she still at heart felt she was happier with Anne than without her.

Ann now decided that she wanted to go abroad again, and Anne writes that on 21 March they decided that they had 'fixed to winter in Italy', no matter what the state of Aunt Walker's health.[8] With this decision made Ann tried to throw herself into sorting out estate matters. A few days later she sent a letter to her sister discussing the issues surrounding Oakview Mill and enclosed a parcel of goodies for the children. In tone Ann's letter gives no indication that anything was amiss, but Anne was seriously beginning to worry that Ann's low spirits were worse now than any time since their marriage, and she acknowledged that they needed to get away from Shibden and the prying eyes of Ann's family and friends.[9] We see Anne changing her routine so that she could eat luncheon with Ann and persuade her to eat. Touchingly, her daily 'to-do' lists include 'soup or sandwich for A'.[10] Anne could easily have left such care to the servants, but she wanted to assure herself personally that Ann was eating. All this care was to little avail and when Catherine Rawson came to visit her, she was shocked to find Ann so weak and unwell.

Ann now felt that she would like to go to Egypt. Anne thought more modestly that Berlin or Paris would be suitable and the initial plan was only to go for a few weeks, 'being off and return in July'.[11] Despite all their troubles, Anne was frantic at Ann's illness and tore around Halifax for weeks, sorting out things for their departure. Ann did not wish for her family to see her like this and so largely stayed out of society, but she tried to keep up something resembling her normal regime. She attended to business, wrote letters to her sister, practised her French, began to learn Russian alongside Anne and rode to Cliff Hill when she felt strong enough.

On 28 March Ann was sitting by her wife, who gently told her that 'if she could not rouse herself out of this lowness she had [to] settle all safely on me that they could throw her property into chancery'. With the use of chancery Anne is referring to the court that dealt with both equity and lunacy, and this is the first time that Anne seems to have seriously thought that this was a possibility. Lowness or melancholia at this time was enough to refer someone, and have them deemed as a lunatic. Both Ann and Anne were well aware that legally Ann's family would be in a position to do this if they wanted – their marriage had no basis in law. Anne would be powerless to protect her wife.[12]

Perhaps it was this knowledge that began to draw them closer once again; the following day they slept in the same bed for the first time since returning to England and Ann slept better for it. Ann was still managing her own estates and meeting with Washington and her tenants, but as April dawned it is noticeable that she is more frequently asking Anne's advice in such matters and allowed Anne to act as a buffer between her and the outside world. On 4 April Ann walked with Anne, ate lunch and then lay down, 'when Messrs Whitely of the village of Stainland and James Harper Walker of the district of Stainland called to see Ann – she sat in [the] blue room and [Anne] went down to them.' They wanted to ask Ann for a donation towards a Methodist church. Anne told them that Ann had a headache but that she would take the papers up for her to see. Ann and Anne then spoke together before Anne then returned with the agreed donation of £20.[13]

Ann acknowledged herself to be very unwell, and on 7 April, perhaps with the knowledge of the legal limitations of her marriage, stated that she was resolved to sign everything she could over to Anne and that she wanted to go to York as soon as possible to sign the legal papers.[14]

Russia was now mentioned for the first time since 1837/8 as a possible travel destination and the necessity of leaving was felt keenly by both women. In the meantime Ann consulted with Dr Jubb, who gave Ann 'pills calomel coleynth and carbonate to dissolve'. He seemed to think that lack of food lay at the heart of her sickness and also advised her to take '3 or 4 glasses of wine a day'. Calomel is a derivative of mercury chloride and today is regarded as a toxin which, when swallowed, suppresses the central nervous system and can lead to breathing difficulties, pain and nausea, so it is hardly surprising that Ann was violently sick upon taking it. As early as 1825 a publication in Virginia issued a poem that warned physicians about the dangers of prescribing Calomel Colynth as a treatment 'Since Calomel's become their boast / How many patients have they lost / How many thousands they make ill / Of poison with their Calomel.' Its use declined as a result; unfortunately for Ann this knowledge had not filtered through to Halifax and she persisted taking the pills despite the side effects.[15]

Ann's world had shrunk when she gave up the school and Anne, on 14 April, blamed her depression on 'this giving up school business ... I blame it much for her present lowness'. This explanation makes sense, all her life Ann searched for meaning and purpose. The school had given that to her – without it she was rudderless and adrift. Ann was utterly miserable and Anne 'grieved' to see her so, but Dr Jubb, when he called the following day, felt her to be better and added 'Hudson's concrete essence of sarsaparilla' to her prescription, which he was sure 'will do her good'. Thankfully, modern medicine has shown that sarsaparilla is not harmful, and can be helpful in reducing inflammation; however, perhaps wary after the Calomel, Ann hesitated to take it.[16]

Alongside these physical remedies Ann began to pray more frequently, but this made her feel worse as thoughts again surfaced about the immorality of her life. She told Anne that she felt herself to be a fornicator and Anne told her that she must not go to church after one sermon in April greatly upset her. Anne was worried and frustrated that nothing seemed to be helping her wife, while Ann for her part kept resolving to do better but was never quite able to manifest her intention. It is possible that having started on Calomel pills Ann might have been experiencing hallucinations, fever and other side effects. Unfortunately it is simply not possible to know for certain, but the worsening of her mental health should be considered in this context. All the while Aunt Anne continued 'bothering' her with numerous demands regarding Cliff Hill, something that Ann confessed to Dr Jubb was playing on her mind.[17]

Ann's mind was also full of the justifiable fear that she might be taken from Anne's care against her will and they made the long planned visit to York secretly on 20 April, staying at the George Inn. Going to York also meant that Ann could consult with Dr Belcombe, but not about her mental health, this time she wished to ask him about her bowels. Her lowness could not be entirely concealed from him however, and he was concerned. On 23 April Anne met with Mr Gray and added him and Ann as an executor to her will, this is curious because it suggests that as worried as Anne was about Ann's health, she did not truly expect that she would be incapable of fulfilling such a task.[18] Ann informed Mr Gray that she would like to move her property into Anne's name. Ann was showing unprompted decisiveness here, demonstrating just how afraid she was. Anne had advised her against mentioning it so soon as she felt sure she would recover her spirits, Ann though was not so convinced. To the intense frustration of both women, Mr Gray advised that Ann could not do this; it turned out that 'Mrs Sutherland's giving all to her husband [was considered] a different thing.' Ann's marriage was simply not recognised by the law and Ann's transfer of property to Anne was not the same as her giving it to a husband. Ann was not going to be able to do as she pleased, but Mr Gray's intentions in blocking her wishes seem to have been motivated by genuine concern: he suspected Anne's motives.[19]

Back at Shibden Ann's life resumed its usual pattern; she read, rode and walked, but she also felt desperately guilty about the impact her illness was having on Anne's life. She told Anne that 'she ought to be in a place of confinement so that she could do no more mischief'. That these were Ann's true feelings is supported by the contents of a letter she sent to her sister in which she laments that she brings upset and inconvenience to those she loves.[20]

On 8 May Ann rode as usual to Cliff Hill for dinner, and drank rather a lot of champagne until Anne was obliged to fetch her coffee.[21] The evening triggered an improvement in Ann's spirits and she 'ate more than she has done for long' at breakfast the next day, and two days later she enjoyed some hot gingerbread after a lunch of beef. Sadly this was a false dawn, and Marian was so worried about Ann that in May she came back to Shibden to help watch over her. By 19 May Anne's concern was such that she dared not let Ann out of her sight. Ann was desperately low and both she and Anne worked towards their departure now with a frantic urgency.[22] On 24 May Ann walked to Halifax with Anne to deal with business which included loaning Anne £100 on top of the £20 she had given her two days before, to be repaid at Christmas. In contrast to this, on 28 May Ann was so weak that Anne had to help her dress and the same day Anne wrote to apply for their passports which state that St Petersburg was to be their destination.[23] Ann asked Anne not to tell her aunt about their plans to travel, as she feared her aunt's objections and her own strength to resist them. In fact, Anne does mention their plans, but keeps the specifics so vague that Aunt Walker had nothing particular to argue against.[24]

They were off on 20 June and we know Ann took a cup of tea at Shibden before they set off at 2.50 am, having altered their plans slightly so that they would travel first to Wakefield rather than Rochdale, before going on to Doncaster. Perhaps Ann watched her wife write the three words 'left Shibden Hall' in her journal.[25] It would prove to be a poignant line.

Chapter 22

Sauntering around Scandinavia

The plan had been for them to head to London and take a ship on 2 July straight to Hamburg, but Ann was beset by thoughts of death and told Anne that she was afraid of the voyage – and Anne herself was hesitant to spend so long afloat so they abruptly changed their plans, deciding to cross from Dover to Calais instead. Quickly heading south, they changed horses at Shooters Hill, London, before travelling on to Gravesend, where Ann told Anne that she was feeling well enough to continue. By 4 pm they were in Dover, where they were lucky enough to catch the *Wigeon* before it departed at 6.50 pm and they rolled straight aboard 'never alighting.'[1] Ann was seasick but less so than her wife, who was once again overcome with nausea. Ann calmly dealt with the 'little surf' present when they went ashore in Calais, her appetite was improving already and she enjoyed a good dinner that night. They left at 4 am and did not stop until reaching Gravelines at 6 am where they changed horses, then drove on until Dunkirk where Ann had bread, butter and strawberries, along with cafe au lait. Relying as we are on Anne's journal, it is testament to her relief that she notes carefully how often Ann was already eating. Quickly they fell into their usual travel routine of consulting guide books and admiring the various towns they passed, while keeping up a brisk pace. They alighted at Bruges on 5 July and Ann peeked into the church of St Jacques and then visited the Grande Place.[2] The next day saw her back in Antwerp, where they reunited with Pierre, the valet they had used the previous year. Ann cashed some money but Anne had miscalculated the exchange rate and so had to send a servant back to get more, only for him to find that the bank was shut. In the meantime they went to the cathedral where they saw paintings by Ruebens and Ann enjoyed a vanilla ice cream.[3]

The next day Ann passed the 'square tall pillar at the roadside [that] marks the limit between the 2 kingdoms [of] France and Belgium', through fields of corn and fir trees. Ann was delighted when she arrived at Breda and found a glorious dinner waiting for her, consisting of no less than 'excellent potage and mutton cutlets, and peas … nice little potatoes browned as if under meat and a fowl and stewed lettuce – 13 plats at desert – including 2 glass jars of sweetmeat ginger and greengages'. Another boat awaited them the next day and Ann sat at the poop of the small boat that was to take them across the river, enjoying the view.[4]

Travel was no magic cure for Ann though and she wanted to rest the next day, but there can be no doubt that her health had dramatically improved, alongside her appetite, as she moved through the Dutch landscape admiring churches and eating copious amounts of fresh and stewed lettuce. It is also worth noting that, judging by Anne's journal, Ann was now taking her medication less regularly and this may have contributed to her improvement. The weather had turned hot and both women found the carriage cooler than many of the buildings in which they stayed. On 8 July Ann was in Amersfoort, where she walked the pretty gardens and happily promenaded along the river. Then it was on through the beech forests to the king's summer palace at Appeldoorn.[5] Ann stayed that night at Deventer and after ordering dinner went with Anne to visit the church. They made the most of the fine evening by walking about the town and buying a loaf of gingerbread at the famous shop there, which had been selling gingerbread to locals and travellers alike since 1593 – Ann declared it delicious.[6]

Ann's physical strength was by now returning. She was well enough to, in Anne's words, 'walk[…] on and on' through ankle-deep sand in Lingen one evening, even though she had already walked a good deal earlier in the day.[7] Ann was feeling better and at Wildeshausen she, rather ironically, told her wife to stop worrying about money when Anne was unable to account for about 5 florins.[8] On 11 July Ann dressed, had 'good coffee and strawberries' for breakfast and then went with Anne to visit the caves at Bremen, where Anne purchased wine, and then to the cathedral with its 'whitewashed ceiling … and side aisles studded sparingly with gold stars'. She also viewed the famous dried bodies there, before promenading around the town's gardens and departing 'pleased with Bremen'.[9] It is very frustrating that we don't know Ann's own thoughts for all the places she travelled to, instead she appears to us in snapshots: eating 'one excellent cold veal cutlet' in Rothenburg;[10] dozing alongside Anne for four hours in Harburg;[11] or in Kiel, attending a soiree that was 'sufficiently en toilette to make [us] apologise'. After which they boarded a boat from Kiel to Copenhagen beneath a blazing sunset.[12]

Hot and bothered, Ann and Anne in their 'heavy carriage' (for it was the heaviest the captain had ever seen) arrived into the city by 5.30pm. They went for a walk on the ramparts of the Roskilde Gate before eating well, Ann ordered a second plate of strawberries.[13] This is all a far cry from the woman who just the previous month had been too weak to dress herself. They were staying at the Royal Hotel, a vast, handsome stone building that was for a while the home of Hans Christian Anderson. In Copenhagen, Anne was anxious to meet up with previous friends and acquaintances and dispatched notes to several people, most of whom were out of the city. Ann, meanwhile, eagerly viewed the cathedral, and climbed up to the top to see the fine view. From there she would have been able to see the castle of Rosenburg, which they visited that afternoon; on the evening of 16 July Ann went to Lyngbye with Anne, where they travelled around some mills with the Count and Countess Blucher.[14] They left Copenhagen on 18 July and made for Roskilde, where they stayed at the Prince Hotel and that evening attended a ball held there with 'fiddling and dancing'. Perhaps this was the high society that Ann had been dreaming of?

While at Roskilde, Lady Harriet Hagemann called on them and they took tea together, before driving to Madame Rosencrantz's, where Ann took a stroll outside with her wife. The next day Ann slept in the carriage while they travelled through Gorlose onto the Frederiksborg Palace.[15] What Ann thought of the famous gold chapel there we can only guess at, but Anne thought it magnificent and surely Ann cannot fail to have been impressed with such a monument to the glory of God.

The Swedish coastline awaited Ann and she climbed 151 stairs to view the island of Wien from the top of Kronborg castle.[16] She was less keen on taking the ferry from Elsinore later that day and for the first time since England was frightened, probably because she had to stand around and wait for the boat as they were early for once. She did not panic however, and stepped aboard happily enough 'and was afterwards well satisfied'. They crossed to Helsingborg where Ann and her wife 'strolled out first to the little harbour and neat new bathing establishment and then to the Borg through the picturesque little town'.[17] From here Ann and Anne were heading north through Sweden and towards Norway, greeted by the sweet smell of stewed juniper, and warm Kaviring, a classic Swedish bread made with rye flour and treacle. Their route took them to Gothenburg where, after some heavy rain, the day of 23 July dawned fine and bright. Ann dressed then went to the booksellers, who gave recommendations for couriers for their journey onwards, the price alarmed them and much of the day was spent in planning and negotiation. They visited the exchange on their guidebooks advice but were disappointed and could not see why it was so recommended.[18] Both women were far more impressed with Kattleburg with its beautiful canals, which they passed as they headed yet further north. Ann admired the falls and locks at Trollhattan, though both she and Anne felt the Devil's Fall was the worst and that the upper ones were finer.[19] The next day found Ann strolling out in Venersborg where she sketched until, as Anne rather dolefully records, 'Adney lost her pencil.'[20]

They barely paused as they travelled deeper into Norway until 27 July, when they were forced to stop as Ann felt faint – due once again to lack of food, for she felt better once she had eaten 'a little of Mrs Todd's rice pancake.'[21] Pancakes had been filling the stomachs of Scandinavian travellers since the earliest record of it in 1328 and Ann liked the mix of oven-baked rice porridge.

Anne was now further north than she had been before and both she and Ann more frequently consulted their guidebook. At Hogdal Ann and her wife sat down and 'inked over their accounts' before discussing how they should proceed with their journey. The guide book suggested the road from Westgaard was the prettiest route and so Ann travelled on through forests of pines and then they took a ferry at Svinesund over the river into Norway proper. Despite the rain both women loved the scenery, their eyes were full of mountains and fjords, and the first night in Norway their bellies were filled with pork pancakes, bread and butter and thick milk.

Ann had evidently managed to borrow a pencil, for the next day found her sketching again in Saner, but they barely paused, before journeying on into Xtania where they took a room at the Hotel du Nord.[22] In Christiana, Ann was careful to insist that she buy more pencils at the cost of '40 skilling for 2 pencils English', before they went to the botanic gardens that were 'well arranged and very pretty'.[23]

They left Christiana on 2 August and travelled to Drammen on good roads. It seems that Ann had quite managed to overcome her fear of water for Anne makes no mention of her being afraid when they took yet another ferry at Hokksund and watched the salmon leap in front of a dramatic mountain vista.[24] The next day was Sunday and Ann read to her wife chapters 5 and 6 from Matthew to Anne while she lay in bed. Ann then sketched the room until they were brought flatbread, butter and coffee. It was a rare quiet day and in the evening Ann sat down with the rest of the household – the mistress, her daughter and two woman servants, her son and three manservants – to a dinner of more flatbread, butter fried bacon and pig's ribs, alongside a sauce made of Dravel. This was followed by fish in butter and sauce before Ann and Anne 'sauntered' off into the kitchen, about the house, and then off for a stroll.[25]

Ann began to take lessons alongside Anne in Norsk, but from Norway it was back into Sweden, and on 13 August Ann was eating Pease soup and boiled salmon in 'very beautiful' scenery on board a ship heading towards Starvern. Ann enjoyed the journey but Anne was violently sick over the side of the boat. Seasickness plagued Ann's wife throughout their journey through the fjords; she was so ill that the captain 'civilly offered [her] a mattress', but she preferred to remain with Ann who, although suffering from some sickness, felt better than Anne and slept fairly well.[26] They were both relieved to reach Gothenburg and be on dry land. 'Adney's portmanteau and her bag' followed her off immediately and they spent the next three days relaxing in Gothenburg. While there Ann visited the public gardens and sketched the 'curule' chairs that she saw everywhere in Sweden. Anne also bought her some new white gloves.[27] By the 17th they were at Sollenbrun, where Ann felt unwell, managing only to take a little bread and tea, though she was well enough the next day to eat plenty of cold rice pudding before they journey through the landscape studded with juniper berries, blueberries and heather. While out walking at Hova Ann foraged and ate wild cranberries, after a breakfast of chocolate, bread, and biscuits.[28] As she stood inhaling the cool, damp Scandinavian air she must have felt a million miles away from her life back at Shibden. Here there was no one to judge, no one to comment; indeed she and Ann were figures to be respected and admired for their bravery and mettle in travelling so far.

The landscape interested Ann and she read throughout this part of their journey from an encyclopaedia of geography, but the weather was not cooperating and as they journeyed on to Lislena, the views they hoped for were obscured by the rain. Nevertheless, they enjoyed the countryside as they made their way back towards Stockholm – arriving there on 22 August. While there they walked around the fish and vegetable markets, bought gooseberries, saw the king go aboard a thirty-gun ship in the harbour, and heard the accompanying thundering guns.[29]

They were not yet done with Sweden and travelled through to Maista, where snow was expected and snow ploughs littered the roads. They arrived at the city of Uppsala on 25 August, where they viewed the magnificent cathedral before Ann sketched the castle from the window of their hotel. She coloured her work a little before they set off on their day's sightseeing, during which she also sketched the church and more of the castle, in between visiting the library and botanical gardens.[30] Heading north once again, Ann witnessed people getting in the harvest, and at Osterby she and Anne went down the Dannemora mine. Anne was involved in an 'uncivil' row about her driving with the locals – she was going much too fast for the roads. By the end of August they were in Strand, viewing the Great Pit in Falun where Ann decided to stay and sketch above ground this time, while Anne went down another mine. It is noticeable that Anne is no longer worried about leaving Ann to shift for herself for a few hours. In fact Ann was quite content to keep sketching even after Anne returned, and continued to draw in peace until Anne fetched her in the afternoon so they could visit a booksellers in town.[31] From Flaun it was on to Ornas, Angelerby, Sater, Grado and Brunback, where Ann walked on the floating bridge and they viewed the typically Swedish red houses that make up the towns and villages of the area.

Ann sat and sketched again as they travelled through Jordbro; the station house was her subject this time as it was 'one of the most picturesque' that they had seen. She could not escape Anne's enthusiasm for pits though and they descended on 3 September into the Sala Silver mine where Ann chose to 'mount by escaliers' on three level, rather than by the bucket. At 155 metres deep, Ann would have seen the magnificent Lake Christina, among the huge haunting caverns.[32]

When they got back to Stockholm this was one of many adventures that Ann related in a letter to her sister and aunt, who she took the opportunity of writing to now they were back in the city. They could not avoid another steamer journey and by 9.15 pm on 6 September they were aboard the steamer the SS *Furst Menschikoff*. The passenger list was published in a Swedish newspaper and Anne and Ann are clearly mentioned; they landed at Abo on 8 September.[33] From there Russia was firmly in their sights.

Chapter 23

Russia

According to legend, on 16 May 1703 Tsar Peter the Great had stood at the mouth of the Baltic, cut two strips of turf from Hare's Island on the Neva river, laid them in a cross and declared 'let there be a city here'.[1] Based in a swamp and built at the cost of thousands of lives, by the time Ann drove over the Neva, the city of St Petersburg was a teeming metropolis, a magnet for travellers and artists alike who saw it as the infinitely fascinating gateway to the East.[2] Maxim Vorobiev's painting *Moonlit Night in St Petersburg* shows a harbour of boats and city of spinning spires looming beneath a golden sky, perfectly epitomising the romanticism with which the city was regarded.[3]

Romance was not the first thing on Ann's mind as she entered Russia though, far from it; she was cold and they had scarcely escaped the border crossing into Russia without having had their books impounded. Her first accommodation in Russia proved to be far from luxurious and Ann decided it would be a good idea to add alcohol to their morning tea. Ann's first view of St Petersburg was 'in the distance ahead right – 2 or 3 towers dimly seen', and she crossed into the city over the Troitski bridge.[4] We know from Anne's diary that she and Ann drove past the Bronze horseman statue of Peter the Great, and saw the Osinovaya Roshcha with its grand classical front.[5] Ann was staying at Mrs Wilson's English hotel and she and Anne engaged an Englishman as their guide, although rather predictably given their past history with guides this man proved to be less than useful and the two women largely fended for themselves. On her first day Ann visited Luke Dixons bookshop, famous for having been patronised by Alexander Pushkin, whose debts to Dixons had only been paid off after his death in a duel twelve years prior to Ann's visit.[6] The next few days were all spent sightseeing, and they shopped for maps, books and sweets. Anne was determined to learn Russian and Ann joined her wife in at least attempting it – but understanding Cyrillic was to prove a step too far for them both. Ann visited the mining university and the botanic gardens, at which they compared the plants with those they had grown at Shibden. Then, on 21 September, Ann rode on Russia's first passenger train to view the imperial palace at Tsarskoye, where she saw the legendary Amber Room.[7]

Ann was not feeling well the next day; they went to church, but on their drive afterwards Ann 'wished to return' to rest. It appears that Ann's illness had once more manifested itself as a rash on her face, and when a Dr Levfevre called in the evening he could offer no opinion but said that he would call again in two days time.[8] Neither woman was convinced about the doctor's qualifications and mused on whether going back to see Dr Double in Paris would be an option. Ann did not allow this rash to stop her though, and was feeling sufficiently well to visit the Hermitage, with which she was very impressed, and the Smolny Monastery. She happily walked around the city the next day viewing the St Peter and St Paul fortress. The Tsar at the time was the reactionary Nicolas I, one of the most autocratic rulers of the day, and in Nicolas' Russia there was no notion of free press, limiting the two women's access to news.[9]

From St Petersburg Ann travelled to Moscow, and they made the journey of 435 miles in only five days. Once there, on 12 October they took rooms at the Howard's Hotel kept by an English family.[10] Mrs Howard was 'very civil' and they spoke with her the first morning in Moscow about their plans before Ann spent half an hour reading her prayers. They engaged another guide, called Leopold, and told him that they particularly wished to see the Treasury at the palace in the Kremlin and to see the Tartar palace. Anne has also given some thought as to how to access society in Moscow and sent a letter of introduction from Lady Stuart de Rothsay to Prince Gallitzin, who was the general governor of Moscow.[11] Ann was keen to see something of the city and she and Ann wandered by themselves to the Cathedral of St Basil. Ann felt that she had seen nothing like it. A greater contrast with her quiet Anglican church in Lightcliffe is hard to imagine. The damp and foggy weather did not deter Ann and Anne from visiting the Kremlin where they saw emeralds the size of blackbirds' eggs, and a painting of Catherine the Great among other treasures. They travelled on to Donskoi convent, where Ann found herself doused in incense. They had made no stop for lunch and Ann was 'half starved' by the time they finally got to eat dinner.[12]

More sightseeing and enjoyable excursions followed over the next few days, but the peace and happiness that had returned to Ann's marriage was threatened when, on 18 October, Prince Gallitzin was announced at their hotel; Anne failed to introduce her wife to the prince and Ann was deeply upset at the slight.[13] It played on all her deepest fears that Anne in fact felt that she was not a worthy companion and was embarrassed by her. Anne doesn't seem to have thought anything was amiss with her conduct and wrote that evening that Ann's only use to her was 'in point of money'.[14] It was a painful reminder that the troubles in Ann's marriage had not gone away entirely. The quarrel was set aside the following day when they visited Arkhangelsky, where Ann viewed 'several valuable botanical English works', and delayed their departure so that she could read and take note of them. Ann at this time was also taking plant samples to dry on paper for later study.[15]

The next day though was a much less pleasant visit for Ann when they went to view the infamous Sparrow Hills prison, where she saw prisoners getting ready to set off that afternoon on the five and a half month journey to Siberia. They were pleased to see that the prisoners were allowed access to religious books and when Dr Hayes gave Anne a New Testament in memory of their visit, it was accompanied by a subtle hint that one Miss Harrison – an English lady who had previously visited – had given £5 to be directed among the prisoners, and had promised the same again as a annual subscription. Ann handed over £5 though she promised no subscription. On seeing just how many prisoners there were, Ann and Anne made Leopold hand over an additional 50 kopek. Perhaps the sight of 'the women's wrists handcuffed together' and setting off without a tear played on both women's minds, for they sat up talking late into the evening.[16] Practical matters were also on their minds, they could not agree on what to do with regards to servants – Ann did not want to send for Joseph Booth as she did not like him, and suggested taking on a Russian girl but Anne argued they still needed another manservant to accompany them back to England.

On 22 October Anne writes that Ann had one of her 'low fits' and her period arrived that evening, more evidence that Ann's moods were affected by hormone fluctuations associated with her menstrual cycle.[17] It is also noticeable that she is bleeding more regularly now that she is eating better. In Moscow they were not short of company and we find again a discrepancy between how Anne views her wife and how others do; at dinner on 24 October, Ann asked Mr Fischer de Walheim about the Mongol Idol in Yamantage, Anne writes that she was embarrassed and thought about how to ensure that Mr Fischer knew that Ann 'did not know what she was talking about'.[18] Fischer, however, spoke with Ann on the subject, promising to look for a paper on the subject for her. A few days later Anne again misjudges Ann's opinion by thinking that she would object to their taking on a girl as a trial. Ann was quite astonished that Anne had thought so and assured her that she would be quite happy to take on one of the girls proposed.[19] Ann was also evidently capable of handling herself in company, and she displayed her understanding of current issues when, at a dinner with the Fischer family and friends on the 27th, she asked, why the emperor would not allow Mr Bremner back into Russia. Mr Bremner's expulsion had been the subject of society's gossip for several weeks, and shows that Ann was well aware of the issues of the day. The evening concluded in dancing and music at which Ann enjoyed herself immensely and found the company 'most agreeable'.[20]

By late October the first snows were falling and Ann was often cold: she buys wool to knit 'muffettees' for her and Anne and discusses with Mrs Fischer how best to buy suitable furs. She walked out with Anne daily, enjoying the gardens and shopping; on 28 October she found herself in a curiosity shop where she admired a room of books that had belonged to Count Razumovsky.[21] They stayed to look at them until late, calling for candles, until darkness eventually forced them to leave.

The steadily worsening weather led Ann to question whether they should not think about heading back. Anne objected, before conceding that they would need to see whether the snowy roads would be passable late in the year. Soon though a worse quarrel was brewing; Anne's letter at last received a formal response and on 7 November Anne and Ann were invited by the Prince Gallitzin, the general governor of Moscow to the governor palace. Suddenly Ann found herself at her wife's side at the highest echelons of Moscow society and despite her natural shyness she enjoyed herself very much and delighted in the company, to start with at least. Anne, meanwhile, was very taken by the Princess Sophia Alexandrovna Radsivilli, who she described as 'one of the finest women I ever saw'.[22] She was quite swept away and acknowledged in her diary that they were 'mutually attracted', and both flirted madly. Is it any wonder that Ann was not impressed? She was left to sit in ignorance while Anne and Sophia laughed and talked in rapid-fire French. Ann was jealous and deeply hurt. On 19 November she was in tears and Anne asserted to the princess that 'the idea of her and [Ann] learning anything together is too absurd', which given their difference in intellect, was not a fair comment by any means. The situation was insupportable and by the end of the month Ann, who was not content to simply sit by and watch Ann court another woman, tried to insist that the 'Princess R [did] not wish for [them] so often.'[23]

She was also worried by Anne's latest travel plans. Anne wanted to visit the Caucasus. Ann knew enough of the destination to have serious concerns. A peace treaty had been signed between Turkey and Russia in 1829, but Russia had not succeeded in subduing the area. Ann's unease was not helped by hearing stories of travellers who had been abducted and killed, nor was Ann alone in feeling this way; several of their new acquaintances felt that the journey would be foolhardy at best − and if taken over winter, suicidal − temperatures in the area plummeted to a murderous -27°C. Ann was also 'very hesitant about the expense of further travelling', especially with the sleigh hire and equipment that would be required.[24] News from home had worried her on this account and Ann tried to discuss their finances properly with Anne, only to be met by Anne telling her that 'she ought to have nothing to do with affairs and decisions', and that perhaps she would go on and leave Ann behind. Ann was very upset at even the idea of such a plan, declaring on 18 December that 'she would rather die on the road than be left here'.[25] She began to think once again of leaving Anne. She mentioned the plan of going to Paris with Jane Chapman again, but conceded that she was miserable at the thought. Ann insisted, though, that she was worried they were spending too much money and that they should not go on. The next morning, following a restless night, Anne − her head full of Princess Sophie − sat Ann down and told her that she thought they should separate if they could not agree.[26] Ann was 'frightened', and under this veiled threat, quickly agreed to do whatever Anne wanted, even to journey on if that was what she wished. Ann's feelings here are hard to know for certain; she must have felt in an impossible situation, stuck at what felt like the edge of the world. Whatever her doubts though, ultimately Ann loved and was bound to Anne.

Onwards they would go.

Chapter 24

The Caucasus

Christmas was a miserable affair; Ann was often left alone while Anne went to flirt with Princess Radziwill and she deeply resented it.[1] She was also being called upon to spend more of her money as they had to buy vehicles in which to continue their journey. They were to travel in a kibitka, a cross between a sledge and a coach with a cabin, doors and windows. Count Panin also advised the addition of a mattress and that they should put hay on the bottom of the kibitka beneath it and the carpet to help insulate it.[2] Wolfskins, furs, books and thick cloaks were also purchased. Their maid Grotza flatly refused to travel on, and so a former serf George Tchaikin and his fiance/wife Dominica were found to accompany them instead.[3]

Ann tried out their new vehicle alongside her wife in early January, when they travelled to Sergiyec Posad, a journey of forty-five miles from Moscow.[4] The conditions were warm enough but cramped and rather claustrophobic – 'we slid along the hardened snow with a tremendous motion and noise like that of being near the engine of a steamboat.' This trip did not convince Ann of the wisdom of their venture and Anne complained that she was 'in the dumps'. Ann resorted to ignoring Anne for the next few days. Anne loathed the silent treatment, which is perhaps why Ann persisted in using it, it was one of the few things that got a reaction from her wife.[5]

The preparations for their departure continued apace despite the frosty atmosphere; Ann wrote to her sister to inform her of their plans and she and Anne bought furs, tea and sugar, alongside other last minute essentials. Then, on 5 February, they were finally off. Their kibitka, 'uncomfortably packed,' was followed by their servants George, Dominica and Gross in a sledge. Ann unfortunately had a draft that carried a bit of snow through the window on her side, but the journey otherwise went well and by the evening of 6 February, having travelled through the night, they were '186 ¾ versts from Moscow'.[6] Ann was hungry, frozen and burst into tears.

Anne was genuinely worried and reluctantly offered to turn back. Not for the first or last time though, food saved the day and after a good breakfast Ann felt much better. That night they stopped at Manacowa where they slept in a 'little log room with broad seams and moss between the logs'.[7] Sitting by the fire, they ate partridge and sent for cream. Ann slept poorly and the road they took from Aleschkowo to Doskino the next day jolted her so violently that she was forced to wake Anne for help when the iron bar holding up her lantern came crashing down. Both women felt rather sick, but Ann at least managed to find a way to plug the draft in her door and window. She also turned her hand to other practical matters and helped Gross to make soup on their portable heater and warmed up the leftover partridge.[8]

Such little snippets give us intimate glimpses into Ann's day to day life on her journey through the snowy landscape. She glimpsed the Mahomedan mosque, but they could not visit as there was too much snow, instead they drove along the Oc until it met the Voga. She saw the Kremlin at Nizhny Novgorod, where she and Ann kept good company and ate good food. Ann also bought some Nijeni boots there, hoping to keep her feet warmer than of late. Despite this the cold continued to plague her, and the phrase 'Ann half starved' appears frequently in Anne's journal, suggesting that Ann was often left hungry. On Saturday 15 February they were warned that they were approaching an area 'that was full of thieves and rogues'; Anne's robust response was to get all the pistols loaded.[9] Other hazards included breaking ice and poor Gross got soaked to his knees in the freezing water of the Volga. Ann's reaction is not recorded, but she was sufficiently impressed by the landscape to request that they open the doors, despite the cold as they approach Kazan.

Ann and her wife's arrival in Kazan caused quite a stir. It was inhabited at the time largely by Tatars and Ann would have found the society very different to that of Moscow. Relations between her and Anne had also improved dramatically once away from the city. That evening for their 'veritable sixth anniversary', they drank champagne and toasted the health of all their friends and family.[10] Even a mix up over timings in the biting cold did not dampen their spirits. The next day Ann visited the university for several hours, and while there met Professor Turnerelli.[11] With her deep interest in art, it was surely a meeting that thrilled Ann.

Outside of Kazan, the standard of their accommodation declined and just a few days later Ann found herself having to shake five white fleas from her nightcap before lying down. Both women had taken to sleeping in their clothes to help keep them warm.[12] The landscape was stunning, but snow continued to fall and some roads they wished to use were fast becoming impassable. The temperature also plummeted reaching –20 °C on a regular basis. It was therefore quite a relief that the temperature on 26 February was only –5 °C and Ann felt able to walk outside for twenty minutes at the 'poor village of Iwanowskoje'.[13] After which they stayed at Elmanka where Ann again showed off her cooking skills, making custard from the eggs that she felt Anne had 'wasted' their money on. Ann had also grown fond of cranberries boiled up with honey, which she made for them on more than one occasion. In fact, more often than not at this point in their journey, Ann can be found making dinner or cups of hot tea for them all. By the 28 February they were at Saratov, where Ann was in such high spirits that they went out for a walk immediately and both women were 'well amused' by the market and traders.[14]

In March they pulled into Saroet, where surely nothing could have prepared Ann for the sight of colourful Kalmyks – who with their distinctive appearance were Buddhists Mongolians. She also visited a yurt whose floor with a fire in the middle was a world away even from the Mosques she had visited. Ann found herself an object of curiosity and she and Anne had to block their doors with chairs so that they might guarantee their privacy. We also know that her family were not far from her thoughts, and she bought a gift of a white and red striped nightcap for Captain Sutherland.[15]

By 12 March they were at Astrakhan, and were forced to ask the chief of police for a room for the night. They remained there for ten days, both women were cold and Ann was concerned for Anne's health – she had contracted a heavy chill; Gross had had enough and demanded to leave.[16]

They went on without him once their kibitka had been repaired and they paid to get a pass to travel to Tbilisi. Anne's diary gives the strong impression that Ann had decided that if she could not dissuade Anne, then she might as well make the best of it. She began to sketch more frequently and found purpose in helping make tea and ensuring everyone was warm. At Mozdok they received their first military escort when two Cossacks accompanied them through the extremely muddy conditions to

Yekaterina Gradskaya where the soldiers were all occupied and so they were forced to stop and wait.[17] As she looked out of the kibitka Ann would have seen the Caucasus for the first time.

Eventually they were permitted to travel on and had cause to be thankful for their Cossack escort on the way to Vladikavkaz. Ann and her wife saw a horseman approach and the cry of 'Techerkess!' went up.[18] Ann's protection at that moment consisted of four Cossacks, four drivers, a Russian officer and servant, the courier, George and Anne. They were not terribly impressive but despite this Anne notes that Ann was not the least afraid.[19] Luckily the Tcherkess decided that they were not worth the trouble and rode off. Ann's nerves had steadied indeed.

By now it was the first week in April and from here on in it was mountainous roads, steep and littered with debris. Ann often found herself travelling by sledge rather than by kibitka, but even in the midst of this she still found time to sketch as they travelled into what is now Georgia, and by the 12 April they were in Tbilisi, having seen Mtskheta.[20] They hoped to stay there a while but the rooms they found were cold and damp. The food was also completely unsuitable so it fell upon Ann again to improvise their meals and she cooked soup, eggs and rice on their spirit cooker, wrapping her fingers around tea cups to keep them warm. This did not, however, stop her from enjoying herself and she walked out about the town with Anne, speaking to a good number of people who were fascinated by the appearance of these strange pale English ladies. At the bazaar in town she ate barley scones with rice and raisins, that were lifted for them out of a cauldron-like oven.[21] Ann found herself welcomed into the homes of the Russian military and while out one evening she met the celebrated Grogain sisters, Nino Chavchavadze and Princess Ekaterina Dadiani, who invited them both to stay.[22] Ann went out and about sketching in the botanic gardens and she walked with Anne the whole length of the old wall, which they declared to be magnificent. Ann made them dinners of eggs and barley cake when they got back to their rooms, and one evening Mr Chavastoff came to talk with them about Russian history, though both women realised that he was not at liberty to speak entirely freely. Anne writes that he implied that 'Peter poisoned Alexis but no one dares say this'. Ann must have been thrilled, she had read about the history of the area and here she was listening to it first hand.[23]

Anne now wanted to go on to Tehran but a furious Ann put her foot down. They were, she said, running low on money and her doubts about the safety of travelling further were reinforced by everyone they met. Even Anne this time had to listen to reason and agreed to put Persia off for now, and she and Ann seriously talked over their plans. Anne wanted to see the Caspian Sea even if Persia was not an option, and Ann felt this was a reasonable compromise.[24]

They left Tbilisi with a much reduced amount of luggage on 13 May and with four Cossacks for protection. The lands they were now travelling though were more contested than those they had passed. The terrain was dangerous, and the rivers were high and fast as they made their way to Baku. Once again Ann seems to have thrown herself into the journey, she allowed women in the area to admire and examine her 'green silk wadded bonnet lined with pink', and slept in a caravan of camels with no complaint.[25] At Baku, Colonel Tchekmarev, the commandant of the city, gave them accommodation and his wife sent them cream, bread and a 'marinade of fowl'. Ann liked Madame Tchekmarev very much, Anne's diary is littered with references to the two women talking and laughing together. Ann loved the beauty of Madame Tchekmarev's Turkish outfit and bought herself Persian silk, from which she sewed herself dresses of the same style with the help of her new friend.[26] We know that Ann was sketched in this outfit but sadly this has long since been lost. Anne's diary rather ironically hints that she was jealous of Ann's new found friendship and confidence. Ann was happier here than at any other point in their travels, she spoke with a naval officer about the shells of the area and along with Anne visited a thickly carpeted harem where they were fed sweetmeats and admired.[27] While in Baku Ann also viewed the ruins of the Shirvanshah palace, which had been founded by Ibrahim I of Shirvan in the fifteenth century when he moved his capital to Baku from Shemakha following an earthquake. Its stunning domes and white stone cannot have failed to impressed her. The Tchekmarevs also took Ann and her wife to view the Absheron peninsula, where the natural gases mean that eternal flames burnt at the Zoroastrian temples, and Ann witnessed a ceremony in which 'the high priest was signed on his forehead with a red tongue between two yellow lines but called himself a worshipper of Krishna'.[28] Ann seems to have delighted in this strange and colourful world. Both women's spirits were also helped by the warming weather as winter gave way to spring.

Ann was less fond of the countryside they met with when they tearfully departed, armed with the meat pie, naphtha, rice, eggs, fowl and bread that Madame Tchekmarev had pressed on her. Anne wanted to journey back via Armenia but they ended up back in Tbilisi as their pass was not approved for another route. Ann's legs meanwhile were 'covered in blisters' from a multitude of flea bites, and she removed her stockings and unbuttoned her boots on Anne's advice.[29] Ann was not thrilled by news they received in Tbilisi of their finances and as usual they quarrelled about the subject, with Ann feeling that they should at least begin to think of going back. Anne, though, was desperate to see the Black Sea and assured Ann that they had enough money to do so and that they would head home after that.

Ann agreed and after three weeks of planning they left once again to go to Gori, where Ann rode to view the Ateni Sioni Church, famous then as now for the beautiful frescoes that Ann sat down to sketch. From there Ann went on what both women felt to be one of the most beautiful drives they had ever taken through the Surami Pass which runs through the Likhi mountain range.[30]

The weather was heating up and they reached Kutaisi by the end of June on a warm, cloying day. They were greeted by the wife of the local Cossack commander, Madame Boujourova, whom Anne called 'very amiable' and who had hastily prepared the government guesthouse for them.[31] Ann was feeling well and happy and told Anne so the next day. She loved the warm weather and liked Kutaisi 'very much'. From Kutaisi they travelled on to view the Greater Caucasus range. Along with a Cossack escort, George and local guides Adam and Moshe, they set off properly on the 9 July, and later that day after a breakfast of cucumber and tea, Ann lay down on her cloak and dozed beneath the mountains, wearing her habit and men's Moscow boots.[32] It was very hot, 27°C in the shade, and the climate seemed almost tropical. The passes with which they had been issued entitled them to accommodation and their guide went ahead everyday to secure it for them. Some accommodation was good, some was beyond primitive, but they were easily distracted by the landscape, viewing bear cubs and beautiful churches.

One night Ann had to sleep out in the open, and between the Cossack and Anne they arranged her a little bed beneath the stars on which she slept, wrote and snacked on an egg. Only the walk to the source of the Rioni river was too much for Ann and she remained behind while Anne went ahead and sketched the scenery around her. Rather to Anne's surprise, Ann was dealing with the swelteringly hot and damp conditions far better than she was, and she seemed to have adapted easily to life in the wilderness. Ann walked in the morning, sketched and rode, impressing the men with her horsemanship. Anne seems impressed by Ann too and we get manifest proof of the regard in which Anne held her wife when she always ensured that Ann was given the most comfortable places to sleep.[33]

Together they talked and admired the landscape, and for once Ann would have been quite happy to keep travelling, but eventually their guides had had enough and refused to go to Svaneti and so they returned to Kutaisi. Anne, though, was keen to be off and they travelled to Zugdidi on 8 August, where they stayed at the Dadianis' palace in an utterly luxurious room carpeted with Persian rugs. They ate well and Ann was treated the next day to the services of a maid who did her hair very nicely. The air though was hot, and so thick with vapour that even Ann began to feel unwell and so they decided to head back towards Kutaisi instead of proceeding as planned towards the Black Sea. They departed on 10 August with supplies of cucumbers, cheese, rolls and wine.[34]

From here we know that Ann and her wife rode northeast where they stayed with a family in Lia. We know Ann did not like it there and was anxious to leave. They had intended to pass through the ravine at Jvair but they got lost before they reached it. The rain came down and they stayed at Jgali for one night in an 'Indian corn barn', and at some point Anne suffered a nasty insect bite. It is at this point in Ann's story that her wife falls silent.[35] Anne wrote what was to be the last entry in her diary on 11 August, but it has been suggested that they had travelled on to Lailashi by the 31st August and then to Kutaisi.[36] Why did Anne not write? We simply don't know, but it is most likely that she was simply too unwell to do so.

Ann's terror is easy to imagine; the danger Anne was in must have quickly become apparent. It seems likely that Anne lapsed into fever immediately and Ann was forced to plan how best to move her disease-ridden wife back to where there was hope of medical aid. However it transpired, and we will never know, Ann watched her wife die of 'La fievre chaud' on 22 September 1840.[37]

Due to the fact that Anne's fever appears to have been a procured one – and lasted five to six weeks judging by the lapse between her last diary entry and her death – and the presence of an insect bite, it seems most likely to have been either typhoid or malaria, both of which were running rampant throughout the area at the time, but the absence of concrete evidence means that further supposition is useless.

What is absolutely certain though, is that for Ann the unthinkable had happened. She was now a widow, in a strange land far from home, with little but her wife's body for company.

Chapter 25

Widow

Given Ann's single-minded determination to bring her wife's body back to England, it seems likely that Anne had told Ann that was what she wanted. To this end, Anne's body was embalmed and almost certainly then placed on sawdust and sealed in a metal coffin. It is extremely difficult to piece together Ann's journey back from Georgia to England, but she would have had to step into her wife's shoes and carry out the bulk of the organisation herself. Here, finally, was a chance to do things exactly the way she wished, but it came at a very high price.

We know that at Tbilisi Ann had found money waiting for her, the money they had sent for on their outward journey and passes were issued so that Ann, Anne's body, and servants could avoid the usual two weeks quarantine.[1]

Ann also sent word of Anne's passing to England where an inaccurate report was run by the *Halifax Guardian* on 31 October, claiming that Ann was bringing her body back via Constantinople, something we now know was not the case as Ann was in Moscow on 17 December, where she wrote to Booth at Shibden instructing him to carry out philanthropic acts on her behalf.[2] Mrs Oddy was to provide Mr Green with a shirt, stocking and five shillings, the woman at Dove House was to be given flour, widow Taylor three shillings and Betty Hodgson five shillings. Even from thousands of miles away Ann was concerned about the people on her estate. She concludes her note by urging Booth to 'go on fearlessly, [and] do your duty'.[3] This was the maxim Ann herself was living by, clinging onto her faith and the duty she had to perform even while the world seemed to be crumbling around her.

According to Phyllis Ransom, Ann could go no further until the winter had passed, and so she had Anne's body temporarily buried.[4] However, this has been contradicted more recently by Steve Crabtree who discovered instead that it was Ann alone who went to Moscow while her wife's body remained in Georgia ready to complete her journey via sea the next year.[5]

It seems almost certain that in Moscow, Ann would have met with some of their previous friends and acquaintances. Perhaps she reminisced with them, or perhaps she preferred to quietly visit the places Anne and she had seen together. That winter was freezing cold and Ann must have been thoroughly miserable. Ann is frustratingly absent until 19 February when we know that she was 'recently returned' to Shibden Hall, alone and without Anne's body, having been left a life interest in the estate under the terms of Anne's will.[6] Ann had returned to England leaving her wife's body to travel to Constantinople unaccompanied and then up through the Mediterranean. The Walker v Grey documents prove this, in that they contain the record for Ann's payment of £57 16s 9d for 'freight of the body of the deceased to England from Treizbond', and the body was apparently sent via the Levant packet, a ship which docked in England on 9 April 1841.[7]

Upon her return Ann went straight to Shibden, where on 20 February she received and replied to a letter from Robert Parker.[8] We can safely assume that she called on her aunt and we know she picked up the reins of managing both estates. Her wife's body finally made its way to Yorkshire on Saturday, 24 April. This attracted a good deal of local attention and was reported in the *Halifax Guardian*. Given this level of local interest we can perhaps assume that Ann had been subjected to a good deal of curiosity since her return.

Anne's coffin was 'of the most splendid description' and bore her coat of arms, as she would surely have wished. It was accompanied by two mourning coaches, in one of which Ann rode. It seems that all of this was arranged at Ann's request, but while the crowds that lined the land would surely have gratified Anne, for Ann they were further evidence of persistent local interest in her. The funeral service was performed by Charles Musgrove, who Ann respected very much.[9]

With Anne laid to rest it seems that Ann's family now expected her to return to the family fold, but Ann was determined to remain at Shibden and from there manage her life and estates.

On the night of 6 June 1841, the first full UK census was taken and it tells us that Ann had achieved that aim and was living at Shibden Hall alongside her servants Susan Oddy, Susan Woodhead, Jane Metcalf,

Henrietta Pomoud, Joseph Buyst, Francis Knight and John Booth.[10] There is circumstantial evidence, though, that that during the latter part of 1841 and early 1842, Ann was sinking into a depression, during which time she feared for her health. This can be surmised from a letter Ann wrote in July 1842 to Robert Parker in which she mentions having been in poor health and the fact that she was now feeling better. The same letter also gives us clues as to how Ann had been acting, she writes that she has 'followed the example of my lamented friend Mrs Lister of making out my own rent accounts ... which I should have claimed sooner had I been aware of them'. Ann's tone in this letter is one of barely veiled annoyance, opening her letter with the words, 'as you did not take the trouble to furnish me with a rent'.[11] It seems that many were surprised by the fact that Ann was intending to take an active part in the management of both estates herself, and that she was frustrated by this reticence to engage with her. Perhaps driven by the memory of Anne, she also sought to carry out the improvements to Shibden that Anne had planned.

In April 1843 Ann had a run in with the local authorities during which she 'sally[ed] forth with a number of men' to challenge an ordnance survey team that were on her land. Unfortunately Ann was in the wrong here as that the law had changed during her travels and ordnance survey teams now had the right to access private land where necessary. For her actions Ann was fined £2 8s 6d for 'obstructing and hindering' the ordnance survey.[12] Ann complained that the men had damaged her property and she wrote to London to complain. All of this caused embarrassment to her family and Elizabeth was asked to give her opinion on Ann's actions.

Ann felt that in the magistrates court she was insulted, the court was presided over by, among others, John Rawson, and Ann was furious that she should be penalised by them for protecting her own land.[13] Unfortunately her loud complaints had the effect of annoying Halifax society and so further isolated Ann. It was not just in society she was becoming isolated either, at some point after her return she argued with Lydia Fenton and stated that she did not wish to see her again.

Ann still wanted to add to her family's legacy, in the same way Anne had wished to. To this end she once again looked to purchase land, and on 27 September 1842 Washington signed on her behalf an agreement to purchase land from Charles Horncastle. The agreement was that Ann was to pay £3,750 for the land and that the purchase would be finalised within eight weeks; if it was not, then Ann would have to pay 4 per cent interest per month in compensation for the delay.[14] The properties Ann wished to buy included the Hoyle House estate and Smithhouse estates, both of which had only been bequeathed to Charles Horncastle by his cousin Charles Radcliffe. Mr Radcliffe's heir, William Towne Radcliffe, was given a life interest in the estate and if he had heirs then it would be they who would inherit. William Radcliffe, however, had been declared a lunatic, which meant that while he was unlikely to have issue, his committee, in place to protect and administer his interests, would still have to be dealt with. Ann claimed that she was not aware of all this and accused Horncastle of trying to sell land that was not legally his, but here she was in error. The lunacy case of William Radcliffe was well publicised and it is impossible that Ann was not fully aware of the circumstances of the sale.[15] By 30 June 1843 Ann had stated that she did not wish to proceed until new clauses were added to protect her, and told Horncastle that he was trying to sell land that was not his; from then on the case went rapidly downhill. Ann began to receive letters that she termed 'threats' from the solicitors Barker and Rose, who escalated the case to the Chancery in view of Ann's actions. There is nothing wild or frantic about the way Ann writes in response to these demanding letters, but the threats against her are now very serious – she could have been arrested.[16]

Having fallen out with Parker and Gray, Ann at some point travelled down to London and appointed Mr Rymer to act for her in legal matters.[17] All this further increased the concerns of Ann's family, especially Elizabeth, who having been told of Ann's actions was now seriously concerned for her sister's health and reputation. She also knew Ann was grieving and feared for her mental health.

Ann soon found herself under huge pressure beset by further legal issues, including the accumulation of debt of £77 3s to Jane Aitkinson; Ann declared that she had never owed her money and that it was Jane Aitkinson who had not paid her rent and so she refused to pay.[18] Jane Aitkinson's case was taken on by George Higham and by August 1843 he had won the case and was given the right to seize property from Ann to sell at auction to raise the money.[19] The case reached its conclusion at the same time as the Horncastle case, an unfortunate coincidence, and Ann's lawyers were growing ever more concerned about her ability to manage her own affairs. Perhaps Ann felt patronised by them for she stopped seeking Gray's legal advice entirely in 1843.

On 17 August a Sheriff's Officer and bailiffs came to Shibden and forced their way into Ann's house. Ann was outraged and went on the offensive; an account of the incident was published in the *Halifax Guardian*, which states that 'a person of the name of Highley forced himself into Miss Walker's house, Shibden Hall, by almost knocking down Miss Walker when she civilly requested him to leave her house'. Needless to say he did not, and Ann then tried to secure herself away from them. She accused them of not producing documents to prove their authority.[20]

As Ann could have easily paid this debt it suggests that she was holding out on a point of principle, but equally she seems to have been either misinformed or ignorant regarding the legalities of the process in which she was now embroiled. Ann declared that having been insulted in Halifax she would now appeal to the court in York. To his credit, Gray does try to advise Ann, despite her hostility, about the best course of action to take. The article in *the Guardian* brought Ann under closer scrutiny and her sister Elizabeth was concerned enough to set out south. Elizabeth ordered Parker to pay on Ann's behalf to prevent the auction of items from Shibden.[21]

It is very difficult to get close to Ann's true thoughts and feelings during this time. One image we get of her is of a woman increasingly isolated as she fought for what she believed was right, but there is another – and that is of an Ann who was once again not eating and who was by now very unwell. She certainly was not helping herself, which suggests that perhaps she was by now unable to, and there was no Anne to help her. Elizabeth claims in her letters that Ann was by now a 'laughing stock' and Ann certainly didn't get any support from her wider family.[22]

Elizabeth and Captain Sutherland did not go to Shibden upon their arrival, but rather stayed at Pye Nest where they consulted Dr Belcombe immediately regarding Ann's state of mind. Whatever she was told, this, and the combination of all the events of the past few months, led to Elizabeth responding to Robert Parker.[23]

The process to have Ann declared a lunatic had been set in motion with frightening speed.

Chapter 26

Epilogue

After her removal from Shibden Hall Ann remained at Terrace House in Osbaldwick, under Dr Belcombe's care, for seven months, during which time her Lunacy Commission hearing took place. We know this because Dr Belcombe was paid by the Chancellor £277.15 for the 'maintenance' of Miss Walker from 19 September 1843–13 April 1844.[1] It seems that after this period Elizabeth wanted her sister at home with her, and when the Sutherlands took a house at 16 Grove End Road, St Johns Wood, London, Ann visited them and Elizabeth sought for her 'the best advice' while she was there. Ann then remained with her sister and family when they removed to Merton in Surrey. They lived at the Abbey Lodge which was situated on the North side of Merton High Street. Surviving photos of the building show a handsome Georgian residence with large bay windows, perhaps offering Ann the ideal place to sit and sketch. Ann was still living there with her sister's family when, as per the law, the Master of the Lunacy checked up on her in November 1844.[2] Unlike an informal committal, the Lunacy Commission kept track of certified 'lunatics' to ensure they were being properly cared for. The idea that Captain Sutherland and Ann's family were now free to access her money freely is simply not the case. Captain Sutherland had to justify any expenditure to Ann's committee. There were also many other legal issues to contend with, not least that of Dr John Lister, a relative of Anne's via a brother of her grandfather, who objected to Ann's claim on the Shibden estate and would ultimately inherit it. In response Captain Sutherland set about portraying Ann, and himself, as victims of Anne's unnatural ambitions.[3]

While staying with her sister Ann would certainly not have been isolated, by this time she had five nieces and nephews: Mary, George, Elizabeth, Evan, and her namesake Ann, and she spent a lot of time with them. Unfortunately, as a lunatic Ann's name only rarely appears on documents during this time, as others acted for her, and she wrote few letters as she was with her family. As such it is very difficult to get an impression of Ann's thoughts and feelings. Did she feel safe? Did she worry about her estate and tenants? We simply do not know, but if she did she was powerless to act. We do know that tragedy for Ann was once again lurking around the corner. In 1842 Ann's nephew George died, aged just 12.[4] The loss of their son must have devastated his family, but worse was to come. In late 1844 Ann suffered what must have felt like a catastrophic blow when, on 28 December, her sister Elizabeth died of tuberculosis.[5] Generally speaking it takes time to die of tuberculosis and Ann may have helped to nurse her sister, but ultimately she would have looked on helplessly as Elizabeth died. We know that Ann often had mixed feelings towards her sister; she loved her, but resented her interference, as well as her dependence and the influence of her husband. It was a relationship that certainly had not been made easier by Elizabeth's actions regarding the Lunacy Commission, but all this notwithstanding, Ann must have been devastated. With Elizabeth's death the last link between her and her siblings had been severed. The only other person who remembered Mary, and recalled their childhood, was gone. For her whole life Ann had had a sister; she had been one of the Crow Nest Walkers, now she was alone.

By the 17 April 1845 we know that Ann was back at Shibden with Captain Sutherland, and that she spent the summer there.[6] Captain Sutherland had written ahead to inform Gray of his plan. In a legal document, she is described as 'Miss [Ann] Walker, a lunatic, the occupier of Shibden Hall', and we know that she remained there until 1847. For Ann this return must have been bittersweet. Shibden was her wife's house, the scene of their lovemaking and of their quarrels, but now it was under the control of Captain Sutherland. Ann could make no decisions, she could only watch as life went on around her. About eight weeks after her arrival Ann's eldest niece Mary died and was buried in St Matthew's Churchyard, where her memorial still stands. Mary was just 15 years old and surely for Ann this brought back memories of her own sister Mary's death twenty years before.[7]

During this time in Halifax, Captain Sullivan remarried Mary Elizabeth Haigh, the daugher of John Haigh, a wool stapler of Savile Hall. The windows of Savile Hall were smashed in the election violence of 1835 that Ann had been caught up in.[8] Ann's feelings on the subject are not known, but the speed with which her brother-in-law remarried could hardly have helped their already tense relationship. George and Mary had a daughter, called Mary Elizabeth, who was born on 17 March 1847, but by the 22 April that same year Ann's brother-in-law was dead and he was followed quickly to the grave by Ann's beloved Aunt Ann.[9,10]

Ann must have felt utterly alone.

Following her aunt's death in 1848 Ann moved into Cliff Hill, with the blessing of her Committee of Person including her Aunt Harriet Dyson, who was now involved in her care.[11] She was in residence there by 29 January 1848. To reside at Cliff Hill had been Ann's wish for many years, she had discussed it endlessly with her family and with Anne, but now she was there it seems she wanted to return to Shibden Hall. A letter from Robert Parker states that:

> Miss Walker is desirous that the place [Shibden Hall] should be ready for the reception of Miss Walker at any time she may take a fancy to return ... Miss Walker may settle down at Cliffe Hill and all feeling of return to Shibden maybe dissipated both as regards herself and her friends.[12]

This letter certainly implies that Ann was being given a fair amount of consideration by the committee that was managing her affairs now that Captain Sutherland and Elizabeth were dead. Her wishes are being taken into consideration and nothing has so far turned up in the archives to suggest that Ann was considered to be a danger to herself or those around her.

An interesting incident occurs when Ann is living at Cliff Hill that was reported in the *Leeds Intelligencer* on Saturday 1 July 1848, under the byline 'premeditated burglary'.[13] It seems that a lad was found 'concealed in the mansion of Miss Walker at Cliff Hill', he had apparently been told to gain admittance and then let in four other men to rob the place. During the incident the 'forewarned inmates of the house' kept watch. One has to wonder if Ann was among this number. The men were not apprehended as they ran off when a pistol shot was fired. Perhaps by Ann following in her wife's footsteps? It is tempting to picture Ann toting a gun Lister-style, but as there is no other evidence regarding the incident we cannot know for certain.

What we do know is that at the time of the 1851 census Ann was still living at Cliff Hill and she had been joined by her old friend Lydia Fenton, who is listed as her housekeeper, their old quarrel evidently patched up. She also had an 'attendant' named Johanna O'Brien, four servants and an Irish coachman John Kelly.[14] For a 'genteel lunatic' such as Ann it would have been usual for gentle exercise and regular meals to have been prescribed. Feminine occupations, such as needlework, music and reading would also have been recommended. Perhaps we should therefore picture Ann during these years sitting by the fire with Lydia Fenton, knitting, listening to music or reminiscing about the past.

By early 1854 Ann's health was failing, on 18 February she suffered a fit and 'her mind has been restored to reason' wrote Robert Parker.[15] The implication being that Ann was indeed insane or not herself prior to this point. We already know that Parker believed Ann to have been insane, but he offers no new evidence in support of this so there is no reason to suppose that Ann's 'condition' had changed in the few years previous to her death. Over the next few days Ann suffered further fits and she died on 25 February 1854 at 50 years of age. Ann's death certificate lists her cause of death as 'Congestion of the brain ... Effusion.'[16] According to Dr Jennifer Wallis this was a cause of death that 'crops up quite a lot and was in use throughout the nineteenth century', and it 'harks back to the long established idea that health relied on a balance of fluids'.[17] It has therefore been suggested that Ann died of a cerebral haemorrhage – in effect a stroke – but the precise definition of these terms cannot be known at a distance of 150 years.[18] Even at the time such a diagnosis was open to a good deal of debate among doctors.[19]

Ann was buried in St Matthew's churchyard on 3 March 1854, and the service was conducted by the same Charles Musgrave who had officiated at Anne Lister's burial.[20] She was laid to rest alongside her Aunt Mary, and probably Aunt Ann too, in the church vault. Ann had not been able to rewrite her will for many years, prohibited by her classification as a lunatic, but her last will made years earlier left her lands and estate to her nephew. There were, however, a few personal bequests, among which was a bequest to Marian Lister, which left her £300 pounds a year for life, to be paid half yearly.[21] It was money that Marian much appreciated. Philanthropic to the end, Ann also instructed among her bequests that

£10 a year be given to the poor of Lightcliffe, something that was still being paid as recently as 1971.[22]

As Jill Liddington in her excellent book *Female Fortune, Land, Gender and Authority* concludes, while Anne Lister is commemorated and celebrated today, inconvenient Ann Walker has suffered a different fate: 'there are no public building to commemorate her nor streets names after her … no trace of the Walkers' splendour or of their later tragedies remain visible … It is as if Ann Walker never was,' and that has remained true for far too long.[23]

It is my fervent hope that by telling Ann's story, in as many of her own words as possible, that I have gone some way to redressing this imbalance. The tragedies of Ann's life and her ultimate fate as a 'lunatic' are incontrovertible, but they are only part of Ann's remarkable story, and not even the larger part. Ann was a woman of extraordinary courage; she loved to laugh, to travel, and she remained loyally at her wife's side when it would have been all too easy to have left. When Ann loved, she loved fiercely and she was willing to court any amount of ridicule and disgrace to do so. She was clever, educated and resourceful, devoted to her family and to her God. That she also suffered from mental health issues in an age when they were poorly understood, and paid the price, does not in my mind lessen any of her achievements. On the contrary it makes them all the more remarkable.

I hope that having read this book people will picture Ann not as a stereotypical nineteenth-century feeble-minded lunatic, pale and wan, but as a traveller, dressed in Persian silks, bathed in the golden light of far off Kutaisi.

The End

Notes

Key:
WYAS Calderdale – West Yorkshire Archive Service, Calderdale.
LMA – London Metropolitan Archive.
BL – British Library.
BNA – British Newspaper Archive.
NYCROA – North Yorkshire County Record Office Archive.
GJ – Steidele, A. Derbyshire, K (trans.) 2018, *Gentleman Jack: A Biography of Anne Lister*. Serpent's Tale: London.
GJ The Real Anne Lister – Choma, A, Wainwright, S. 2019, *Gentleman Jack: The Real Anne Lister*, BBC Digital: London.
FF – Liddington, J. 1998. *Female Fortune, Land, Gender and Authority. The Anne Lister Diaries and Other Writings 1833–36*, Rovers Oram Press: London and New York.
ND – Liddington, J. 2019, *Nature's Domain: Ann Lister and the Landscape of Desire*, Pennine Pens: Yorkshire.
IKMOH – Whitebread, H. 1988, *I Know My Own Heart: The Diaries of Anne Lister*, Virago Press: London.
HG – The Halifax Guardian.

Introduction

1. *The Secret Diaries of Miss Anne Lister* was first broadcast on 26 May 2010. Written by Jane English. Directed by James Kent. It stars Maxine Peake as Anne Lister, Anna Madeley as Mariana Belcombe/Lawton, and Christine Bottomley as Ann Walker.
2. Mariana Belcombe 1790–1868 was the daughter of Dr Belcombe, a York based doctor. She met Anne Lister in 1812 and they became long term lovers. In 1816 she married Charles Lawton.
3. Eliot, G. 2007 ed. *Middlemarch: A Study of Provincial Life*, Vintage Books: London. p.396.
4. Referencing an email conversion with Pat Metcalfe on 31 December 2021.
5. *Gentleman Jack* was first broadcast on 19 May 2019. Created by Sally Wainwright. It stars Suranne Jones as Anne Lister and Sophie Rundle as Ann Walker.

Chapter 1

1. WYAS Calderdale – MAC: 73/3 Draft letter from Robert Parker to Elizabeth Sutherland.
2. *Parliamentary Papers*, Volume 18, 1844.
3. Hartog, H. 'Mrs Packard on dependency' *Yale Journal of Law and the Humanities*, 1 (1989), pgs.79–103.
4. Collins, W. 1975, *The Law and the Lady*, Chatto and Windus: London.
5. WYAS Calderdale – MAC: 73/4 Letter from Elizabeth Sutherland to Robert Parker.
6. WYAS Calderdale – MAC: 73/6 Letter from Elizabeth Sutherland to Robert Parker.
7. WYAS Calderdale – CC00183 MAC: 73/17 Letter from Dr Belcombe to Robert Parker.
8. WYAS Calderdale – MAC:73/22-23 Letter from Dr Belcombe to Robert Parker.
9. WYAS Calderdale – MAC: 73/26 Robert Parker notes on what he saw at Shibden.
10. BNA Yorkshire Gazette February 1837. Advertisement for Terrace House.
11. NYCROA QAL (MIc 1757/158).
12. Parry-Jones William, 1972, *The Trade in Lunacy: A study of Private Mad-Houses in England in the 18th and 19th Centuries*. Routledge: London.
13. Edington, B. 'The York Retreat' *Victorian Review Vol 39*. No. 1. Pgs.9–13, http://jstor.org/stable/24496989 Further information on William Tuke: Kibria, A.A Metcalfe, N. A biography of William Tuke (1732–1822) Founder of the modern mental asylum. *Journal of Medical Biography, Vol. 24, Issue 3, (2014)*
14. NYCROA QAL (MIC 1757/158) Returns of Private lunatic asylums 1832–1887. Includes list and details of inmates. With thanks to Anne Boyens.
15. Ibid.
16. Ibid.
17. Elmer, J. 1844, *An Outline of the proactive in lunacy under commission in the nature of Writs de Lunactie Inquirendo*, London: V&R Stevens and G.S. Norton. The reference to Ann Walker is in the appendix.
18. NA: C/211/28/W249 Inquisition of Lunacy Document.
19. NA: C/211/28/W249 Inquisition of Lunacy Document.

Chapter 2

1. The Walker family motto.
2. Data from www.statistica.com – in 1800 there were 329 deaths per 1,000 births for children under 5, taking a mean average.
3. Gould, A, 'Alexander Goron, puerperal sepsis and modern theories of infection control – Semmelweis in perspective' *The Lancet Infectious Disease*, 10,4 (April 2010) pgs.275–8.

4. https://janeausten.co.uk/blogs/landscape-and-property/developements-in-childbirth-in-regency-and-victorian-england

5. Developments in Childbirth in Regency and Victorian England at www.janeausten.co.uk discussed this issue.

6. Tomalin, C. 2012, *The Life and Death of Mary Wollstonecraft*. Penguin Books: London. p. 76.

7. On the evening of 4 November 1847 Dr John Simpson, Professor of midwives at Edinburgh University, was experimenting and realised that chloroform caused a 'safe' loss of consciousness. Simpson, D. 'Simpson and the Discovery of Chloroform' *Scotland Medical Journal*, 35, 5 (October 1990) pgs.149–153.

8. Vickery, A. 1999, *The Gentleman's Daughter: Women's Lives in Georgian England*, New Haven: Yale University Press.

9. Hallett, C. 'The Attempt to understand puerperal fever in the 18th and 19th centuries: The influence of inflammation theory.' *Medical History* 2005 January 1:49(1) pgs.1–28.

10. Email conversation with Mr Ian Philp, Chair of the Friends of St Matthew's Churchyard, regarding Ann Walker's place of birth 3 June 2021, with thanks.

11. The Morgan Library and Museum Archive: LHMS MA 2696.36 Record No. 28365. A letter from Charlotte Brontë to W.S. Williams dated 1848.

12. Adams, S and S. 1825, *The Complete Servant*, London p.257.

13. Commons Chamber Records Volume 1 www.hansard.parliament.uk

14. Holmes, R., 2019, *The Napoleonic Wars*, Welbeck Publishing: London.

15. Account of the Murder of Mr Dighton, the excise officer of Halifax 1769. Unknown author. Handbill. Doc ID: 100419 Halifax Library ID: P343R563.

16. Wragg, B. Worlsey, G. (ed.) 2000, *The life and works of John Carr of York*, Oblong Creative Ltd: London.

17. Japhet Lister of Northgate House was the great uncle of Anne Lister. 'The Calderdale Companion' Ref: 58–146.

18. Glover, D., 2007 *Wilberforce in Halifax*, BBC Bradford and West Yorkshire Archive.

19. Prerogative and Exchequer court of York Probate Index 1688–1858. Extracted from Barker, D.M. 2018 *The Walkers of Crow Nest* www.lightcliffechurchyard.org

20. Frank, K. 1992, *A Chainless Soul: A life of Emily Brontë*, Battatine Books: London. p.64.

21. Sugden, K. Cockerill, A. *The Wool and Cotton textile industries in England and Wales up to 1850*. www.campop.geog.cam.ac.uk

22. Barker, D.M. 2018 *The Walkers of Crow Nest* www.lightcliffechurchyard.org

23. Stuart, J. 'The Halifax Piece Hall: The 2017 refurbishment and history'. *The Yorkshire Journal* Vol.1 2018 p.9.

24. *The Walkers of Lightcliffe* www.lightcliffehistory.org.uk

Chapter 3

1. WYAS Calderdale – WDP53/1/1/8
2. Rousseau, J-J (Author) Bloom, A. (trans) 1979 (ed) *Emilie: Or on Education*, Basic Books: London.
3. Myers, M. 'Impeccable governesses, Radical dames, and Moral mothers: Mary Wollstonecraft and the female tradition in Georgian childrens books', *Children's Literature* Vol. 14 1986 pgs.31–50 Project MUSE.
4. Newbury, J. 2009 (reprint) *A Little Pretty Pocket Book*, Dodo Press – Illustrated edition.
5. McHale, S.M, Updegraff, K.A., Whiteman, S.D., 'Sibling relationships and influences on childhood and adolescence', 2012 *Journal of Marriage and Family*, October 1 74(5) pgs.913–30 p.913.
6. WYAS Calderdale SH:7/ML/E/6/0023
7. Frazer, E., 'Mary Wollstonecraft and Catharine Macaulay on Education', *Oxford Review of Education*, Vol. 37. No. 5 October 2011 pgs.603–17.
8. Shoemaker, R. 1998, *Gender in British Society* 1650–1850, Routledge: London. p.6
9. Barker, D.M. 2018, Ann Walker, Anne Lister and St Matthew's Church, Lightcliffe. www.lightcliffechurchyard.org.uk
10. Benson History of Education York p.87 In: 'Schools and colleges', in *A History of the County of York: The City of York*, ed. P M Tillott (London, 1961), pgs.440–60. British History Online http://www.british-history. ac.uk/vch/yorks/city-of-york/p440-460
11. Hargrove History of York ii 390–1 *Minutes of Managers 1812–1822*, York Public Library.
12. Ancestry.com, 'Oxford University Alumni 1500–1886' Vol.4 p.1485. John Walker at Oxford.
13. WYAS Calderdale SH:7/ML/E/5/0037
14. WYAS Calderdale SH:7/ML/E/3/0068
15. The Governess in the Age of Jane Austen www.janeaustenworld.com
16. WYAS Calderdale SH:7/ML/E/3
17. WYAS Calderdale SH:7/ML/E/2 Transcription PDF pgs.55–6.
18. ibid.
19. WYAS Calderdale SH:7/ML/E/2 Transcription PDF pgs.52–4.
20. WYAS Calderdale SH:7/ML/E/2/0032
21. WYAS Calderdale SH:7/ML/E/2/0045
22. ibid.
23. ibid.
24. WYAS Calderdale SH:7/ML/E/4/0121
25. Baines, E. 'History, Directory and Gazetteer of Yorkshire' 1, (West Riding, 1822), accessed via University of Leicester special online collection, ID: LUL8005.
26. Bentley, G.E., 'The Edwardses of Halifax as Booksellers by Catalogue 1749–1835' *Studies in Bibliography* Vol. 45 Bibliographical Society of the University of Virginia 1992 pgs.187–222.

27. WYAS Calderdale retrieved via Ancestry FHL Film No: 1542105 Ref ID: 1-2p10n73

28. Gaskell, E, 1866, *Wives and Daughters,* Elder and Company: London.

29. King, H. 2009, *The sickness of Virgins: Green sickness Chlorosis and the Problems of Puberty,* Routledge: UK. p.2.

30. ibid.

Chapter 4

1. WYAS Calderdale SH:7/ML/E/2/0030 Anne Lister's account of the evening.

2. WYAS Calderdale SH:7/ML/E/2/0040-0041

3. wwwlightcliffehistory.org Auction Photographs of Crow Nest.

4. Kay. E. 2014, *Dining with the Georgians: A delicious history,* Amberley Publishing: London.

5. V&A Museum Archive Acc. No. T.51-1934 and Shep, R.L (ed) 1997 reprint, *A Lady of Distinction: Regency Etiquette* 1811.

6. WYAS Calderdale SH:7/ML/E/2/0037

7. WYAS Calderdale SH:7/ML/E/2/0031-0032

8. *Halifax Courier* 15 April 2010 retrieved via press reader.

9. Now called the Grange.

10. *Halifax Courier* 15 April 2010 retrieved via press reader.

11. WYAS Calderdale SH:7/ML/E/2/0053

12. WYAS Calderdale SH:7/ML/E/2/0055

13. Shorter, E. 1984, *The History of Women's Bodies,* Penguin: London. p.53.

14. Sharp, J. 1671, *The Midwife's Book or The Whole Art of Midwifery discovered in 6 books.*

15. Corsets and Drawers: A look at Regency underwear www.janeausten.co.uk

16. Hollilck, F, 1847, *The Diseases of Woman. Their causes and cure familiarly explained: With practical hints for their preservation and for the preservation of the female health,* T.W.Strong: New York. p.17.

17. WYAS Calderdale SH:7/ML/E/12/0088

18. WYAS Calderdale SH:7/ML/E/12/0090

19. E. Showalter, 'Victorian women and Menstruation' Volume 14,1 (1970) pgs.83–9 (p.85).

20. WYAS Calderdale WDP53/1/3/7

21. Woolson, D. 2021, Lydia Fenton (née Wilksinson) writing for www.insearchofannwalker.com

22. Holland, N. The Story of Anne Brontë's godmothers www.anneBrontë.org

23. University of Sheffield Library – MS58 Elizabeth Frith's Diary.

24. ibid.

25. ibid.

26. Pride and Prejudice had been published five years earlier in 1813.

27. GJ p.102.

28. FF p.31

29. IKMOH pgs.14,100,122-3.
30. WYAS Calderdale SH:7/ML/E/11/0057
31. www.who.int Section on adolescence.
32. IKMOH p.169.
33. ibid p.206.
34. ibid.
35. www.calderdalecompanion.co.uk Walker Priestley Ref 39–158. John Preistly Ref 39–172 Thorpe Mill Ref 15–59.
36. Ancestry England Select deaths and burials 1538-1991 FHL Film No. 1542105 Ref ID: 1-2p68n544.
37. WYAS Calderdale WDP 47/1/4/1
38. WYAS Calderdale SH:7/ML/E/6/116
39. WYAS Calderdale SH:7/ML/E/7/0082
40. WYAS Calderdale SH:7/ML/E/7/0083
41. WYAS Calderdale CM/89/25
42. *The Fancy Ball at the Upper Rooms, Bath 1825* by Isaac Cruikshank in Blackmantles, The English Spy.
43. Wilson, T. 1816, *A Companion to the Ballroom*, Button, Whittaker and Co: St Paul's London.
44. Almack's Assembly Rooms www.janeausten.co.uk Lady Jersey.
45. Anne Lister writes at this time that she did not call at Crow Nest very often anymore as John Walker had not called upon her father first to pay his respects, and so she felt awkward.
46. Portrait held by the Regimental Museum of the Argyll and Sutherland Highlanders.
47. National Records of Scotland, Old Parish registers. Births 069/10166 p.166.
48. Henry Edwards on Elizabeth and Captain Sutherland. WYAS Calderdale CN:103/1-4
49. Deed Book 1801 British Library EAP 688/1/1/21 p.77.
50. FF p.35.
51. WYAS Calderdale WDP471/2/1
52. Captain Sutherland did not have a good reputation locally.

Chapter 5
1. Steyning, Sussex Church Records 1803 FHL Film No. 1068527 item 1.
2. Steyning, Sussex Church Records 1803 FHL Film No. 1068527
3. WYAS Calderdale WYC/1525/7/1/5/1/p.68
4. www.janeausten.com/blogs/arts-and-entertainment/the-regency-wedding-breakfast
5. Beckford, W. Gemmett, R.J (ed) 2007 (reprint), *Dreams, Waking Thoughts and Incidents*, London: Dodo Press.
6. Redlich, Fritz. 'Jacques Laffitte and the Beginnings of Investment Banking in France,' *Bulletin of the Business Historical Society*, Vol 22 (December 1948).

7. Walker, M. 18/4/2021 William Rawson & Co and the birth of Rawson's bank on www.insearchofannwalker.com and WYAS CN:99/2 CN:99/7 – John Walker's bank account records.
8. www.uploadsknightlab.com
9. James, H. Edel, L (ed) 1987 *Henry James Selected Letters*, Harvard: HUP p.51.
10. Talbot, M. Heaford, M. (ed) 2012, *Life in the South: The Naples Journal of Marianne Talbot 1829–32*, Cambridge: Postillion books.
11. WYAS Calderdale WYC/1525/7/1/5/1 p.68
12. www.uploadsknightlab.com Caroline Walker diary entry provided by Martin Walker.
13. ibid. Also see: Borrelli A. 'Medicina e organizzazione sanitaria a Napoli tra fine settecento e decennio francese' [Medicine and health services in Naples (1750–1810)]. *Med Secoli*. 2011;23(3):593–640. Italian. PMID: 23057196.
14. Lapham's Quarterly Roundtable 'A Riot of the Dead' A German poet reports from the Paris cholera outbreak of 1832 by Henirch Heine 25/3/2020 www.laphamquarterly.org Le Ministerie Attaque du Choléra Morbus by Grandville 1831 Bibliothèque nationale de France.
15. WYAS Calderdale WYC/1525/7/1/5/1 p.68
16. Archivio di Stato di Napoli, *Stato civile della restaurazione quartieri de Napoli Chiaia Morti 1830* Ref. Immagine 85. Death record discussed in an email exchange with Lucia and Francesca from Anne Lister Italia. 3 April 2021.
17. WYAS Calderdale CN:99/2 CN:99/7 Also see: www.uploadsknightlab.com Fanny's Return.
18. WYAS Calderdale WYC/1525/7/1/5/1 p.68.
19. WYAS Calderdale SH:7/ML/E/12/0170 transcribed by Leila Straub.
20. WYAS Calderdale CN:99/7 Also see: www.uploadsknightlab.com Paris and Dover.
21. Diane Halford, In Search of Ann Walker Family Tree Ancestry.com
22. Cavallo, S. Warner, L (ed) 1999 *Widowhood in Medieval and Early modern Europe*, Harlow: Longman. p.235.
23. Philp, I. 2020,The Walker and Sutherland Walker Estates www.lightcliffehistory.com
24. ibid.
25. The monument can still be seen at St Matthew's Church, Lightcliffe.
26. FF p.37.
27. Caledonian Mercury Saturday 12 November 1831. They are listed as staying at MacKenzies Hotel.
28. WYAS Calderdale CN/93/3

Chapter 6

1. For a comprehensive overview of Lidgate House, see www.lightcliffe churchyard.org.uk The Walker property known as Lidgate House or Farm, Ian Philp and Dorothy Barker, Friends of St Matthew's Churchyard 2020.

2. WYAS Calderdale SH:2/M/1/2 Estate maps drawn by Washington.
3. WYAS Calderdale SH:7/ML/E/15/0126-0127
4. WYAS Calderdale SH:7.ML/E/15/0087-0088
5. GJ The Real Anne Lister p.61.
6. WYAS Calderdale SH:7/ML/E/14/0118
7. WYAS Calderdale SH:7/ML/E/14/0171-0172
8. WYAS Calderdale SH:7/ML/E/15/0065-0066
9. FF p.36, 73 etc. Ann's finances are discussed.
10. The proposal seems to have lingered, it was still being put to Ann in February 1833 See. WYAS Calderdale SH:7/ML/E/16/0018
11. WYAS Calderdale SH:7/ML/E/15/0104
12. ibid.
13. WYAS Calderdale SH:7/ML/E/15/0106-0107
14. WYAS Calderdale SH:7/ML/E/15/0105
15. GJ The Real Anne Lister p.70
16. WYAS Calderdale SH:7/ML/E/15/0106-0107
17. GJ The Real Anne Lister p.93
18. WYAS Calderdale SH:7/ML/E/15/01113
19. ibid.

Chapter 7
1. WYAS Calderdale SH:7/ML/E/2/0128
2. WYAS Calderdale SH:7/ML/E/15/0112-0114
3. Wordsworth, W. 1835 (5th edition) *A Guide through the District of the Lakes.*
4. Barker, J. 2021, *Wordsworth: A Life*, Lume Books: London p.454 – on Wordsworth's popularity.
5. Wordsworth, W 'Lines composed a few miles above Tintern Abbey on revisiting the banks of the Wye during a tour July 13 1798' www.poetryfoundation.org
6. Sir Walter Scott met his wife when touring the lakes, Tennyson spent time near Bassenthwaite whose lake is said to have been his inspirations for the lake into which Excalibur is thrown, and Carlyle was a frequent visitor to Mirehouse.
7. WYAS Calderdale SH:7/ML/E/15/0114
8. Charlotte Deans (1768–1859), *A Commentary on the Story of a Travelling Player,* Frances Marshall commentary, Kendal: Titus Wilson, 1984.
9. Martin, J.D. 'Wasdale Hall In: Cumberland and Westmorland' *Antiquarian and Archaeological Society Transactions*, Cumberland and Westmorland Society (2015), pgs.269–282 (p. 271).
10. ibid pgs.271-2.
11. The Coat of Arms remains above the door today, the building is used as a Youth Hostel.
12. WYAS Calderdale SH:7.ML.E.15/0124-0125
13. WYAS Calderdale SH:7/ML/E/15/0121

14. ibid.
15. ibid.
16. WYAS Calderdale SH:7/ML/E/15/0122
17. ibid.
18. ibid. Anne was considering hiring Eugenie Pierre to be her lady's maid, but she wanted to make sure that she would be up to the rigours of travelling.
19. WYAS Calderdale SH:7/ML/E/15/0122
20. ibid.
21. ibid.
22. ibid.
23. WYAS Calderdale SH:7/ML/E/15/0123
24. ibid.
25. ibid.
26. ibid.
27. ibid.
28. Anne carefully does not mention to Ann about the plans she had initially made to entertain Vere or other women there.
29. WYAS Calderdale SH:7/ML/E/15/0123
30. ibid.
31. ibid.
32. ibid.
33. WYAS Calderdale SH:7/ML/E/15/0124-0125
34. ibid.
35. Anne knew she would inherit all the Shibden estate and wealth upon the death of her father and aunt.
36. WYAS Calderdale SH:7/ML/E/15/0124-0125
37. ibid.
38. ibid.

Chapter 8
1. WYAS Calderdale SH:7/ML/E/15/0126-0127
2. Euler, C.A. 1995 *Moving between worlds: Gender, Class, Politics, Sexuality and Women's Networks in the Diaries of Anne Lister of Shibden Hall, Halifax, Yorkshire 1830–1840* Unpublished PhD thesis. Discussed pgs.133–8.
3. Clark. A 'Anne Lister's constriction of Lesbian Identity' Journal of Sexuality, 7,1 (1996) pgs.25–50.
4. WYAS Calderdale SH:7/ML/E/15/0126-0127
5. ibid.
6. ibid. Also discussed in GJ The Real Anne Lister p.134.
7. WYAS Calderdale SH:7/ML/E/15/0126-0127.
8. ibid. No letters have to date been found.
9. ibid.
10. WYAS Calderdale SH:7/ML/E/15/0127-0128.

11. ibid. Also see: Crabbe, George, 1754–1832. *The Poetical Works of the Rev. George Crabbe: with his letters and journals, and his life, by his son. In eight volumes.* Vol. II. [poems only] London: John Murray, Albemarle Street. MDCCCXXXVIII., 1838. 8 volumes.
12. ibid.
13. GJ The Real Anne Lister p.146.
14. WYAS Calderdale SH:7/ML/E/15/0128-0129
15. WYAS Calderdale SH:7/ML/E/13/0071 Anne Lister discusses the use of pocket holes.
16. GJ The Real Anne Lister p.148.
17. GJ The Real Anne Lister p.153.
18. WYAS Calderdale SH:7/ML/E/15/0129-0130
19. ibid.
20. ibid.
21. ibid.
22. WYAS Calderdale SH:7/ML/E/15/0130
23. ibid.
24. ibid.
25. WYAS Calderdale SH:7/ML/E/15/0133
26. ibid.
27. WYAS Calderdale SH:7/ML/E/15/0130-0133
28. WYAS Calderdale SH:7/ML/E/15/0133
29. WYAS Calderdale SH:7/ML/E/15/0134-0135
30. ibid.
31. WYAS Calderdale SH:7/ML/E/15/0132-0133
32. WYAS Calderdale SH:7/ML/E/15/0134-0135.
33. Passages from 'the English note books of Nathaniel Hawthorne' Volume 1 1875
34. GJ The Real Anne Lister p.172.
35. ibid.

Chapter 9
1. WYAS Calderdale SH:7/ML/E/15/0136-0137
2. ibid.
3. ibid.
4. WYAS Calderdale SH:7/ML/E/15/0142-0143
5. WYAS Calderdale SH:7/ML/E/15/0136-0137
6. WYAS Calderdale SH:7/ML/E/15/0137
7. WYAS Calderdale SH:7/ML/E/15/01378-0138
8. WYAS Calderdale SH:7/ML/E/15/ 0138-0139 and GJ The Real Anne Lister p.190.
9. ibid.
10. ibid.
11. WYAS Calderdale SH:7/ML/E/15/0139-0140

12. WYAS Calderdale SH:7/ML/E/15/0139-0141
13. WYAS Calderdale SH:7/ML/E/15/0142. See also GJ pgs.66–7.
14. WYAS Calderdale SH:7/ML/E/15/0143
15. ibid.
16. WYAS Calderdale SH:7/ML/627/1 and WYAS SH:7/ML/628/1.
17. WYAS Calderdale SH:7/ML/E/15/0143-0150 See also discussion in GJ The Real Anne Lister Chapters 8 and 9 for a detailed discussion of these events.
18. WYAS Calderdale SH:7/ML/E/15/0145 13 November 1832.
19. In addition Ann prevents Harriet from going to Pye Nest during her visit, feeling that she would gossip about her and Anne.
20. WYAS Calderdale SH:7/ML/E/15/0155
21. *Leeds Mercury News* 1 June 1833 retrieved via the BL Board. See also Lydia Fentoné Wilkinson by Deb Woolson www.insearchofannwalker.com.
22. ND pgs.72–3.
23. WYAS Calderdale SH:7/ML/E/15/0154-0155
24. WYAS Calderdale SH:7/ML/E/0157-0158 Dr Sunderland diagnosed *'some little excitement of the mind'* on 17 January 1833.
25. WYAS Calderdale SH:7/ML/646/1
26. WYAS Calderdale SH:7/ML/E/15/0158-0159
27. WYAS Calderdale SH:7/ML/E/15/0162-0163
28. WYAS Calderdale SH:7/ML/E/15/0165-0166
29. WYAS Calderdale SH:7/ML/646/1
30. WYAS Calderdale SH:7/ML/E/15/0177
31. WYAS Calderdale SH:7/ML/E/15/0178
32. WYAS Calderdale SH:7/ML/E/15/0177
33. GJ The Real Anne Lister p.214.
34. WYAS Calderdale SH:7/ML/E/16/0010-0011 GJThe Real Anne Lister p.214.
35. WYAS Calderdale SH:7/ML/E/16/0012

Chapter 10

1. WYAS Calderdale SH:7/ML/E/16/0013
2. WYAS Calderdale SH:7/ML/E/16/0018
3. GJ The Real Anne Lister p.214.
4. Contemporary notes collated on the Edinburgh 1832 Cholera outbreak can be found in *The Edinburgh Medical Journal* 1933 Vol.39 and www.scottishmining.co.uk
5. WYAS Calderdale SH:7:ML/E/16/0021-0022
6. WYAS Calderdale SH:7/ML/E/16/0024 Anne received a letter from Captain Sutherland.
7. They are recorded in the Resolis Communicant Rolls there in 1831–32.
8. Jim MacKay www.kirkmichael.info 'Sutherland of Flowerburn and Sutherland of Udale.' Also reference email conversation with Jim Mackay on the subject 7 April 2021.

9. WYAS Calderdale SH:7/ML/E/16/0035
10. Letter transcribed in GJ The Real Anne Lister pgs.265–7.
11. FF pgs.83–4.
12. WYAS Calderdale SH:7/ML/E/16/0155
13. WYAS Calderdale SH:7/ML/E/16/0156
14. WYAS Calderdale SH:7/ML/E/16/0157
15. WYAS Calderdale SH:7/ML/E/16/0158
16. FF p.88.
17. FF. pgs.91–2.
18. WYAS Calderdale SH:7/ML/E/16/0174

Chapter 11
1. WYAS Calderdale SH:7/ML/E/16/0174
2. WYAS Calderdale SH:7/ML/E/16/0176-0177
3. WYAS Calderdale SH:7/ML/E/17/0007
4. FF p.91.
5. WYAS Calderdale SH:7/ML/E/17/0014-0015
6. WYAS Calderdale SH:7/ML/E/17/0014
7. WYAS Calderdale SH:7/ML/E/17/0015
8. WYAS Calderdale SH:7/ML/E/17/0015 – transcription by www.woollylisterblog.tumblr.com
9. WYAS Calderdale SH:7/ML/E/17/0016
10. ibid.
11. FF pgs.110–11.
12. Helena Whitbread in *No Other Priest but Love*, suggests that Anne's STI was in fact trichomoniasis rather than Syphilis as originally thought.
13. WYAS Calderdale SH:7/ML/E/17/0020
14. ibid.
15. Marian was engaged in 1834 to John Abbot, a rug maker but they never married.
16. WYAS Calderdale SH:7/ML/E/17/0022-0023
17. WYAS Calderdale SH:7/ML/E/17/0023-0024

Chapter 12
1. WYAS Calderdale WYC:1525/7/1/5
2. WYAS Calderdale WYC:1525/7/1/5/1/2
3. WYAS Calderdale SH:7/ML/E/17/0041
4. ibid.
5. WYAS Calderdale WYC:1525/7/1/5/2
6. Boland, M. *Handbook of Invalid Cooking*.
7. WYAS Calderdale WYC:1525/7/1/5/1/2
8. ibid.
9. WYAS Calderdale SH:7/ML/E/17/0041
10. WYAS Calderdale WYC:1525/7/1/5/1/3

11. WYAS Calderdale SH:7/ML/E/17/0041
12. WYAS Calderdale SH:7/ML/E/17/0041-0042
13. WYAS Calderdale WYC 1525/7/1/5/1/3
14. ibid.
15. WYAS Calderdale WYC:1525/7/1/5/1/4 and SH:7/ML/E/17/0042
16. WYAS Calderdale SH:7/ML/E/17/0042
17. WYAS Calderdale WYC:1525/7/1/5/1/4
18. WYAS Calderdale WYC:1525/7/1/5/1/4-6
19. ibid.
20. ibid.
21. WYAS Calderdale WYC:1525/7/1/5/1/6
22. WYAS Calderdale SH:7/ML/E/17/0043
23. WYAS Calderdale WYC:1525/7/1/5/1/6
24. WYAS Calderdale SH:7/ML/E/17/0043
25. WYAS Calderdale WYC:1525/7/1/5/1/6
26. WYAS Calderdale SH:7/ML/E/17/0043
27. ibid.
28. WYAS Cadlerdale WYC:1525/7/1/5/1/7
29. WYAS Calderdale SH:7/ML/E/17/0043
30. WYAS Calderdale WYC:1525/7/1/5/1/7
31. ibid and SH:7.ML.E.17/0044
32. WYAS Calderdale WYC:1525/7/1/5/1/7-8
33. WYAS Calderdale SH:7/ML/E/17/0044
34. WYAS Calderdale WYC:1525/7/1/5/1/7-8
35. ibid.
36. WYAS Calderdale WYC:1525/7/1/5/1/8 and SH:7/ML/E/17/0044-0045

Chapter 13
1. WYAS Calderdale WYC:1525/7/1/5/1/8
2. ibid.
3. WYAS Calderdale SH:7/ML/E/17/0045
4. WYAS Calderdale WYC:1525/7/1/5/1/8-9
5. ibid.
6. WYAS Calderdale WYC:1525/7/1/5/1/9
7. WYAS Calderdale WYC:1525/7/1/5/1/9-10
8. WYAS Calderdale SH:7/ML/E/17/0046
9. WYAS Calderdale WYC:1525/7/1/5/1/9-10
10. Green, M. 1992, *Miss Lister of Shibden Hall: Selected Letter 1800–1840*, Lewes: The Book Guild. The letter was mistakenly identified as one of Anne Lister's.
11. WYAS Calderdale WYC:1525/7/1/5/1/10-11
12. WYAS Calderdale SH:7/ML/E/17/0046
13. WYAS Calderdale WYC:1525/7/1/5/1/11-12
14. WYAS Calderdale WYC:1525/7/1/5/1/12

15. WYAS Calderdale SH:7/ML/E/17/0047-0048
16. ibid.
17. WYAS Calderdale SH:7/ML/E/17/0048-0049
18. ibid. Anne notes this in the margin.
19. WYAS Calderdale WYC:1525/7/1/5/1/12-13
20. WYAS Calderdale SH:7/ML/E/17/0048-0049
21. WYAS Calderdale WYC:1525/7/1/5/1/13
22. ibid.
23. Shelley, M and P.D. 1817, *History of a 6 weeks' tour through a part of France, Switzerland, Germany and Holland with a preface by Percy Bysshe Shelley with letters descriptive of a sail around lake Geneva*, BL: C.58.b.12. p.27.
24. WYAS Calderdale SH:7/ML/E/17/0050-0051
25. Shelley, M. 1818, *Frankenstein*, Reader's Library Classics: London. Chapter 10.
26. WYAS Calderdale WYC:1525/7/1/5/1/13
27. WYAS Calderdale WYC:1525/7/1/5/1/13-14
28. ibid and WYAS Calderdale SH:7/ML/E/17/0051-0052.

Chapter 14
1. WYAS Calderdale WYC:1525/7/1/5/1/14
2. Lister, A and Green, M.M. 1992 *Miss Lister of Shibden Hall: Selected Letters (1800–1840)* Lewes: Book Guild. Originally mislabelled as having been written by Anne Lister. With thanks to www.mypb0813.wordpress.com for the discussion.
3. WYAS Calderdale WYC:1525/7/1/5/1/14
4. ibid.
5. WYAS Calderdale WYC:1525/7/1/5/1/15
6. WYAS Calderdale WYC:1525/7/1/5/1/15-16
7. ibid.
8. WYAS Calderdale WYC:1525/7/1/5/1/16
9. Lister, A and Green, M, M. 1992 *Miss Lister of Shibden Hall: Selected Letters (1800–1840)* Lewes: Book Guild. As #2.
10. Benavides, A. 8/4/21 *A Ladies Tale: The First Women up Mont Blanc* www.explorersweb.com
11. WYAS Calderdale WYC:1525/7/1/5/1/16
12. WYAS Calderdale WYC:1525/7/1/5/1/17
13. ibid.
14. WYAS Calderdale WYC:1525/7/1/5/1/17–18
15. WYAS Calderdale WYC:1525/7/1/5/1/18 and WYAS SH:7/ML/E/17/0063-63
16. WYAS Calderdale WYC:1525/7/1/5/1/18
17. WYAS Calderdale SH:7/ML/E/17/0063
18. WYAS Calderdale WYC:1525/7/1/5/1/19
19. WYAS Calderdale SH:7/ML/E/17/0064

20. WYAS Calderdale WYC:1525/7/1/5/1/19-20
21. WYAS Calderdale SH:7/ML/E/7

Chapter 15
1. WYAS Calderdale WYC:1525/7/1/5/1/19-20
2. ibid.
3. WYAS Calderdale WYC:1525/7/1/5/1/20
4. WYAS Calderdale SH:7/ML/E/17/0065
5. WYAS Calderdale WYC:1525/7/1/5/1/20
6. WYAS Calderdale SH:7/ML/E/17/0066
7. ibid.
8. WYAS Calderdale WYC:1525/7/1/5/1/21
9. ibid.
10. WYAS Calderdale SH:7/ML/E/17/0066-0067
11. ibid and WYAS Calderdale WYC:1525/7/1/5/1/21-22
12. ibid.
13. WYAS Calderdale WYC:1525/7/1/5/1/22
14. ibid.
15. WYAS Calderdale WYC:1525/7/1/5/1/22-23 and SH:7/ML/E/17/0068-0069
16. WYAS Calderdale WYC:1525/7/1/5/1/22-23
17. WYAS Calderdale WYC:1525/7/1/5/1/23
18. WYAS Calderdale WYC:1525/7/1/5/1/24
19. WYAS Calderdale SH:7/ML/E/17/0071
20. WYAS Calderdale WYC:1525/7/1/5/1/24–25
21. ibid.
22. WYAS Calderdale WYC:1525/7/1/5/1/26 and SH:7/ML/E/17/0072
23. WYAS Calderdale WYC:1525/7/1/5/1/26 and SH:7/ML/E/17/0073
24. WYAS Calderdale SH:7/ML/E/17/0073
25. WYAS Calderdale WYC:1525/7/1/5/1/26
26. WYAS Calderdale WYC:1525/7/1/5/1/28-29 and SH:7/ML/E/17/0075
27. WYAS Cadlerdale WYC:1525/7/1/5/1/29
28. WYAS Calderdale WYC:1525/7/1/5/1/29-30
29. WYAS Calderdale WYC:1525/7/1/5/1/31 and SH:7/ML/E/17/0078
30. WYAS Calderdale WYC:1525/7/1/5/1/31
31. WYAS Calderdale SH:7/ML/E/17/0080
32. ibid.

Chapter 16
1. WYAS Calderdale SH:7/ML/E/17/0081
2. ibid.
3. ibid.
4. WYAS Calderdale SH:7/ML/E/17/0082
5. WYAS Calderdale SH:7/ML/E/17/0083-0083 and FF p.112.

6. WYAS Calderdale SH:7/ML/E/17/0084-0086
7. WYAS Calderdale SH:7/ML/E/17/0087
8. WYAS Calderdale SH:7/ML/E/17/0089
9. FF p.118.
10. Letter transcribed in FF pgs.119–21. Reproduced FF p.58.
11. ibid.
12. WYAS Calderdale SH:7/ML/E/17/0096
13. WYAS Calderdale SH:7/ML/E/17/0100-0101
14. James Stuart Wortley www.historyofparliamentonline.org
15. FF pgs.139–41.
16. FF pgs.122–3.
17. WYAS Calderdale SH:7/ML/E/17/0106-0107
18. WYAS Calderdale SH:7/ML/E/17/0116-0117

Chapter 17

1. WYAS Calderdale SH:7/ML/E/17/0136
2. www.calderdale.gov.uk Halifax Election 1835 and Handbill Doc. No. 102228.
3. Leeds Mercury 10 January 1835 BNA
4. WYAS Calderdale SH:7/ML/E/17/0141-0142
5. WYAS Calderdale SH:7/ML/E/17/0147
6. FF p.148.
7. WYAS Calderdale SH:7/ML/E/16/0171
8. Ian Philp at www.lightcliffechurchyard.org.uk discusses the division of Ann Walker's estate in detail.
9. WYAS Calderdale SH:7/ML/E/18-0017-0018
10. WYAS Calderdale SH:7/ML/E/18/0018-0019
11. WYAS Calderdale SH:7/ML/E/17/0183-0184
12. WYAS Calderdale CN: 103/1-4
13. Ann's mistreatment in Scotland as discussed by David Glover's Illustrated History Talk, Ann Walker's in-laws. September 2018 Square Chapel Arts Centre.
14. FF pgs.164–5.
15. Letter from Captain Sutherland 18 February 1835 transcribed in FF pgs.165–6.
16. McAuliffe, M and Tieman, S. (ed) 2009 *Tribades, Tommies and Transgressives; History of Sexualities*, Cambridge Scholars Publishing: Cambridge p.124.
17. WYAS Calderdale SH:7/ML/E/18/0031-0032. See also FF p.172 and 192.
18. ibid.
19. WYAS Calderdale SH:7/ML/E/18/0048
20. WYAS Calderdale CN:103/1-4
21. WYAS Calderdale SH:7/ML/E/18/0056
22. ibid.

23. ibid. See also FF p.183.
24. Brontë, C. 1897 (ed) *Jane Eyre,* London: Service and Paton p.150.
25. WYAS Calderdale SH:7/ML/E.18/0071-0072
26. WYAS Calderdale SH:7/ML/AC/25
27. WYAS Calderdale SH:7/ML/E/18/0081-0082
28. WYAS Calderdale SH:7/ML/E/18/0092
29. WYAS Calderdale SH:7/ML/E/18/0098
30. WYAS Calderdale SH:7/ML/E/18/0099 and GJ The Real Anne Lister p.190.
31. WYAS Calderdale SH:7/ML/E/18/0103-0104
32. ibid.
33. ibid
34. WYAS Calderdale SH:7/ML/E/18/0118-0119
35. FF p.197 discusses Ann's expenses.
36. ibid.
37. WYAS Calderdale SH:7/ML/E/18/0109
38. WYAS Calderdale SH:7/ML/E/18/0113-0114
39. ibid.
40. WYAS Calderdale SH:7/ML/E/18/0147
41. WYAS Calderdale SH:7/ML/E/18/0149
42. FF p.202.
42. WYAS Calderdale SH:7/ML/E/18/0151

Chapter 18
1. WYAS Calderdale SH:7/ML/E/18/0154
2. ibid. Gives an example of Anne monitoring her wife's diet.
3. ibid.
4. WYAS Calderdale SH:7/ML/E/18/0154-0155
5. WYAS Calderdale SH:ML/E/18/0154-0157
6. FF pgs.205–207 discusses these figures.
7. WYAS Calderdale SH:7/ML/E/18/0162-0163
8. ibid.
9. WYAS Calderdale SH:7/ML/E/18/0176
10. FF. p 209.
11. WYAS Calderdale SH:7/ML/E/19/0010
12. WYAS Calderdale SH:7/ML/E/19/0010-0012
13. WYAS Calderdale SH:7/ML/E/19/0011
14. FF p.214.
15. WYAS Calderdale SH:7/ML/E/19/0012-0013
16. WYAS Calderdale SH:7/ML/E/19/0012
17. FF pgs.216–18.
18. WYAS Calderdale SH:7/ML/E/19/1116-0017
19. FF pgs.220–1.
20. Gottke, F. 2021, *Burning Images: A History of Effigy Protests,* Valiz. P.14.

21. WYAS Calderdale SH:7/ML/E/19/0020
22. WYAS Calderdale SH:7/ML/E/19/0021-0022
23. WYAS Calderdale SH:7/ML/E/17/0117 Marian moved to Market Weighton.
24. WYAS Calderdale SH:7/ML/E/19/0121-0122

Chapter 19

1. Anne's diary is littered with references to Ann being at the school, for example: WYAS Calderdale SH:7/ML/E/20/0025 – 'Ann not in bed til 2 ½ or later last night and off to the school about 8 ½ this morning in the market cart.' SH:7/ML/E/20/0032 – 'Ann was to be at the school at 9 – off without my seeing her.'
2. WYAS Calderdale SH:7/ML/E/20/0026
3. ibid.
4. ibid.
5. WYAS Calderdale SH:7/ML/E/20/0026-0027
6. WYAS Calderdale SH:7/ML/E/20/0027
7. WYAS Calderdale SH:7/ML/E/0/0028
8. WYAS Calderdale SH:7/ML/E/20-0027-0028 – Anne's account of their Bolton Abbey trip.
9. WYAS Calderdale SH:7/ML/E/20/0035 Anne makes marginal note in her diary – 'Thieves in house.'
10. Dr Shaikh, J. 2/12/2021, *How does Belladonna work?* www.medicinenet.com
11. WYAS Calderdale SH:7/ML/E/20/0039
12. WYAS Calderdale SH:7/ML/E/20/0040
13. WYAS Calderdale SH:7/ML/E/20/0044
14. ibid.
15. ibid.
16. WYAS Calderdale SH:7/ML/E/20/0046
17. WYAS Calderdale SH:7/ML/E/20/0044
18. WYAS Calderdale SH:7/ML/E/20/0120-0121
19. ibid.
20. WYAS Calderdale SH:7/ML/E/21/0025-0026
21. WYAS Calderdale SH:7/ML/E/21/0027-0028

Chapter 20

1. WYAS Calderdale SH:7/ML/E/21/0089
2. WYAS Calderdale SH:7/ML/E/21/0090
3. WYAS Calderdale SH:7/ML/E/21/0091
4. WYAS Calderdale SH:7/ML/E/21/0091-0092 Transcribed by Dorjana Sirola March 2020 1838 Tour of France www.knightlab.com
5. William Tyndale was a leader to the Protestant Reformation. He was convicted for heresy under the authority of the Holy Roman Empire and was executed.

6. WYAS Calderdale SH:7/ML/E/21/0093-0094
7. Scottish British Army officer. He was famously killed at Waterloo while speaking to Wellington.
8. WYAS Calderdale SH:7/ML/E/21/0095-0097
9. WYAS CalderdaleSH:7/ML/E/21/0100-0101
10. WYAS Calderdale SH:7/ML/E/21/0103
11. WYAS Calderdale SH:7/ML/E/21/010
12. WYAS Calderdale SH:7/ML/E/21/0108
13. WYAS Calderdale SH:7/ML/E/21/0111-0112
14. WYAS Calderdale SH:7/ML/E/21/0118-0119
15. WYAS Calderdale SH:7/ML/E/21/0128-0129
16. WYAS Calderdale SH:7/ML/E/21/0129-0134
17. ibid.
18. The First Carlist War was fought between the supporters of the late king's brother Carlos de Bourbon, and those of the regent Maria Christina. The conflict cost over 140,000 lives.
19. WYAS Calderdale SH:7/ML/E/21/0138-0139
20. WYAS Calderdale SH:7/ML/E/21/0144-0145
21. ibid.
22. WYAS Calderdale SH:7/ML/E/21/0150
23. WYAS Calderdale SH:7/ML/E/21/0159
24. WYAS Calderdale SH:7/ML/E/2/0160
25. WYAS Calderdale SH:7/ML/E/21/0166-0167
26. WYAS Calderdale SH:7/ML/E/21/0175
27. WYAS Calderdale SH:7/ML/E/22/0017
28. ibid. See also GJ The Real Anne Lister p.144.
29. WYAS Calderdale SH:7/ML/E/22/0017-0020
30. WYAS Calderdale SH:7/ML/E/22/0032 Diveira, M. Pauline, M and Labate, L. April 2020. Pyrenees 1838 Anne Lister is mistaken for a man www.packedwithpotential.com
31. WYAS Calderdale SH:7/ML/E/22/0055-0056
32. WYAS Calderdale SH:7/ML/E/22/0063-0064
33. WYAS Calderdale SH:7/ML/E/22/0066

Chapter 21
1. WYAS Calderdale SH:/7/ML/E/22/0072-0073
2. WYAS Calderdale SH:7/ML/E/22/0073-0074
3. ibid.
4. WYAS Calderdale SH:7/ML/E/22/0083-0084
5. WYAS Calderdale SH:7/ML/E/22/0090-0093
6. WYAS Calderdale SH:7/ML/E/22/0099
7. WYAS Calderdale SH:7/ML/E/22/0138
8. WYAS Calderdale SH:7/ML/E/23/0006
9. WYAS Calderdale SH:7/ML/E/23/0009

10. NA C106/60
11. WYAS Calderdale SH:7/ML/E/23/0009-0010
12. ibid.
13. WYAS Calderdale SH:7/ML/E/23/0013
14. WYAS Calderdale SH:7/ML/E/23/0016
15. Schwarcz, J. PHD 2019 'A Little Mercurial History' www.mcgill.ca
16. WYAS Cadlerdale SH:7/ML/E/23/0017 – The medicine from Dr Jubb makes Ann sick.
17. ibid.
18. WYAS Calderdale SH:7/ML/E/23/0026
19. WYAS Calderdale SH:7/ML/E/23/0026-0028
20. WYAS Calderdale SH:7/ML/E/23/0034
21. WYAS Calderdale SH:7/ML/E/23/0037
22. WYAS Calderdale SH:7/ML/E/23/0046
23. WYAS Calderdale SH:7/ML/E/23/0052
24. WYAS Calderdale SH:7/ML/E/23/0057
25. WYAS Calderdale SH:7/ML/E/23/0066 – Anne writes these words vertically in the margin and underlines them.

Chapter 22

1. WYAS Calderdale SH:7/ML/E/23/0074-0075
2. WYAS Calderdale SH:7/ML/E/23/0075-0076
3. WYAS Calderdale SH:7/ML/E/23/0076-0077
4. WYAS Calderdale SH:7/ML/E/23/0077-0078
5. WYAS Calderdale SH:7/ML/E/23/0078-0079 The summer residence of the House of Orange-Nassau until the mid-twentieth century.
6. ibid.
7. WYAS Calderdale SH:7/ML/E/23/0079-0080
8. WYAS Calderdale SH:7/ML/E/23/0080-0081
9. WYAS Calderdale SH:7/ML/E/23/0081
10. ibid.
11. WYAS Calderdale SH:7/ML/E/23/0081-0082
12. WYAS Calderdale SH:7/ML/E/23/0082
13. WYAS Calderdale SH:7/ML/E/23/0082-0083
14. WYAS Calderdale SH:7/ML/E/23/0083 The Bluchers were old friends of Anne's whom she met in 1833.
15. WYAS Calderdale SH:7/ML/E/23/0084-0085
16. WYAS Calderdale SH:7/ML/E/23/0085-0086
17. WYAS Calderdale SH:7.ML/TR/12/0002
18. WYAS Calderdale SH:7/ML/TR/12/0005-0008
19. WYAS Calderdale SH:7/ML/TR/12/0009
20. WYAS Calderdale SH:7/ML/TR/12/0010
21. ibid.
22. Transcription by Yvonne Haugen 2019 www.annelisternorway.com 29 July.

23. ibid. 31st July.
24. ibid. 3rd August.
25. ibid. 4th August.
26. WYAS Calderdale SH:7/ML/TR/12/0026-0027
27. WYAS Calderdale SH:7/ML/TR/12/0035-0037
28. ibid.
29. WYAS Calderdale SH:7/ML/TR/13/0004
30. WYAS Calderdale SH:7/ML/TR/13/0007
31. WYAS Calderdale SH:7/ML/TR/13/0016
32. WYAS Calderdale SH:7/ML/TR/13/0021-00

Chapter 23
1. Luhn, A. 'The Guardian' Wednesday 23 March 2016 Story of Cities #8 St Petersburg www.guardian.com
2. This assertion is opposed by writers such as Alexsandr Gorsanin – 23/3/2017 Did the Swedes make up the myth that St Petersburg was built on bones? www.russklymir.ru
3. Painted 1839, held by the Pushkin Museum, Moscow.
4. Green, M. 1992, *Miss Lister of Shibden Hall: Selected Letters 1800–1840* p.194 Letter from Anne to Vere Cameron.
5. WYAS Calderdale SH:7/ML/TR/14/0012-0014
6. Alexander Pushkin Biography www.saintpetersburg.com
7. It was created in the Catherine Palace of Tsarskoye Selo and called the Eighth Wonder of the World. The Nazis dismantled it when they occupied the city and the original room was lost.
8. Today facial rashes are often associated with stress. Kandola, A PHD 2020 How does stress affect the skin? *Medical NewsToday*. Vol. 3.
9. Woodburn, S. 2000 'Reaction reconsidered, Education and State in Russia 1825–1848', *Consortium of Revolutionary Energy 1750–1850*, Selected Papers pgs.423–31.
10. WYAS Calderdale RAM 11-12
11. ibid.
12. WYAS Calderdale SH:7/ML/E/23/0101-0102
13. WYAS Calderdale SH:7/ML/E/23/0106-0107
14. ibid.
15. Preserved plants were a growing field of study, Ann would have known this. See discussed in www.ladyscience.com Floral Fixation, 12/3/2020.
16. GJ p.149.
17. WYAS Calderdale SH:7/ML/E/23/0110-0111
18. WYAS Calderdale SH:7/ML/E/23/0112
19. WYAS Calderdale SH:7/ML/E/23/0112-0113
20. WYAS Calderdale SH:7/ML/E/23/0113
21. WYAS Calderdale SH:7/ML/E/23/0115
22. WYAS Calderdale SH:7/ML/E/23/0121

23. WYAS Calderdale SH:7/ML/E/23/0131
24. GJ p.150.
25. WYAS Calderdale SH:7ML/E/23/0154-0155
26. WYAS Calderdale SH:7/ML/E/23/0162-0164, Transcription courtesy of www.annelister538400391.wordpress.com

Chapter 24

1. 26–7 December 1839 GJ p.460.
2. Ramsden, P. Ingham, V. Typescripts inWYAS Calderdale RAM 12,3
3. WYAS Calderdale SH:7/ML/E/23/0241
4. An important Orthodox Monastery.
5. Ramsden, P. Ingham, V, Typescripts in WYAS Calderdale RAM 5,1.
6. WYAS Calderdale SH:7/ML/E/24/0006-0007
7. WYAS Calderdale SH:7/ML/E/24/0007
8. ibid and WYAS Calderdale SH:7/ML/E/24/0008
9. WYAS Calderdale SH:7/ML/E/24/0016
10. WYAS Calderdale SH:7/ML/E/24/0016-0017
11. WYAS Calderdale SH:7/ML/E/4/0018, He had been royal sculptor to George III. Later he spent eighteen years in Russia under the patronage of Tsar Nicholas I, who he knew well.
12. WYAS Calderdale SH:7/ML/E/24/0023-0024 transcription Oliveira, M. http://anne-lister-adventures.tumbler.com/archive
13. WYAS Calderdale SH:7/ML/E/24/0026 ibid.
14. WYAS Calderdale SH:7/ML/E/24/0027-0028 ibid.
15. WYAS Calderdale SH:7/ML/E/24/0032-0034 ibid.
16. WYAS Calderdale SH:7/ML/E/24/0043-0044 ibid.
17. WYAS Calderdale SH:7/ML/E/24/0068-0069 ibid.
18. WYAS Calderdale SH:7/ML/E/24/0070-0072 ibid.
19. ibid.
20. WYAS Calderdale SH:7/ML/E/24/0082-0084
21. WYAS Calderdale SH:7/ML/E/24/0085
22. GJ p.159.
23. WYAS Calderdale SH:7/ML/E/24/0088
24. WYAS Calderdale SH:7/ML/E/24/0090
25. WYAS Calderdale SH:7/ML/E/24/0095
26. WYAS Calderdale SH:7/ML/E/24/0108
27. GJ p.160.
28. WYAS Calderdale SH:7/ML/E/24/0110-0114
29. WYAS Calderdale SH:7/ML/E/24/0120-0121
30. www.pleiades.stoa.org OSM location and map of Surami Pass.
31. WYAS Calderdale SH:7/ML/E/24/0137
32. WYAS Calderdale SH:7/ML/E/24/0145-0146
33. WYAS Calderdale SH:7/ML/E/24/0165-0166
34. WYAS Calderdale SH:7/ML/E/24/0174

35. ibid.
36. GJ p.167.
37. Green, M 1992, *Miss Lister of Shibden Hall: Selected Letters 1800–1840*, Lewes: The Book Guild. p.206.

Chapter 25
1. GJ p.167.
2. Halifax Guardian 31st October 1840.
3. WYAS Calderdale SH:7/LL/406 Transcription by Anne Choma July 2019.
4. Ramsden, P. Higham, V. Typescripts in the WYAS Calderdale, Halifax 43–4.
5. Crabtree,S.March2020Ann'sReturntoShibdenwww.insearchofannwalker. com. Also with thanks to Diane Halford for the conversation on Ann's life after her return to England.
6. WYAS Calderdale WYASC/106/60 retrieved by Diane Halford 18 July 2021.
7. NA C 14/619/W106 researched by Diane Halford.
8. NA C 106/60
9. WYASC WDP53/1/4/3 – No. 1621 Anne Lister burial record. See also: *Leeds Times* 1 May 1841.
10. www.ancestry.com 1841 census entry for Shibden Hall.
11. Letter dated 6 July 1842 Horncastle v Walker published www. packedwithpotential.com January 2020 written and transcribed by M. Oliceria, L. Labate and J. Dobson.
12. Crabtree, S. March 2020 1843 Ann Walker and the Durnford Incident www.insearchofannwalker.com
13. ibid.
14. WYASC CN/103/2/30 See 11.
15. WYAS Calderdale CN/103/2/82 See 11.
16. WYAS Calderdale CN/103/2/65 See 11.
17. Kobevko, A 2/5/21 John Snaith Rymer www.insearchofannwalker.com
18. Crabtree, S, 2020 Aitkinson vs Walker, www.insearchofannwalker.com
19. WYAS Calderdale MAC 73 – letters and paper relating to the case. See also: Steve Crabtree 2020 August 1843 Aitkinson v Walker www. insearchofannwalker.com in which he has researched the case extensively.
20. ibid. With thanks to David Glover for the transcription of WYAS Calderdale MAC 73. See also: Halifax Guardian 19 August 1843.
21. ibid.
22. WYAS Calderdale MAC 73
23. WYAS Calderdale MAC 73 – See notes for Chapter 1.

Chapter 26
1. WYAS Calderdale CN 103:2/101
2. WYAS Calderdale RW:120/31

3. GJ p.523.
4. www.ancestry.com GRO Death Index April ¼ 1842 Vol.22 p.202 Yorkshire.
5. ibid. October 1/4m1844 Vol.22 p.178 Wimbledon. She is buried in St Mary's Churchyard, Merton. www.findagrave.com/memorial/203846907/elizabeth-sutherland
6. FW: 120/51/1
7. WYAS Wakefield WDP47/1/4/2
8. WYAS Leeds WDP53/1/3/41
9. WYAS Wakefield WDP53/1/2/9
10. www.ancestry.com GRO Death Index April ¼ 1847 Vol.22 p.203.
11. WYAS Calderdale CM:100/2 and NAC 14/905
12. WYAS Calderdale SH:7/DRL/33/1 Transcribed and analysed by Diane Halford and Steve Crabtree www.insearchofannwalker.com
13. *Leeds Intelligencer* 1st July 1848 discovery credited to S. Riocain.
14. www.ancestry.com 1851 census for Cliff Hill.
15. WYAS Bradford 68D 82/5/241
16. www.ancestry.com GRO Death Index January ¼ 1854 9a 258
17. Referencing an email conversation with Dr. Jennifer Wallis 9 January 2022.
18. Halford, D and Daleen, L. ed. Godley, L. 24 Feburary 2021, The Last Days of Ann Walker www.insearchofannwalker.com
19. For example discussed in: Boyd Mushet, W. 1866, *A Practical Treatise on Apoplexy (cerebral haemorrhage) its Pathology, Diagnosis, Therapeutics and Prophylaxis: With an essay on so called Nervous Apoplexy on congestion of the brain and serous effusion,* Churchill and Sons: London
20. WYAS Wakefield WDP47/1/4/2
21. NA PROBII/2192/68 Ann Walker's Will and WYAS CN99/5 evidence of Marian Lister's collection.
22. NA IR26/433/91 WYAS Wakefield WDP47/Box 9. Research undertaken by www.insearchofannwalker.com Today ISOAW fundraise for the Brighouse Foodbank in Ann's name.
23. FF p.241.

Select Bibliography

Primary Sources
West Yorkshire Archives, Calderdale.
   Crow Nest Records:
   WYC:1525/7/1/5 – Ann Walker's diary.
   CN:89 – Walker Family Papers.
   CN:93 – Wills etc.
   CN:103 – Letters.
   MAC:73 – Robert Parker's and other contemporary correspondence.
Shibden Hall Records:
   SH:1/SHA – Shibden Hall Accounts.
   SH:2.SHE/CN – Papers relating to Shibden Hall and Crow Nest.
   SH:7/ML – Anne Lister letters etc.
   SH:7/ML/E – Anne Lister's journals.
RAM – Phyllis Ramsden Papers.
North Yorkshire County Records Office QAL MIC 1757/158 – Returns of private lunatic asylums 1832–1887.
The Morgan Library and Museum Archive MA 2696.36. Record Number. 28365 – Charlotte Brontë Correspondence.
Parliamentary Papers for 1844.
University of Sheffield Library MS58 – Elizabeth Firth's diary.

Books
Adams, S and S. 1825, *The Complete Servant; Being a practical guide to the peculiar duties and business of all descriptions of servants from the housekeeper to the servant of all-work and from the land steward to the foot-boy with useful receipts and tables,* Knight and Lacey: London.
Barker, J. 2021, *Wordsworth: A Life,* Lume Books: London
Beckford, W. Gemmett. R.J. (ed) 2007, *Dreams, Waking Thoughts and Incidents,* Dodo Press: Moscow.
Boyd Mushet, W. 1866, *A Practical Treatise on Apoplexy (cerebral haemorrhage) its Pathology, Diagnosis, Therapeutics and Prophylaxis: With an essay on so called nervous apoplexy on congestion of the brain and serous effusion,* Churchill and Sons: London.
Brontë, C. 1897, *Jane Eyre,* Service and Paton: London.
Carvallo. S. Warner, L. (ed) 1999, *Widowhood in Medieval and Early Modern Europe,* Longman: Harlow.

Choma, A. 2019, *Gentleman Jack: The Real Anne Lister*, BBC Digital: London.

Collins, W. 1875, *The Law and the Lady*, Chatto and Windus: London.

Eliot, G. 2007 ed. *Middlemarch: A Study in Provincial Life*, Vintage Books: London.

Elmer, J. 1844, *An Outline of the proactive in lunacy under commission in the nature of Writs de Lunactie Inquirende*, V&R Stevens and G.S. Norton: London.

Frank, K. 1992, *A Chainless Soul: A LIfe of Emily Brontë*, Battatine Books: London.

Gaskell, E. 1866, *Wives and Daughters*, Elder and Company: London.

Green, M. (ed) 1992, *Miss Lister of Shibden Hall: Selected Letters 1800–1840*, The Book Guild: Lewes.

Hollilck, F. 1847, *The Diseases of Woman. Their causes and cure familiarly explained: With practical hints for their preservation and for the preservation of female health*, T.W.Strong: New York.

Holmes, R. 2019, *The Napoleonic Wars*, Welbeck Publishing: London.

James, H. Edel, L (ed) 1987, *Henry James Selected Letters*, HUP: Harvard.

Kay, E. 2014, *Dining with the Georgians: A delicious history*, Amberley Publishing: London.

King, H. 2009, *The sickness of Virgins: Green Sickness, Chlorosis and the Problem of Puberty*, Routledge: London.

Liddington, J. 1998, *Female Fortune, Land, Gender and Authority: The Anne Lister Diaries and Other Writings 1833–36*, Rovers Oram Press: London and New York.

Liddington, J. 2019, *Nature's Domain: Anne Lister and the Landscape of Desire*, Pennine Pens: Yorkshire.

Lim, A. 2021, *In the Footsteps of Anne Lister Volume 1: Travels of a remarkable English gentlewoman in France, Germany and Denmark 1833*, Independently Published.

McAuliffe, M and Tieman, S. (ed) 2009 *Tribades, Tommies and Transgressives: History of Sexualities*, Cambridge Scholars Publishing: Cambridge.

Newbury, J. 2009 (reprint) *A Little Pretty Pocket Book*, Dodo Press: Moscow.

Parry-Jones, W. 1972, *The Trade in Lunacy: A study of Private Mad-Houses in England in the 18th and 19th Centuries*, Routledge: London.

Rousseau, J.J. and Bloom, A. (trans) 1979 (ed) *Emilie: Or on Education*, Basics Books: London.

Shelley, M. 1818, *Frankenstein*, Reader's Library Classics: London.

Shoemaker, R. 1998, *Gender in British Society 1650–1850*, Routledge: London.

Shorter, E. 1984, *The History of Women's Bodies*, Penguin: London.

Steidele, A. Derbyshire, K (trans) 2018, *Gentleman Jack: A Biography of Anne Lister*, Serpent's Tail: London.

Talbot, M. Heaford, M (ed) 2012, *Life in the South: The Naples Journal of Marianne Talbot 1929–32*, Postillion Books: Cambridge.

Thompson, D. 1984, *The Chartists*, Smith: London.

Tillott, P.M. 1961, *A History of the County of York: The City of York*, Dawson: London.

Tomalin, C. 2012, *The Life and Death of Mary Wollstonecraft*, Penguin: London.

Vickery, A. 1999, *The Gentleman's Daughter: Women's Lives in Georgian England*, Yale University Press: New Haven.

Whitebread, H. 1988, *I Know My Own Heart: The Diaries of Anne Lister*, Virgo Press: London.

Wilson, T. 1816, *A Companion to the Ballroom*, Button, Whittaker and Co: St Paul's London.

Wragg, B. Worsley, G (ed) 2000, *The Life and Works of John Carr of York*, Oblong Creative Ltd: London.

Articles

Bentley, G.E. 'The Edwardses of Halifax as Booksellers' by Catalogue 1749–1835 *Studies in Bibliography* (1992) Volume 45 pgs.187–222.

Bretton, R 'Walkers of Crow Nest' *THAS* (1971).

Clark, A. 'Anne Lister's construction of Lesbian Identity', *Journal of Sexuality* (1996) Volume 7 Number 1 pgs.23–50.

Edington, B. 'The York Retreat', *Victorian Review*, Volume 39. Number 1, pgs.9–13.

Frazer, E. 'Mary Wollstonecraft and Catharine Macaulay on Education', *Oxford Review of Education* (2011) Volume 37 Number 5 pgs.603–17.

Gould, A. 'Alexander Gordon, puerperal sepsis and modern theories of infection control – Semmelweis in perspective', *The Lancet: Infectious Disease* (2010) Volume 10 Number 4 pgs.272–8.

Hallett, C. 'The Attempt to understand puerperal fever in the 18th and 19th centuries: The influence of inflammation theory,' *Medical History* (2005) January 1:49 pgs.1–28.

Hartog, H, 'Mrs Packard on dependency' *Yale Journal of Law and the Humanities* Volume 1. (1989) pgs.79–103.

Kandola, A., 'How does Stress Affect the skin?' *Medical News Today* (2020) Volume 3.

Kibria, A.A. Metcalfe, N.A. 'A Biography of William Tuke (1732–1822) Founder of the modern mental asylum', *Journal of Medical Biography* (2014) Volume 24. Issue 3.

McHale, S.M. Updegraff, K.A. Whiteman, S.D. 'Sibling relationships and influences on childhood and adolescence', *Journal of Marriage and Family* (2012) October 1 74 95) pgs.913–30. Myers, M. 'Impeccable governesses, Radical dames and Moral mothers: Mary Wollstonecraft and the female tradition in Georgian children's books', *Children's Literature* (1986) Volume 14 pgs.31–50.

Redlich, F. 'Jacques Laffitte and the Beginnings of Investment Banking in France', *Bulletin of the Business Historical Society* (1948) December Volume 22.

Showalter, E. 'Victorian women and Menstruation' *Victorian Studies* (1970) Volume 14 Number 1 pgs.83–9.

Simpson, D. 'Simpson and the Discovery of Chloroform', *Scotland Medical Journal* (1990 reprint) October 35 Number 5 pgs.149–153.

Stuart, J. 2018, 'The Halifax Piece Hall: The 2017 refurbishment and history,' *The Yorkshire Journal* (2018) Volume 1.

Websites

www.ancestry.co.uk
www.britishnewspaperarchive.co.uk
www.calderdalecompanion.co.uk
www.insearchofannwalker.com
www.janeausten.co.uk
www.lightcliffehistory.org.uk
www.packedwithpotential.org
www.stmatthewslightcliffe.co.uk